AF564691

# TRIBAL FOLKTALES OF INDIA

*(A STUDY IN ANTHROPOLOGICAL PERSPECTIVE)*

# TRIBAL FOLKTALES OF INDIA

## *(A STUDY IN ANTHROPOLOGICAL PERSPECTIVE)*

***By***

**Sarita Sahay**

*Lecturer*

*Department of Anthropology*

*Ranchi University*

*Ranchi (Jharkhand)*

*(India)*

**DISCOVERY PUBLISHING HOUSE PVT. LTD.**

**NEW DELHI-110 002**

*Published by:*
**Tilak Wasan**

**DISCOVERY PUBLISHING HOUSE PVT. LTD.**
4383/4B, Ansari Road, Darya Ganj
New Delhi-110 002 (India)
*Phone* : +91-11-23279245, 43596064-65
*Fax* : +91-11-23253475
*E-mail* : discoverypublishinghouse@gmail.com
sales@discoverypublishinggroup.com
parul.wasan@gmail.com
*web* : www.discoverypublishinggroup.com

*First Edition:* **2013**

**ISBN: 978-93-5056-357-1**

**Tribal Folktales of India (*A Study in Anthropological Perspective*)**



*Printed at:*
Aditi Fine Art Press
Delhi

# Preface

It is a common practice to publish folktales as compilation of tales. When I published my first article on folktales of Bihar in anthropological perspective, it received favourable response from the readers as well as the reviewers. It appeared to me that presentation of folktales in an anthropological perspective makes sense as such and the idea of writing present book came to my mind. Thus, I was not satisfied when Lourdusamy and I published the compilation of folktales of Bhil, Barela, and Korku in Hindi language. I felt, there upon, it would be a nice idea to publish folktales of important tribes of India with anthropological analysis. Such analysis helps formulate the ethnographic study of the tribal community. I hope the present work will meet the requirement and will be of interest to the researchers of anthropology, folklore, psychology, sociology and literature.

I would like to express my deep sense of gratitude for Late Rev. Fr. S. Lourdusamy, former Director, Centre for Applied Culture Research, Indore (Madhya Pradesh, India), with whom the folktales of Bhil, Barela and Korku were collected, co-edited and published in Hindi language. Authorizing me to pursue the studies related to folktales of these three tribes further Fr. Lourdusamy wound up and left for the south India to take up the new role at Centre for Dialogue and Communication, Hyderabad (India). I came to Melbourne (Australia) and joined Monash Asia Institute of Monash University as Honorary Research Fellow. I published articles on Folklore of Bhil tribe and adolescent studies during my stay in Melbourne. Rev. Fr. Lourdusamy expired while I was abroad. Subsequently I came down to Jharkhand and undertook the job of collection of folktales of Munda, Oraon and Santhal tribes. I also undertook the task of presenting the folktales of all the six tribes in anthropological perspective. My links with Monash University has continued as Adjunct Research Fellow at the School of Political and Social Inquiry.

I do thank the authorities as well as the library staffs of the institutions I visited in respect of collecting information for the present book: Centre for Applied Cultural Research, Indore (M.P., India), Dr. Babasaheb Ambedkar National Institute of Social Science, Mhow (M.P., India), Matheson Library, Monash University, Melbourne (Victoria, Australia), University Department of Anthropology, Ranchi (Jharkhand, India).

I wish to express my deep sense of gratitude to all the people who shared the folktales of their communities with the Research Investigators and with me.

I would thank all the Research Investigators to have collected data in accordance with my guidelines and suggestions.

I wish to express my love and affection for my son Vatsal whose habit of hearing story during his bed time helped me in preserving the store house of the tales in my memory. Secondly he would not allow me to sit idle any time. He would bring pen, paper and my glasses and then force me to get down to the business of writing. Without his involvement and insistence this project would have stretched longer.

Above all I am very much obliged and grateful to my spouse who although went on lending full support to me in this endeavour.

I do hereby recall with a sense of deep love and respect the contributions of my parents at the both personal as well as professional fronts during the past several years. Mummy always had a word of encouragement and Papa lent a positive support during the writing of this book. Both of them taught me to face the hard times with enormous courage and capacity.

I sincerely thank Discovery Publishing House Pvt. Ltd., New Delhi, for bringing out the book elegantly.

**—Sarita Sahay**

# Contents

*Preface*

1 **Introduction** 1

About Folktales; Studies on Tribal Folktales; The present Book; Locale of the Study; Methodology; Organization of Data

2. **Folktales of Bhil** 7

The Damors; Bhada Gardan; Halun Sorya; Dharmi Raja; Anna Raja; The Cow Named Rupan; The Hag and Her Daughter; Khokha and Kassumar Dev; Jahma Mata; Megh Raja and Sawan Mata; Bhola Ishwar; Saat Bhowani Mata; Bapsi Dev; Bhilji Bhil; The Moving Room; Baniser Raja and Onkha Kumari; Dudi Megh and Bhada Gardan; The Bhil Boy and the King; The Bhil Farmer and the God; Somara; The Rabbit and the Girl; The Cunning Step Mother; In Search of Fortune; The Clever Girl; The Boom of Jal Mata; Hura and Pura; The Trick of a Woman; After the Cataclysm

3. **Folktales of Barela** 85

Ringiya and Jingiya; The Boy named Raju; The Frarmer, the Bull and the Justice; Abba Kulchi; The Bull and the Tiger; Seven Brothers; The Monkey; The Old Couple and Seven Children; Gappa and Sappa; Ganga Teli and Bhilat Dev; Clever Sablu; Dhinchiri; The Death of a Demon; The Flying Cot; The Parrot and the Sparrow; The Rat and the Female Mouse; The Pewit and the Thieves; Bhola and Bhunda; Bhondu Barela and His Son; Ramiya and Shaymiya; The Teaching of a Brahmin; The Girl Named Sonbai; The Golden Haired Boy

4. **Folktales of Korku** 118

The Seven Fruits; The Game of Luck; The Brave Prince; Realization of the Mistake; To Solve a Riddle; Kalua and the Barber; The Ill-begotten Earnings; The Conceited; The Fight; The Cursing of a Cow; The Greedy Brothers; The Clever Farmer; Four Fools; Waiting for the God; The Fox; Death of a Demon; Two Brothers; The Veracious

**5. Folktales of Munda** **147**

The Creation of Land; Sohrai Festival; The Wild Buffaloes; The Old Couple; The Stupid Tortoise; The Plough; The Well Wisher Parrot; The King and His Four Sons; The Wise Jackal; The Milkman; The Huniputi Clan; The Seventh Queen; The Great Drummer; The Old Couple and The Jackal; Somara and Budhna; The Asur; The Sohrai Festival Two; The Boy, the Dragon and the Monkey; The Old Woman; The Monkey Friend; The Wicked Sisters-in-Law; The Foster Parents; The Imposturous Exorcist; The Frog and the Fish; The Helpful Wolf

**6. Folktales of Oraon** **182**

The Creation of World; The Shining Dark Hair; The Foolish Man; Two Friends; The Ogre; The Brother in Mandolin; The Dancing Mouse; The Animal Friends; Bhola Oraon; The Gullible Man; The Greedy Tigress; The Boy named Son-in-Law; Karma Raja; The Revenge of a Jackal; Four Friends; The Running Dog; The Snake and the Girl; Budhna Oraon; Cattle Worship; The New Pair of Shoes; The Cunning Jackal; The Brother Born Again; The Lion and the Jackal; To Guard a Corpse

**7. Folktales of Santal** **215**

The Tiger and the King; The Clever Chicks; A Day Dreamer; Ramu and Shamu; Sabai Grass; The Trick of a Father; The Origin of the World; The Oilman; The Dream of a Potter; The Girl inside a Drum; The Gift; The Younger Brother; The Crocodile and the Jackal; The Girl Refused to Marry; The New Exorcist; The Judgement; The Deceitful Rabbit; Saubhagya; The Darling Sister; The Clever Boy and the Bear; The Cotton Tree; Karma and Balma; The Speaking Bed; The Sal Tree; The Banana Tree; The Cunning Jackal

**8. Nature and Forms of the Folktales** **246**

***Bibliography*** **253**

***Glossary*** **259**

***Botanical Index*** **261**

***Index*** **265**

# 1 Introduction

The term folklore was coined by William. J. Thomas in 1846. It includes all myths, legends, folktales, ballads, riddles, proverbs and superstitions in it (Dundes, 1989). Folklore, like any other products of man's artistic endeavour, is an ideological manifestation of human creativity. Folklore of any society is related with the culture of that society and it reflects the cultural characteristics of that society (Sahay 2001). Since folklore and culture are deeply related no scientific study of the social and religious customs of that society could be complete without studying the folklore of that society. Social scientists (Malinowski 1926, 1948, Redcliffe-Brown 1933, Deva 1972, Chettiar 1973, Punia 1993) claiming folklore very essential and integral element in a living culture have underlined the importance of this heritage. Like other elements of human culture, folklore is not merely the creation of chance. It exists in time and space, and is present in people's linguistic and social contacts, during the passage of years and accompanying historical change (Thompson 1946).

The folktale is an important constituent of folklore. It is one of the principal forms of entertainment and education for a large portion of the world's inhabitants. Characterised by improbable background, folktales usually emphasise a moral at the end of the story. In India millions of people narrate folktales for entertainment and aesthetic purposes. Folktales are orally transmitted from one generation to another; often, especially in recent times, this may also occur in written form. The folktales of different regions represent the thoughts, ideas, mental states, traditions, manners and customs and even wit and wisdom of the people of that region (Sahay 2004). Apart from their entertainment value, they provide an insight into the present and the past traditions and culture of that region from which they originate.

These days especially in city areas when children are much more interested in television and computer games, seldom do they flock round their grandparents to hear stories or riddles or humorous poems, yet for a large proportion of the population in India hearing and telling folktales is one of the principal forms of entertainment. Children are very fond of it. If some one tells them any story they tell that story to others and this way once being entertained by some one, they play the role of entertainer. When an elderly person tells story, young children think he is entertaining them. The story teller thinks children are close to him. Both the story teller and the listeners spend hours with such feelings and develop emotional relation as well as family feelings. If a story teller does not find any story to tell he/she narrates personal experiences in dramatic way. The effect of his/her gesture and voice makes children laugh or feel sorrow. Virtually in all societies, people experience the need to express their feelings and ideas in an artistic medium. Folktales just like other aspects of expressive culture reflect the feelings, needs, and conflicts that people acquire as a result of growing up in their culture (Ember and Ember 1993). Being moved by the artistry in folklore W. Bascon (1953) had termed it as Verbal Art.

The objects of folktales are panoramic: they may be romantic, imaginative, and humorous, based on local traditions, bizarre and even protest against injustice committed in the past (Sahay 2001). Each category of folktales is important for emotional and psychological health of the people.

The tribal society of India possesses a rich and vast variety of folkloric materials. Their folktales help in studying their way of life easily because their folktales reflect their ecological and cultural setting more faithfully. Their folktales bring solidarity, continuity and consistency in their cultural group. A sacred tale, for example told in justification of a ritual is of importance in that it systematises the belief of the community members and regulates their conduct. During festival occasions one can always hear some type of story. Whether it is *Karma, Sarhul* and *Sohrai* festivals of the tribes Munda, Oraon and Santhal or *Jhapa Puj, Gai- Goheri* and *Nawai ki Jatar* festivals of the tribes Bhil, Barela and Korku each festival has a story behind it. The festivals of tribal people are mostly connected with ancestor story. In their society legends are believed to be true and to contain important factual information. The study of folktales of any tribe gives us excellent nucleus of historical facts of that tribe. The present day social scientists fear that folktales which are essential oral literature will not be able to stand the onrush of the rapid changes we are in the midst of. Therefore, it is important to document the folktales in the published form as far as possible. The present book contains the folktales of six major Indian tribes namely Bhil, Barela, Korku, Munda, Oraon and Santal.

### The Rationale Behind Selection of Tribes

The Santal, the Bhil, and the Oraon form the three major tribal groups according to population. The Barela constitutes a mixed tribe of Bhil and non-tribal Rajput (upper caste Hindu) population. The Munda tribe has its origin in the south-east Asia according to Genetic Drift theory. The Korku tribesmen claim to have originated from the Naga tribe of the Mahabharata period. However, they worship Ravana the enemy of mythological character Rama of the Ramayana period. It may be possible that they belong to the Ramayana period. In a nutshell the six tribes constitute an important segment of tribal population of India hence, it was anticipated that the study of the folktales of these six tribes would represent the folk life not only of the bulk population of the tribal people but the multiplicity of their folk culture as well.

## Studies on Tribal Folktales

Folktales of Indian tribes were first published in the journal of Royal Asiatic Society of Bengal, which was established in 1774. During those periods the number of researchers interested in the studies of folklore or folktales was very small. This study got momentum in 1886 when Indian Antiquary after its establishment started encouraging and supporting the scholars economically for collection of folkloric materials. A few researchers published their work in local languages such as Bengali, Marathi, Hindi, Maithili, Tamil, Rajasthani, Telgu and Kannada. Later on many journals such as Mythic Society, Bangalore; Man in India, Ranchi; Journal of Bihar and Orissa, Patna devoted their volumes to folklore. With this beginning, a tradition of folkloric studies was initiated and the researchers started collecting folk songs and folktales of different tribes in different parts of India. The establishment of Indian Folklore Association in 1957 further helped the researcher in publishing their work in its journal Folklore.

On summarising the work done for the collection of the tribal folktales in India we find some of the initial studies on this subject of different tribes such as Manipuri Tales (Damat 1857, 1877), Lushai Tales (Hougton 1893, Anderson 1895), Kashi (Rafy 1920, Narayan 1942), Naga (Goswami 1949, 1955), Garo (Elwin 1958, Ranganathan 1960, Kabiraj 1962) and Bodo (Brahma 1960) were collected from the north eastern region of India.

The folk songs and folktales of Garhwal (Gariola 1926, Bhandari 1946, Bhatt 1962, Babulkar 1964), Gaddi (Majumdar 1950, Satyarthi 1953), Kamra (Kedarnath 1958), Kumau (Pandey 1962) and Tharu (Srivastava 1949a, 1949b,, 1958) were collected from northern part of India.

The folkloric materials of Munda (Roy 1916, Hoffman 1937, Parkin 1992), Birhor (Mitra 1922, 1928), Santhal (Cole 1875, Campbell 1891, 1916; Bompass 1909, Bodding 1925, Archer 1943, Patnaik 2002), and Oraon (Hohan and Archer 1934, 1937; Elwin 1954, Dutta Gupta 1929; Adrashi 1960; Dash 1964, Dhan 1972), Lodha (Bhowmik 1957) were collected from eastern part of central India.

From the western Madhya Pradesh folkloric materials of tribes like Gond and Baiga (Elwin 1944), Bhil (Venkatachar 1933, Avari 1957, Kopper and Jungblut 1976, Sahay 2000, 2010), Bhil, Barela and Korku ( Lourdusamy and Sahay 2003, 2004), Muria and Ojha (Archer 1943, Grifth 1944, Dube 1947, Satyarthi 1951, Shekhgulab 1964, Fuchus 1960) were collected.

The folklores of the tribes of Jharkhand (then Bihar) were also collected by eminent scholars (Mishra 1956, Trigunayat 1957, Edm and Toppo 1959, Vidyarthi 1963, Sahay 2001, 2005). The folklore of the tribes Toda and Kota (Emaneeru 1965, Smith 1946), Chenchu (Reddy 1948), Korgas (Venkatraman 1956), and Savara (Raman Rao 1956) were collected from south India.

This is to be pointed out that the folklore collected by early authors included all the aspects of folklore where folktales formed only one segment. The major part of the published material is not available now. Moreover, the tribes have such a rich store house of folktales that the previous studies were not exhaustive enough to do justice to the work of compilation of tribal folktales.

## The Present Book

Though the phase of collection of folktales of Indian tribes has been continuing for many years, analytical researches in this field have been attempted by a few scholars only recently and are scarce. The earlier scholars, who pioneered the study of folktales in all the Indian languages of this subcontinent, have more or less performed the jobs of collector (Islam 1985). The folktales demand a thorough assessment then only they can help in understanding the culture of the tribe they belong to. Therefore, it was felt necessary to present the folktales with analytical remarks in the form of a brief critique at the end of each tale as far as possible.

The subject is by its nature of great importance to all serious students of literature, anthropology, psychology, and art in general. It is of interest to all those readers who like to bring enjoyment to their leisure time through reading story books. The technical terms from anthropology, psychology, biology and other disciplines of arts have been presented with their meanings at the end of the book to enable common readers to understand the matter. In the present book the presentation of folktales of six tribes enables delineation of the cultural characteristics of the tribes on a comparative basis.

The present book differs from the books written in past on the folktales because it present folktales in the perspective of tribal culture and life. The book attempts to examine structural forms of the folktales. Serious attention has also been paid to understand the motif behind each folktale.

## Locale of the Study

The folktales were collected mainly from Jhabua and Khandwa region in Madhya Pradesh and Ranchi in Jharkhand.

### Jhabua

Jhabua is the western most district in Madhya Pradesh state in central India. It is a predominantly tribal district and suffers from high rates of illiteracy and poverty. According to the 2011 Indian Census report almost half of the population in the tribal region lives below the poverty line (Indian standard income less than Rs. 11001 per annum). The tribes like the Bhil, the Bhilala, and the Patelia inhabit the interior of the district and contribute more than 84 per cent of the total population there. The Bhil men have since long adorned the *Teer-Kaman* (bow and arrow), which has been their symbol of chivalry and self defence. Religious practices of tribe men have been influenced by the Hinduism and Christianity; however, belief in shamanism and witchcraft also dominates. The Bhil tribesmen of one village may differ from the tribesmen of another village because of the degree of influence by the dominant neighbouring culture yet one thing is common among them: They all are similar in terms of holding their traditional beliefs and practices.

### Khandwa

Khandwa is a town in the Nimad region of Madhya Pradesh in India. Khandwa is famous for its local crops of cotton, wheat, soyabean and a variety of seasonal fruits and vegetables. Khandwa is also credited for inventing coloured cotton in late 90s. The name of the city is derived from *Khandav van* which literally means Khandav Forest.

According to the Ministry of Panchayati Raj (2006) Khandwa is one of the most backward districts in India, which is currently receiving funds from the Backward Regions Grant Fund Programme (BRGF). As per Indian Census report, the population of Khandwa is 1, 309, 443 and its literacy rate is 67.53 per cent.

### Ranchi

Ranchi is located centrally in the mineralized belt of the Chotanagpur plateau, Jharkhand state in India. Starting its journey from a small tribal town in 1834, mainly due to the efforts of Captain Wilkinson, the first agent to the Governor General, and followed by the establishment of an administrative Cathedral and business centre, Ranchi is today a rapidly growing industrial city (Vidyarthi 1969).

The local as well as the tribal migrant population from nearby areas, the non-tribal population from all parts of the country, the refugees from Pakistan and Burma (Myanmar) have all contributed to the present day composite socio-cultural configuration of the city, in which migrants have outnumbered the tribal population (Sahay 2002). As per 2011 Indian Census Report, Ranchi has population of 1,126,741. Males constitute 51.3 per cent of the population and female 48.7 per cent. It has an average literacy rate of 77.1 per cent, which is higher than the national average of 74.04 per cent.

### *The Rationale behind Selection of Locale*

Jhabua is a strong hold of the Bhil and the Barela tribes and majority of the Korku population is found in Khandwa. Both Jhabua and Khandwa are districts in Madhya Pradesh (India) with low literacy rate and are under developed. Ranchi on the other hand is the state capital of the tribal dominated Jharkhand province. Munda, Oraon and Santhal tribes are found in Jharkhand. Ranchi has a better than national average literacy rate presumably because of non-tribal migrant population. It was assumed that selection of these locations would be appropriate for data collection on these six tribes.

## Methodology

This study involved extensive field work to collect folktales of six different tribes in India. The folktales were collected with the help of trained Field Investigators of local areas. The participants were chosen randomly without paying serious attention to their age and gender. However, people belonging to both the sexes and of different age group participated in the study.

The stories told by them were recorded and later on written carefully. Some of the stories were also recorded at the time when the authorities concerned were reciting those during festival times. The stories collected from Bhil, Barela and Korku tribes have already been published in Hindi language by the author of the present book with a co-author. It was noticed at the time of collection of the stories of Munda, Oraon and Santhal tribes that they have adopted many popular stories of non-tribal people of Bihar as their own folktales. It was not possible to decide which story belonged originally to the tribal people. The narrations were recorded as told to the Field Investigators. All the narrations were in Hindi language, which were translated into English by the present author. Extensive use of books, journals, and periodicals was also made in this study.

## Organisation of Data

The entire study is presented in eight chapters including introduction. The introduction begins with a short note on folklore and its segment folktale. It is followed by a brief note on the studies conducted by different scholars on this subject in the past. How and where the folktales were collected is also given in the introduction. It also deals with the reason as to why the six tribes were considered for this study and how the present book is different from the other published works on the different tribes of India.

The second, third, fourth, fifth, sixth, and seventh chapters deal with the folktales of different tribes such as Bhil, Barela, Korku, Munda, Oraon and Santal with a brief introduction of each tribe in the beginning. A brief critique is presented at the end of each folktale as far as possible.

The chapter eight examines the structural forms of the folktales and attempts to understand the motif behind each folktale in detail.

# Folktales of Bhil

## BHIL: AN INTRODUCTION

Bhil, the third largest tribal group in India inhabit in the western part of the country particularly in the northern Gujarat, southern Rajasthan, and northern Maharashtra. They also reside in Madhya Pradesh, Chhattisgarh and in Tripura (Shukla 1986). Their language is Bhili, an Indo-Aryan language. However, they also speak the language of the region they reside in such as Gujarati, Marathi, Gujarati, and Hindi. The word Bhil is derived from the Sanskrit word *billi* which means bow. The bow is the weapon of the tribesmen, and the men usually carry their bows and arrows with them.

Bhil tribesmen possess a unique style of self-representation. Myths collected by various scholars (Bannerman 1902; Crooke 1909; Venkatachar 1933; Kopper and Jungblut 1976) as well as written in *Puran* (Vishnupuran 1990) explore the origins of the tribe that include stories of wicked deeds, incestuous unions, foolish acts and misfortunes. The most popular myth of the origin of Bhil tribe narrates that the first man and the woman of the present day human race were brother and sister. During *jal-pralay* (cataclysm) only two of them managed to survive with the help of a fish named *Rohit*. God told them to repopulate the world and they married. They had seven sons and seven daughters. God presented a horse to first-born son and asked him to rule the world. Being unable to ride the horse the son abandoned that and went to forest. He and his sons became foresters and started Bhil tribe. The second popular myth explains that one day god *Bhairo Dev* gave his favourite bull named *Vrishbha* to one of his sons and asked him to plough the earth. Instead of obeying his father, the son killed the bull and ate that. Angry *BhairoDev* dispelled his son to the dense forest. While living in forest the son married a forest woman. The descendents of that son became the Bhil tribesmen. It seems that the first myth is influenced by the myth of Hindus of India but the second myth is independent from any influence.

The Bhil tribespersons are found mentioned in the famous Indian epics like Ramayana and Mahabharata. The popular Bhil figure in Ramayana is Sabri, who offered half-eaten berry fruits to Rama and Lakshmana when they were searching for Sita in the forest. Matanga was a Bhil sage who became a Brahmin. In the Mahabharata there is a popular story of Ekalavya, a Bhil boy who devel̆oped his archery skill as equal to that of Arjuna, and Drona asked for his right hand thumb in *Guru-Dakshina* (the fee paid by the disciple to his preceptor at the conclusion of his studies).

Over the years, a caste, which was considered above them named the Rajputs (Hindu) as well as Muslims, influenced the Bhil tribesmen yet they had been able to retain their own distinct customary ways of living and rituals (Mann 1978; Nath 1960; Tod 1920; Vidyarthi and Rai 1985; Vyas, et al. 1978). In feudal and colonial times, many Bhil tribesmen were employed by the ruling Rajput Kings because of their knowledge of the terrain. Many had even become warriors in their armies. They were expert in *gorilla* war fare, which the Mughal Empire had so much trouble handling.

Until the 19th century, Bhil tribesmen practised a shifting cultivation. With the advent of British rule in India, they were forced to settle down and are now settled cultivators (Ghurye 1973). The lands of the Bhil are mainly unproductive barren slopes. Cultivated year after year they are so eroded that production is minimal. The bulk of the population can barely meet the minimum necessities of life from the agrarian income available to them. Both government and NGO groups are aware that the Bhil tribesmen face economic crisis but disagree on a solution.

## THE DAMORS

(The Damors constitute one of the important clans of the Bhil tribe)

The people of Damor clan say that many years ago, one day all of a sudden, numerous oyster shells appeared on the water surface of a sea. Those oyster shells started growing in size and within ten months of time obtained the size of big earthen pots. Finally those shells burst out and hundred and twenty five dark coloured males belonging to Damor clan came out and after some time they were followed by their wives. The couples started living happily in the sea.

One day Jahma Mata (goddess of water) told them, "Go and live in the place where your forefathers were living There is no place for human beings in the water." The Damors with their belonging moved towards Godra (a place near Gujarat). On the way they met a Pathan who was coming from Godra.

"Who are you? Where are you going?" The Pathan asked the Damors.

"Oh! We are in search of that place where our forefathers used to live." The Damors replied.

"Give me some *charas* (an intoxicating drug prepared from the flowers of hemp) to smoke." The Pathan requested.

"We don't have any." The Damors replied and moved from there.

The goddess Sawan Mata was watching the activities of all the Damors. She came to them and asked, "Who are you? Where are you going?"

All the Damors introduced themselves to Sawan Mata one by one and asked, "Mother! Please tell us where is our land? Where did our forefathers live?"

Sawan Mata replied, "Your forefathers used to live across the sea. The land of that place was white in colour. Even the rats and the crows of your place were white."

All the Damors singing songs moved from there in search of white land which they could not find and reached a place which was under the control of Dholka (chieftain of a village). They erected their tents there and started living peacefully. One day they found lots of iron-rods which they sold and became rich. One night a female Damor dreamt about a musical instrument. In the morning she told about the dream to her husband. The husband Damor called his five friends and taking an axe they all climbed on a small mountain. There was a tree of teak on that mountain. The husband Damor with the help of his friends cut the tree into three pieces. They made a *dhol* (a large drum), from the lower part of the tree, a *mandal* (a kind of drum) from the middle part, and a *damru* (a small musical instrument narrow in the middle and wider at the ends) from the upper part. Now they were in need of animal-skin to cover their *dhol*, *mandal*, and *damru*.

The husband Damor said, "Let us go to settlement of *chamars* (cobblers). From there we will take leather and will give final touches to our musical instruments". Singing songs, laughing, and joking they all moved towards the *basti* of *chamars* (settlement of cobblers).

"We want to cover our musical instruments with animal-skin, give us some", they requested the cobblers. When the cobblers refused to oblige them they went to grazing ground where the cattle of cobblers were grazing.

The husband Damor said, "The cobblers have not given us the animal-skin to cover our musical instruments. We will teach them a lesson. We will make their animals sick." Using their magical powers the Damors made the animals sick. When the cobblers found their cattle sick they became nervous. The wife of one the cobblers, was very clever. She understood the reason for sickness of their cattle. She said, "Since you people had refused to give skin of dead animal to the Damors, they have made our cattle sick." She suggested to her husband to give the animal-skin to the Damors for the welfare of the cattle. After calling back Damors the cobblers gave leather to them. The Damors made their cattle normal. They covered their musical instruments with leather and returned home. Other Damors gave warm welcome to them on their achievements.

The Bada Damor (eldest Damor among them) said to others, "At the time of need one will play the *dhol*, hearing the sound of which every one should come near the person and should help him." One day the wife of Bada Damor wanted to eat pork. She told her husband that last night she had seen a pig in her dream. The Bada Damor understood the desire of his wife. He played the *dhol* and other Damors came near him.

"Why did you play the *dhol*?" They all asked the Bada Damor.

"Your *Bhabhi* (sister-in-law) wants to eat pork." The Bada Damor replied.

"All right! Any five Damors among us will help you in hunting the pig." All the Damors said to the Bada Damor.

Taking bow and arrows made of bamboo as well as some bread and water with them six Damors got ready to go with the Bada Damor who was ready with his gun. They all proceeded towards a forest. Their children followed them. When they reached near the forest they saw an old woman carrying a bundle of dry wood over her head.

"You can not hunt any prey in this jungle, because no animal resides here. It would be better if you go to some other place," the old woman told them.

On the advice of that old woman they did not enter the jungle and climbed on a hillock. There were numerous partridges on that hillock. In the middle of that hillock there was a tree of *Palash* (butea frondosa). The partridges had made their nests on that tree.

"Go and hang the bundles of bread and pots of water from that tree". The Damors told their children. The Damors applied many tricks but could not capture any partridge there. They decided to kill rabbits and went to the area where rabbits were in plenty. There also they could not succeed in their endeavour. Sad and tired Damors moved towards the land of does. There they found only one doe grazing in the field. They did not kill that doe and proceeded towards the nearby jungle. They found that jungle suitable for hunting pigs. In the jungle they reached near a gum tree.

"Go and hide behind the gum tree. We are going to drive away the herd of pigs. When the herd will cross from here kill any one with your gun", other Damors told Bada Damor. Bada Damor agreed for this and leaving Bada Damor there they all went to drive the pigs. Bada Damor was addicted to consumption of opium and had forgotten to bring that with him. When the other Damors went to drive the pigs, Bada Damor leaving his gun on the ground, climbed on the tree and started eating gum for relief. He did not notice the herd of pigs crossing from there because he was busy eating gum. By chance one of the pigs hit the piece of a stone which hit the trigger of the gun.

"Tha"!! The gun made the noise. When the other Damors, who were driving the pigs, heard the firing of the gun they thought that Bada Damor might have killed the pig. They all came to him. Seeing them Bada Damor told a lie, "I fired on the pigs but missed the target." They all decided to give another chance to Bada Damor to kill the pig. They all came near a *temru* (a kind of fruit) tree and leaving Bada Damor near the tree they all went to drive the pigs again. This time, too, Bada Damor did not kill any pig and remained busy eating the fruit.

All the Damors were hungry and thirsty. They went near the tree where they had hung their bread and water. They found that crows had eaten the bread and squirrels had drunk all the water. They all were thirsty. Following a heron they reached near a lake. They erected their tents near the lake and started taking rest.

"When thirsty animals will come here to drink water we will kill any one", Bada Damor told others. While they were taking rest the daughters of Megh Raja (the king of clouds) came there to fetch water.

"Fill your pots without making noise otherwise animals will run away from here", the Damors told the girls. But the girls did not listen to Damors. They took bath there laughing, joking, and making noise. After taking bath they put their wet clothes on the tent of the Damors to dry. After fetching water they all left the place but forgot to collect their wet clothes. The Damors waited long but no animal came to drink water.

"It seems that due to noise made by the girls the animal sensed the danger and did not come here to drink water", Bada Damor said. They all were angry with the girls. On the midway the girls recalled that they had forgotten their clothes near the lake. They all returned to take their clothes. Angry Damors were waiting for them. They misbehaved with the girls and refused to give clothes to them. The girls returned home crying and narrated the incidents to their mother. Angry mother went to Megh Raja and told him what had happened with their daughters.

Megh Raja called his brothers and sisters and asked them to get ready to attack the Damors. Megh Raja had twelve brothers and thirteen sisters. When they all got ready to attack the Damors it started thundering and lightening. They were going to attack the Damors aggressively. They saw an old woman who was collecting cow dung cakes.

Megh Raja said, "Mother! Please go home. It is not safe to stay here because we are going to attack the Damors."

The old woman said to them, "if any one of you dies in this attack the draught will come in one part of the earth and if all of you get killed then the earth would be dry forever. Damors are very brave and wealthy. They have lots of weapon. So in order to punish Damors use your brain and not your power."

Megh Raja agreed with that old woman and sent a message to Damors to face twelve years of drought as punishment for their misdeeds.

"Only twelve years for punishment? Why not for twenty four years? We will not suffer. Even one quarter of our grains will not be finished", the Bada Damor, twisting his big moustache, said proudly. However, within two years of drought they all started starving and went to their in-law's house for help. The in-laws of the Damors were not in a position to help them because they, too, were facing the same situation. Frustrated Damors returned home.

At last they all went to Narsingh Yodha who was the relative of one of the Damors. Narsingh Yodha said, "You all can live here as long as you wish. I have lots of edible with me." All the Damors started living there peacefully. Megh Raja was keeping an eye on every movement of the Damors. When he came to know about the new habitant of the Damors he used his magical power and Narsingh Yodha, too, lost every thing. The Damors started eating Mahua (fruits of bassia latifolia) and abusing Narsingh Yodha who had promised them to feed for ever.

"What can I do? I, too, have lost every thing. My status has become the same like yours", Narsingh Yodha said.

The Damors wanted to return to their home but had lost the way. On the way they asked a person, "Do you know where we were living. Can you please help us in searching our land?" The person had no idea about the land of the Damors. Seeing the black farmers he thought they were from Karnataka (one of the south Indian states). He advised them to move towards the south India. The Damors were not ready to move towards the south and continued wandering here and there. They all reached Dahod (Madhya Pradesh) and in a remote place erecting their tents started living there.

One day one pregnant woman among their group wanted to eat curd. Narsingh Yodha and his friend Halun Sorya said, "No problem. We will bring milk. Not only the milk, we will bring the milk giving animals as well." Both of them reached the place where Lapa, the milkman was grazing his cattle. Narsingh Yodha and Halun Sorya played a trick with Lapa and sent him to a far away pond for fishing. When Lapa left the place both of them ran away with the cattle of Lapa. Seeing the cattle all the Damors became very happy. They enjoyed the milk of buffaloes for twelve years. After twelve years, one of the buffaloes stopped giving milk.

"Look! This buffalo does not give milk. Let us kill it and enjoy the beef", one of the women among the group of Damors said. All the Damors agreed with the decision. However, Nava Damor was not happy with the idea of killing the buffalo; he kept mum. Narsingh Yodha went to jungle with his friends to kill the buffalo. As soon as they wanted to kill the buffalo she started crying and entered into the earth. Narsingh Yodha became a leaper because of his misdeeds.

Seeing the sufferings of Narsingh Yodha the wife of Nava Damor said to him, "you are suffering due to your misdeeds. For atonement you will have to visit seventy eight religious places, failing which you will die."

Nava Damors and his friends decided to leave Dahod and settle anywhere in Malwa (Madhya Pradesh). In Malwa when Nava Damor and his friends were roaming in search of job they came in contact with the Patel (the village official who maintains land record) of that region.

"Who are you and why have you come here?" The Patel asked them.

"We have come here in search of job", Nava Damor replied.

"Can you harvest my gram fields?" Patel asked.

"Why not? We are ready to harvest your field but we are hungry. We will eat the grams while harvesting", the Damors said.

"All right you can eat the grams", the Patel agreed.

Nava Damor with his friends started harvesting the field. They ate all the grams and kept the dry branches, leaves, and skins of grams in the godown. When the Patel saw this he started crying.

"Oh!! Do not cry. We were hungry so we ate all the grams. However, next time we will not repeat the same mistake. We will work hard and your profit would be double", Nava Damor said to Patel.

The Damors started ploughing the field. They worked hard but unfortunately the land had become barren and not even a single plant grew in the field.

"It seems some one has done black magic in the field. Call the *Barwa* (shaman)", the Patel said to Nava Damor.

"I am the grandson of a Barwa. I can find out the reason of infertility of your field", Nava Damor replied to Patel.

After worshipping and chanting some *mantras* Nava Damor said, "The land became infertile because we ate new crops before worshipping our gods and sacrificing animals near the field. This time we will harvest after tying clothes in our mouths. After harvesting we will worship the gods and sacrifice five cocks and one goat near the fields".

The field yielded good crop and the Damors filled the godown with grams. Happy Patel gave one goat and five cocks to them. The Damors sacrificed the animals in the name of various god and goddesses and enjoyed the meat with their family members.

In search of new job they all proceeded towards the city of Dhar (Madhya Pradesh). The king of Dhar saw them; he wanted to know who were they and why had they come to his city. He sent his *mantari* (minister) Duda to inquire about them.

"Who are you? Why have you come here?" Duda asked them.

"We have come here in search of job", Nava Damor replied.

"Our king will give you land to plough and home to live", Duda gave assurance to them.

Before taking the decision to settle there, they all wanted to know whether that place was auspicious for them or not. Nava Damor closed his eyes and chanted some mantras and looking on the leaf of a tree said, "Rupela *titar* (partridge) is telling us to leave the place whereas the bird Rupila is telling us to stay here but with care." They all were in dilemma whether to stay there or not. Finally they all decided to stay there. Some of them started ploughing the field given to them by the king. A few took to the job of labourers. Khalun Damor became the watchman of the house of a businessman name Meegal Moti Seth.

One day all the Damors went to jungle. There they met a watchman named Sudiya who was in search of a job. Khalun Damor sent him to king to ask for a job.

The king asked the Sudiya, "What can you do?"

"I can eat twelve kilo rice and can waste six kilo", Sudiya replied proudly. The king kicked him out. Now the Damors sent the watchman Hudiya to the king.

The king repeated the same question, "What can you do?"

"Oh king! I can eat twelve kilo rice and can waste twenty four kilo". The king kicked him, too.

At last the Damors sent the queen of ants to the King.

"What can you do?" The king asked the queen.

"We can fill your godown with the grains", the queen of ants replied. The king made the ants the guard of his godown.

During rainy season the Damors wanted to perform *Bowni* (seeds sowing ceremony) in their field. They went to Meegal Moti Seth and said, "Give us some seeds of paddy and maize corns. We want to perform *Bowni* in our field." Meegal Moti Seth gave good quality seeds to them. Seeing the good crops of paddy and corn plants the Damors were very happy.

One day Heezmal Damor was guarding his field. He was tired and was very irritated with the behaviour of his oxen. At the same time god the Rama came to him and asked, "What have you sown in your field?"

"Penis", irritated Heezmal replied.

The god wanted to teach Heezmal a lesson. He turned the crops of the field in numerous penises. When Heezmal Damor saw penis every where in his field, he became nervous. However, he understood that the person who had asked question from him was not an ordinary man. He started crying in front of god and asked for forgiveness. Rama forgave him and made his field as it was earlier.

Heezmal was hungry. He cooked some maize corns in an earthen pot and made *daliya* (porridge). He put some porridge on the leaves of *Palash* (butea frondosa) as *naivedya* (oblation) in the name of gods and goddesses and satiated his hunger eating the remaining porridge. When Khalun Damor came to know that Heezmal Damor had eaten the new crops without worshipping the gods and goddesses properly he went to him and said, "You have not done right. First we will install the deities of Sawan Mata as well as Howan Mata and after worshipping those deities with our new crops we will take the new crops."

All the Damors installed the deities of Sawan Mata and Howan Mata under the tree of *Palash* (butea frondosa) and started worshipping the deities with their new crops. While worshipping, Nava Damor got the power of Sawan Mata. He predicted, "Live here carefully. Be prepared for the misfortune. Some one is going to behead all of you."

This prediction of Nava Damor made Khalun Damor angry. In anger he kicked Nava Damor and occupied the post of *Barwa* (shaman) forcefully. After some time he, too, got the power of Sawan Mata and predicted the same as the Nava Damor had predicted. After worshipping the deities with new crops, (the celebration is known as *Nawai ka Jatar* in their language), they started eating the crops. Meanwhile, the king of Dhar Satra Joshi came to know that the Damors had not paid tax of the land. He sent his minister Duda to collect the tax. Seeing Duda all the Damors ran away to a remote place. But Khalun Damor remained there. He said to Duda, "Do not worry. We will give the tax soon." Satra Joshi was not happy with the behaviour of the Damors.

During *Diwali* (festival of light) Meegal Moti Seth went to another city in connection with his business. In his absence Khalun Damor, the watch man of Seth's house, developed relationship with Veerma Sethani (the wife of Meegal Moti Seth), and she became pregnant. Khalun Damor returned to other Damors with Veerma. The Damors were not happy with the deeds of Khalun Damor but they gave shelter to both of them and accepted Veerma as their group-member. When Meegal Moti Seth returned from his business trip he complained to the king Satra Joshi about Khalun Damor and asked for justice.

The king Satra Joshi was already angry with the Damor because they had not paid tax to him. He attacked the Damors with his army and beheaded every one. Khalun Damor was also killed. The prediction made at the time of *Nawai ka Jatar* came true. Veerma Sethani flew away from there. Though all the Damors were killed, their progeny was safe in the womb of Veerma Sethani.

By examining this story we find:

1. A group of people of Damor clan, one of the important clans of the Bhil, came out from the sea and started searching for their land and homes.

Possibly they had escaped from flood and had lost every thing in that. Bhil tribesmen, too, agree with this possibility.

2. They suffered from drought for twelve years. Their imagination did personification of cloud. They say that they suffered because they made the Megh Raja (the cloud god) their enemy by misbehaving with his daughters. If they were able to contact the cloud why did they not try to please him and tried to come out from their sufferings? Did their ego come in between them and the cloud? Did they consider it better to suffer rather than to ask for forgiveness? Bhil people have no answer to these questions. They simply say that their forefathers were like that.
3. Whenever they got a chance they never hesitated in doing mischief; for example they fooled Lapa the milkman and stole his cattle. They ate all the grams of the Patel of the village and filled his godown with hey. If we inquire Bhil people laugh and say that they are like this. We think about quick gain and not about the long term consequences.
4. They had some supernatural power. They were able to make the cattle sick as well as cure them within a few minutes. How did they get this power? Why not they utilized their power for the welfare of the cattle? Bhil tribesmen have no idea about it all.
5. They influenced non-tribals with power through their shamanic knowledge. Many times their predictions came true. If they were able to see the future why did they not take proper steps to protect them? Bhil tribesmen say that even today they do not think much about their present day action.
6. They came in contact with non-tribal people while they were searching for their livelihoods. They got employed by non-tribal people in various capacities such as agricultural labourers and watchmen. They gained food and shelter from the non-tribal people but suffered as well for their misdeeds. At the end of this story many of them were killed by non-tribal people. Bhil tribesmen of today say that they have no bad feelings for the non-tribal people. Their forefathers suffered because they did wrong.
7. Narsingh Yodha became a leper and to get cured he was ready for the pilgrimage of 78 religious places. Going for the pilgrimage is not common among the tribal people. Perhaps this change in thinking was due to their relation with non-tribal people. Bhil tribesmen do not disagree with this possibility.
8. They welcomed their new crops and decided they would not eat that before offering the crops to their gods and goddesses in future. Bhil tribesmen guess that perhaps their suffering had made them god fearing and they did not want to take any risk.

Bhil tribesmen believe this story. They sing and tell this story to their younger generation while they celebrate any festival or during evening time when they remain free. This story reveals how they suffered due to natural calamity the drought and moved from one place to another place in search of food and livelihood. In this process they lost their occupied land and faced economic hardship.

## BHADA GARDAN (THE FEMALE VULTURE)

One day the sky was covered with black clouds and it was raining heavily. Bhada Gardan (a female vulture) came out from the black clouds and flew away on a mountain where a Bhil boy Duda Dutiya was playing with his catapult. When Dutiya saw the Bhada Gardan, he started hurling stones on her.

"Oh. This boy will not allow me to take rest here peacefully. It would be better if I go to some other place", Bhada Gardan thought. She flew to a cow shed where the cow named 'Rupan' was chewing the cud. Bhada Gardan pecked some insects there and reached near a pond to drink water. She quenched her thirst and sat on a tree.

Lapa the milk man and his wife Malka were grazing their cattle near the pond. Bhada Gardan also wanted to engage herself in some work. She went to her *Bhabhi* (elder brother's wife) Ratna Meghan and asked for some work. Ratna Meghan told her to find a life partner for her in a symbolic way. She used the word 'dry wood' instead of 'life partner'.

"My *Bhabhi* has given me some work to perform", Bhada Gardan was very happy. She went near a *babool* (the acacia) tree and after picking up a dry branch of that tree returned to Ratna Meghan.

"Thud". Bhada Gardan dropped the dry branch in the courtyard of the house making a loud noise. Ratna Meghan was taking rest at that time. Hearing loud sound she jumped out of her bed and running fast came in the courtyard. She saw Bhada Gardan was sitting on the dry branch and was very happy.

"Oye Nandi (husband's sister) what are you doing there?" Ratna Meghan asked the Bhada Gardan.

"*Bhabhi* (brother's wife), you had asked me to bring dry wood", Bhada Gardan whimpered.

"*Buddhu* (stupid), she did not understand my word and took every thing literally", Ratna Meghan uttered smilingly.

"Go and search a male vulture for yourself", this time Ratna Meghan told Bhada Gardan clearly.

Bhada Gardan flew away to the mountain where her brothers Khokha and Kassumar Dev were residing. She learned the magic of making the animals sick from her brothers. After that she came to a field where cattle were grazing. She made the cattle sick. Many of them died and a number of vultures started hovering there to eat the flesh of dead animals.

"When they come down, I will capture any one of the male vultures", Bhada Gardan thought. After some time many vultures came down to earth and flew away after eating the flesh but Bhada Gardan did not succeed in capturing any one. She was about to return from there, but suddenly saw that one old male vulture was still eating the flesh. She overpowered that male vulture but found that he was half blind and half deaf.

"Why did you capture me?" The male vulture asked Bhada Gardan.

"I am accepting you as my husband", she replied smilingly.

The vulture couple flew to a banyan tree and made their shelter there. In the morning Bhada Gardan went to an ant hill. In that ant hill a snake was living. The snake wanted to come out but due to fear of Bhada Gardan he was not doing so.

"I want to come out. Will you capture me?" The snake asked innocently the Bhada Gardan.

"Absolutely not", Bhada Gardan replied wickedly.

"Come out without any fear", she said further.

When the snake came out Bhada Gardan killed him and cut into three pieces. She returned to banyan tree and started cooking the pieces of snake in an earthen pot. When half of the cooking was over Bhada Gardan told the male vulture, "I am going to fetch fresh water. In my absence do not see what is cooking in the pot."

The male vulture did not listen what Bhada Gardan had said and peeped into the pot to see what was cooking on. When Bhada Gardan returned she asked the male vulture, "Have you looked into the pot?"

"No", the male vulture told a lie.

After cooking the snake, Bhada Gardan added some magical power into the cooked food and gave that to male vulture to eat. When the male vulture finished eating she asked, "Tell me how long you can see and what can you see?"

"I am able to see the ants carrying eggs on the mountain and I am hearing the croaking of frogs living under the sea", the male vulture replied.

Bhada Gardan understood that her partner had gained power. She spent one night with the male vulture and flew away to a pond where the girls of Damor (Bhil) clan were fetching water. But, before leaving the tree she told the male vulture to build a watch-hut on the tree which was at a central place where the seven roads were meeting. Bhada Gardan was irritated when she found that the male vulture followed her within half an hour.

"Did you make the watch-hut?" Bhada Gardan asked the male vulture.

"Yes. I did", the male vulture replied.

Both of them flew towards the watch-hut. Seeing the watch-hut Bhada Gardan became angry.

"What rubbish you have made?" Bhada Gardan told in angry tone.

Offended male vulture left the place immediately.

"Uh. Get lost. I will make my watch-hut myself", Bhada Gardan uttered.

She went to a paddy field where a number of black farmers were ploughing their field. She took the form of an old woman and started eating *laddu* (an Indian sweet meat) sitting near the tree. The greedy farmers came near her and asked, "Mother. Who has given you the *laddu?*"

"The king Of Dhar Satra Joshi is distributing laddu to every one", the old woman (Bhada Gardan) replied rolling her eyes.

All the farmers, leaving their ploughs under the care of old woman (Bhada Gardan) went to city to take *laddu*. Bhada Gardan flew away with all the ploughs. She made a watch-hut with those ploughs on the banyan tree. After that taking some dust from her claw, she made bed-bugs and put those bugs into the bed of the king Gaihlot. In night when the king Gaihlot went to sleep, the bed-bugs did not allow him to have a sound sleep. In the morning he put his bed in the sun-light to dry up. Bhada Gardan flew away with the bed and put that on her watch-hut. She was happy and satisfied with her watch-hut.

She laid a chain of eggs on the watch-hut in the name of Ravan, Kalka Bhowani Mata, Howan Mata, Sawan Mata, Salar Mata, Lal Bai Mata, Phool Bai Mata and Puja Bai Mata. She started incubating those eggs sitting on them.

Nine months were over and the babies were not coming out of the eggs. Bhada Gardan took some dust from her claw and made an image similar to her. She said to that image, "Go to the settlement of Damors (Bhil tribesmen). Eat the vegetable of their garden. Eat the grains and curd kept in their kitchen. Gnaw the moustaches of the males and excrete in their hearth."

The image of Bhada Gardan did exactly as told to her and sitting on the roof of the hut of Heezmal Damor, started flapping her wing.

Makhna Damoran, the wife of Heezmal Damor woke up in the morning. She noticed the deeds of the image of Bhada Gardan and reported to her husband, "One bird has eaten every thing kept in the kitchen and has excreted in the hearth."

"A bird? Wow. The prey has come to me. I will kill that with my arrow", Heezmal Damor jumped happily. He wanted to twist his moustache but noticed that that was missing as well. He chased the bird in the forest but sensing danger returned home.

Bhada Gardan started shedding tears and flapping her wings.

After a few days she made a doe from the dirt of her claw and said to her, "Go to the settlement of Damors (Bhil tribesmen). Eat the vegetable of their garden. Eat the grains and curd kept in their kitchen. Gnaw the moustaches of the males and excrete in their hearth."

The doe followed the instruction given to her and ran away to jungle.

Makhna Damoran complained to her husband, "One animal bird has eaten every thing kept in the kitchen and has excreted in the hearth."

This time Heezmal Damor got angry. Taking his bow and arrow he went to jungle to kill the doe. But, the doe was not an ordinary doe; he disappeared. Heezmal Damor was thirsty and he was moving here and there in the jungle in search of water. He saw 'Nandiya' the heron on a banyan tree. If 'Nandiya' is there water must be there, Heezmal Damor thought and went to the tree. When he reached near the tree he saw that Bhada Gardan was crying and her tears had got collected making a pond.

"Why are you crying?" Heezmal Damor asked Bhada Gardan.

"I am not getting success in hatching my eggs and my babies are not coming out", Bhada Gardan replied.

"I am a powerful man. I will break the chain of your eggs with my bow and arrow", Heezmal Damor gave assurance to Bhada Gardan. However, he tried a lot but could not succeed in breaking the chain of eggs.

"You can not break the chain with arrow. Find out the way of hatching the eggs through your *barwaism* (shamanism). I will give you some more power so that you can break a watch-hut with one arrow, can kill frog under the sea water, and can pierce seven layers of wall with one arrow", Bhada Gardan told Heezmal Damor.

Heezmal Damor agreed for this. Taking some leaves in his hand he started chanting some *mantras* and said, "For hatching the eggs you will have to put a little bit of the heart of Doliya Pithora Dev on the burning perfumed saw dust".

Instead of the heart of Doliya Pithora Dev, Bhada Gardan put the heart-bit of a young buffalo on the burning perfumed saw dust and worshipped the god. The chain of eggs broke down and her babies came out. After the birth Ravan went to Lanka, and Kalka Bhowani Mata, Howan Mata, Sawan Mata, Salar Mata, Lal Bai Mata, Phool Bai Mata and Puja Bai Mata made the watch-hut crowded. Bhada Gardan was happy to see all of them.

In his story we find:

1. The cloud, the bird, and the human being understand the language of each other. It happens only in story.
2. The vulture was not an ordinary vulture. She had magical powers. She was able to take human form. She was powerful but she was not able to hatch her eggs. She was not even able to find out why her eggs were

not breaking. She called a man of Damor (Bhil) clan to find out the reason as to why her eggs were not breaking through his shamanic power. Does it mean that only the people of Damor clans had the knowledge of shamanism? Bhil tribesmen claim that in previous years only they had the knowledge of shamanism.

3. The vulture became the mother of Ravan (a human) and seven Bhowani Mata (goddesses). Bhil tribesmen do not believe in incarnation. They claim that no one can come to this earth without a mother and a father. God and goddess are no exception. They make any bird, animal, seed or fruit the parents of the god and goddess.

Bhil tribesmen sing this story as a song during celebration of any festival.

## HALUN SORYA

(Bhil tribesmen believe that Megh Raja (the king of clouds) is the *Mama* (mother's brother) of Halun Sorya, a folk-hero who belongs to Damor (Bhil) clan).

"Since long I have not gone to my *Mama's* (mother's brother's) house, Halun Sorya uttered silently. He decided to go to his Mama's house but it was not an easy task. There were a number of villages, mountains and rivers in between his and his *Mama*'s house. After making every arrangement he started his journey and after travelling a month reached his desired destination.

"Mami (wife of Mama)! Oye Mami! I am here. I am not seeing my Mama. Where is he?" Halun Sorya asked her Mami Ratna Meghan.

"Your Mama has gone to some other place and will return after a week", Ratna Meghan replied.

"You take rest. I am going to cook for you", Ratna Meghan said again.

Halun Sorya was a thief by his nature. While Ratna Meghan was cooking, Halun Sorya looked every where in the house and noticed many expensive things there. After cooking, Ratna Meghan served food to him in a gold bowl. Halun Sorya planed to steal every thing. After having the lunch Ratna Meghan slept.

"I have got a good chance to commit theft here", Halun Sorya thought. He took the ornaments of Ratna Meghan as well as the gold utensils and ran away from there. Since he had to travel a long distance he was running fast. He crossed villages, mountains, and rivers and finally reached the mountain where he was living. He hid all the stolen materials in the sediments of the mountain and started taking rest.

When Megh Raja returned he came to know about the theft in his house.

"Who had come here in my absence?" Megh Raja asked Ratna Meghan.

"Your nephew Halun Sorya had come here", Ratna Meghan replied.

"After the lunch I had kept the gold bowl here", Ratna Meghan said further.

Megh Raja told every one of his kingdom to search for the stolen goods. He called the *Barwa* (shaman) and asked him, "Find out who is the thief?"

The *Barwa* closed his eyes and after sometime said, "Your nephew Halun Sorya is the culprit."

Megh Raja with his brothers (they all were twelve in number) proceeded towards the home of Halun Sorya. They all crossed a number of villages, mountains and rivers and finally reached the house of Halun Sorya. When Halun Sorya saw all of them he turned into a small baby and started swinging in the cradle.

"Have you seen Halun Sorya? Is he here?" Megh Raja asked Halna, the sister of Halun Sorya.

"No". Halna replied.

"Who is in the cradle?" Megh Raja asked further.

"My son", Halna replied.

"You are not married. It is not your son", Megh Raja said. He understood that Halun Sorya is hiding himself. He started beating Halun Sorya with the tail of a monkey. Halun Sorya returned to his normal form and said, "Yes. I had stolen the goods from your house. I will return every thing but do not beat me any more."

"Mama I will take revenge from you for this beating", Halun Sorya decided.

"Will you steal any more?" Megh Raja asked him.

"No *Mama*. *Never*", Halun Sorya replied.

"I will become an expert thief. What can you do my *Mama?*" Halun Sorya uttered silently.

Halun Sorya returned every thing to Megh Raja and Megh Raja returned home.

One day Halun Sorya went to his mother and said, "Mother, find out whether the day is auspicious to start any new job or not?"

"Son today is a very good day to start any new job", the mother replied.

"Oh mother I am going for theft to Malwa (Madhya Pradesh)", Halun Sorya told his mother.

Halun Sorya crossing Rampur reached Pithampur (a place near Indore) but could not steal any thing there. Then he went to nearby city of Dhar. On the mountain of Dhar milkmen were cutting grass for their cattle. Halun Sorya cut a heap of grass and made a big bundle of grass.

"Keep this bundle on my head", Halun Sorya asked the milkmen.

All the milkmen could not lift the bundle. Halun Sorya put the bundle on his head by his own and started moving in the market of Dhar.

The cattle of king Gaihlot of Dhar were hungry. When the king saw the bundle of grass on the head of Halun Sorya he sent his minister to find out the price of the grass.

"What is the price of your grass? How many coins will you take for it?" Duda asked.

"For my grass I will take hundred thousand coins", Harun Sorya replied.

Duda reported about the price to his king.

The king said, "Duda, let us agree to give one hundred thousand coins to Halun Sorya. When he feeds grass to our cattle, we will send him to the horse named Kaliya Khet. That dangerous horse is locked in the room which has seven doors. Kaliya Khet will kill Harun Sorya and we will not have to pay one hundred thousand coins to him."

Duda went to Halun Sorya and said, "Our king is ready to give coins to you. Feed all the cattle first and then go to feed the horse Kaliya Khet."

Halun Sorya gave grass to every cow, horse, and donkey of the king. At last he went to give grass to Kaliya Khet. He unlocked seven doors one by one and reached near the Kaliya Khet. When he reached near the horse he recalled the enmity between the king and the people of Damor clan.

"Who has killed our ancestors?" Halun Sorya asked the Kaliya Khet.

"King Gaihlot", Kaliya Khet replied.

Halun Sorya gave him grass, patted on his back and returned to Duda. The process of opening and crossing the seven doors had made Halun Sorya sick.

"Keep a burnt coal on my stomach", Halun Sorya requested Duda. Duda did exactly that.

Halun Sorya went to the market. He searched the man who used to make keys.

"Build a key as big as the burnt mark on my stomach", Halun Sorya asked the key man. Taking the key he went to a blacksmith and took a shovel from there.

He started digging a tunnel by the shovel and reached near the room of Kaliya Khet. With the key he opened the door and ran away with the horse through the tunnel. In a hurry to reach home soon he was riding the horse very fast. When he reached near the garden of Megh Raja he recalled the incident of receiving substantial beating from the Megh Raja. He had decided to take revenge from the Megh Raja. He made the foot marks of Kaliya Khet in the garden and left the place immediately. He reached home safely.

"I have made our horse free from the clutches of our old enemy. Now the horse is with me", Halun Sorya said to his sister.

"I have brought one hundred thousand coins with me", he said to her mother.

He was happy. After taking food he slept peacefully.

Before analysing this story it would be better to make certain things clear. The forefathers of Bhil tribesmen suffered badly due to drought and famine. They considered the cloud, responsible for rain, their enemy. In their folk tales they did personification of the cloud and tried either to maintain relation with cloud or to teach that a lesson. In this story we find:

1. They made the cloud one of their relatives. Megh Raja (the cloud king or the god of cloud) was the maternal uncle of Halun Sorya, one of the legends of Bhil tribesmen. Who was the mother of Halun Sorya? They have no idea about it.
2. Why did Halun Sorya steal in his own maternal uncle's house? Bhil tribesmen say that out of jealousy he did so. They claim that even today a Bhil can not see more wealth than him, in his relative's or in his neighbour's house. Second thing they say is that Halun Sorya was a thief.
3. The king of Dhar took grass from Halun Sorya and instead of paying for that he wanted to kill him. Why? The Bhil tribesmen say that in previous years some times the non-tribal people used to exploit them. They also say that possibly Halun Sorya was asking excessive amount for the bundle of grass.
4. Kaliya Khet was the horse of Damor people. When did the king of Dhar capture that horse? Possibly when the army of the king killed the group of Damor living in Dhar (see the story The Damors). Bhil tribesmen, too, agree with this possibility.
5. Why did Halun Sorya want to take revenge from Megh Raja? He had stolen the goods of Megh Raja and in turn had received beating from his maternal uncle? Megh Raja had told him good things, 'not to steal again'. Bhil tribesmen say that they do not care about the reason and never forget their insult.

## DHARMI RAJA

(Bhil tribesmen believe that Dharmi Raja, their supreme god, is the god of cattle).

Dharmi Raja, the well wisher of cattle, is the son of Baba Dev and Kalka Rani. When Dharmi Raja reached the age of puberty, his parents called a Brahmin to find a bride for the son. The Brahmin selected Dholka Rani for Dharmi Raja.

After marriage, as a custom, bride's parents offered food to the newly wed couple. They refused to take food.

"Give me the cow Rupan, otherwise I am not going to eat anything", Dharmi Raja told the father of Dholka Rani. The bride's parents presented Rupan cow to them.

After having their meal, Dharmi Raja started his return journey home with his wife and the cow. On the way, Dharmi Raja came to know that the cow, named Rupan was not physically fit. She was a lame cow.

"Why did you not tell me that the cow is lame? You were living with this cow in your parents' house. You must be aware of the fact", he became angry and scolded his wife for accepting the lame cow.

Not only this, he refused to take that lame cow with him and said to his wife, "If you want to take the cow there is no need to follow me".

Helpless Dholka Rani was looking here and there and wondering what to do. She saw an anthill where Wasing Cobra (Snake God) was lying. She asked the Cobra what to do with that lame cow.

"Pour a few drops of blood of little finger of your right hand on the stone near you", Wasing Cobra advised her.

After cutting the little finger of her right hand, Dholka Rani poured a few drops of blood on the stone. Suddenly the stone, on which the blood was poured, turned to one side and a big ditch was created. Dholka Rani, after pushing that lame cow into the ditch, followed her husband.

One night Dharmi Raja dreamt that someone was telling him to pour some blood from the little finger of his right hand on the same place and stone which Dholka Rani had doused earlier. He was told that by doing so he would get twelve hundred cattle. Dharmi Raja had to lead the cattle holding a red flag. Furthermore, he was warned by that man not to look back.

When Dharmi Raja followed his dream, cattle started coming out one by one from that ditch. Dharmi Raja started running fast leading those cattle. In this process, some of the cattle stepped on the body of Dharmi Raja, thus hurting him badly. In agony he wanted to know how many cattle were still coming, hence he looked back. The flow of the cattle coming out of that ditch stopped. Dharmi Raja found one bull was left in the ditch.

Thus, it is believed by the Bhil tribesmen that owing to that very act, the number of bulls is less than cows, even today.

By examining the myth we find:

1. It is father's responsibility to select a bride for his son. In the society of Bhil, the youths have the freedom to select life partners of their own choice. However, shouldering the responsibility of selecting bride for their son is equally common among the parents of the tribe. For selecting a girl the father of the son sends an intermediary known as *bhanzgerio* and not a Brahmin. How and when a Brahmin actually crept into their mythological story Bhil people are yet to explain.

2. Dharmi Raja ordered his wife not to follow him and threatened to abandon her in the forest. This speaks of the helplessness of a bride else she should always obey her husband.
3. Dholka Rani might know about the super power of the Rupan cow, because both of them were living in the same house, yet she was not able to convince her husband and became ready to leave the cow only for the sake of happiness of Dharmi Raja. This shows wifely devotion and respect for the tradition.
4. In Bhil society, the bride's father takes bride price and gives any thing of his own desire to the couple. There is no provision for asking for any gift by the groom. Here Dharmi Raja makes demands for a gift. This shows the influence of dominant non-tribal culture where dowry system is prevalent, in their mythological story.
5. If the gift is not able to satisfy a husband, he can abandon his wife. He takes revenge from his wife and not from the in-laws who present the gift. This again shows the helplessness of a wife.
6. Dharmi Raja who is responsible for the welfare of cattle banished a cow, so sacred one in the Bhil society only because she was a lame. Why did he do so? Bhil people are not able to answer. Possibly only after this incidence (receiving numerous cattle from a lame cow), he became the well-wisher of the cattle, Bhil tribesmen keep guessing.
7. Why the cow that Dharmi Raja neglected provided so many cattle to him?

   Possibly to give a lesson to him not to neglect any cow, because even a lame cow can produce so many cattle or wealth. Possibly to please Dharmi Raja for the welfare of Dholka Rani, after all both of them were reared in the same house. Possibly to show her power to Dharmi Raja. Bhil people again keep on guessing like this.
8. How can a cow remain alive in a ditch and produce so many cattle. Bhil people believe 'God is almighty and He can do miracle'.
9. No punishment for Dharmi Raja for his cruel behaviour, instead a reward. Bhil tribesmen are not able to justify.

Despite many 'whys' and 'hows' Bhil people do believe in this story and celebrate *'Gai-Goheri'*, as part of *Deewali* (festival of lights) celebration imitating the act of Dharmi Raja with full faith as well as devotion. During celebration the Bhil tribesmen in religious mood prostrate before the hundreds of running cattle and get seriously hurt. They think their action will increase the number of their cattle.

## ANNA RAJA (THE GOD OF GRAINS)

Once all the gods and goddesses gathered in the house of the supreme god, the Dharmi Raja. Dharmi Raja welcomed all of them but gave more importance to the god Anna Raja (the god of grains). He offered him a seat which was made up of gold, whereas other gods and goddesses sat on ordinary seats.

When the gods and goddesses noticed this difference they started talking with each others. One of them said, "Dharmi Raja has made Anna Raja sit on the chair which is made up of gold. Why did he do so? We are not less than Anna Raja in any way".

Anna Raja said, "Yes, you all are true. We all are equal. May be Dharmi Raja will offer the gold-seat to any one of you next time. May be today is my day."

However, all of them did not agree with the explanation given by Anna Raja. They abused Anna Raja with some bad words such as sycophant and flunkey.

Offended Anna Raja left the heaven and started living in a secret place. The absence of Anna Raja created havoc. People on earth started starving and facing scarcity of grains. This situation made all the gods and goddesses perturbed. They all went to Dharmi Raja and requested him to do something to come out of this situation. Dharmi Raja asked them to search for the displeased Anna Raja and to persuade him to return.

All of them told a crow, "Go and search whereabout of Anna Raja."

The crow flew away in search of Anna Raja and after travelling to lots of places reached Mumbai (Maharashtra, India). He saw some light was coming from a house of the settlement of Harizans (low caste people).

"In the atmosphere of gloominess it is dark and silent every where. People are starving. But I see light in that house and hear some sound as well. I should find out the reason", the crow thought.

The crow sat on a tree nearby the house. He found that family members of that house were eating food. The crow understood that Anna Raja was hidden in that house. When the family members finished eating the woman of the house threw the leaf made plates out. The crow pecked some grains which were left on the plates.

"Why should I tell others about the whereabout of the Anna Raja? I will come here daily to eat and will go back. This way I will make sure of my own food. Let the world starve. It is not my problem", the crow thought.

He flew to heaven. Dharmi Raja and the other gods and the goddesses were waiting for him.

"Did you find whereabout of Anna Raja?" Dharmi Raja asked the crow.

"No, I did not", the crow replied.

"You are telling a lie. There is still one grain stuck on your beak", Dharmi Raja said.

The crow told them whereabout of Anna Raja.

"Mahadeva, the Sun, and the Moon will go to the house of that Harizan. They will please the Anna Raja and will bring back him to heaven", Dharmi Raja said.

The three gods, The Mahadeva, the Sun, and the Moon reached the door of that Harizan's house where the Anna Raja was hiding. At that time except the daughter of the Harizan no one was present in the house. The daughter of the house was booming in the courtyard of the house. When she saw the three persons were standing at the door she covered her face with the part of her *sari* and be seated them on a cot. She offered them water to drink.

"I am a girl of untouchable caste. How can I cook for you? I am giving you utensils, you people cook your food yourself", the girl said to them.

"When the colour of blood of all of us is same, how can you say that you are an untouchable? Cook the food, we are sitting here", the Mahadeva said to that girl.

While cooking that girl wanted to urinate and excrete. She felt ashamed in going out to the bushes for this purpose because she had three guests sitting at the door. She urinated excreted in an earthen pot and covered the opening of that pot with a cloth. She put that pot in one corner of the room. After taking bath she finished cooking and offered foods to the three gods. While eating the food, Mahadeva looked at pot which was covered with a cloth.

"What have you kept in that pot?" Mahadeva asked from the girl.

"I want to eat the things kept in the pot", Mahadeva said.

"Oh, what should I do now? How can I save my face? Oh, god please help me", the girl started thinking like this.

When Mahadeva asked again and again to show what was there in the pot the girl removed the cloth.

She was surprised to find that instead of urine and excreta there were radish, onion and the leaves of coriander in the pot.

All the gods ate well. After that they went to the Anna Raja who was in the store room of that house. Anna Raja was sitting there in a sulky mood. The three gods requested the Anna Raja for the welfare of the earth. They all went back to Dharmi Raja. Dharmi Raja gave a warm welcome to the Anna Raja. When Anna Raja returned to his place all became very happy. People started dancing with joy.

Bhil tribesmen believe that human beings, the Sun, and the Moon eat Anna Raja but in turn do not give any thing to him. Due to this human beings suffer from many diseases and the Sun and the Moon face eclipse.

1. All the incidents of this story are the imagination of Bhil tribesmen.

When the forefathers of the Bhil tribesmen suffered from drought and famine, they thought some thing wrong had made the Anna Raja (the god of grains) angry and he had gone for hiding.

2. It was not possible for them to search the whereabout of Anna Raja, they took help of gods, goddesses, and the birds. Bhil tribesmen believe that a crow can search one grain easily in the heaps of dry grass.
3. Mahadev (lord Shiva), the Sun and the Moon (planets), and the human talk with each other. Bhil tribesmen believe that in previous years when the people were free from sin and crime gods, goddesses, and the planets used to roam on the earth.
4. An untouchable (person belonging to lower caste according to Hindu caste system) girl cooked food for Mahadev, the Sun, and the Moon. The caste system is not prevalent in the Bhil tribe. Who was that girl? The tribesmen are unable to clarify.
5. Through this story they also explain why human beings suffer from diseases, and the Sun, and the Moon from eclipse.
6. Bhil tribesmen never insult grains and do not step on that.

## THE COW NAMED RUPAN

(Bhil tribesmen believe that Dharmi Raja is their supreme god and the Rupan is a heavenly cow.)

Dharmi Raja was blessed with a son. The new born baby declared, "I will drink only the milk of the cow Rupan. I will starve, I will die but I will not take even the breast milk of my mother."

Three days were over and the baby had not drunk milk. Worried Dharmi Raja called Narsingh Yodha (a folk hero of Bhil tribesmen) and said, "Go and search for Rupan, the cow and call her here."

"Only Brahmin Guru can perform this task of searching and calling Rupan here. Others can not do so", Narsingh Yodha said.

Dharmi Raja called the Brahmin Guru and said, "Go and search for Rupan. Call the cow here; otherwise my starving son will die."

Riding on a horse the Brahmin Guru searched everywhere but could not succeed in finding the cow. At last he reached *Kajali Van* (the forest named Kajali). An old woman was collecting cow dung cakes near the forest.

"Son where are you going?" The old woman asked the Brahmin Guru.

"Mother, I am searching for the cow Rupan. The son of Dharmi Raja is starving but he is not drinking milk. It is his inflexible demand that he will drink only the milk of the cow Rupan otherwise he will die. I am going to search Rupan in this forest."

"If you will enter in this forest you and your horse will die. This forest is not safe for any living being", the old woman replied.

"What should I do now? Where should I go to search Rupan? It seems the son of Dharmi Raja will not survive", frustrated Brahmin Guru said.

Wasing Cobra (the king of snakes), sitting on an ant hill was listening to their conversation. He said to Brahmin Guru, "Come with me I will take you to the cow Rupan."

Brahmin Guru agreed to go with Wasing Cobra. The cobra removed a big stone, which had covered the opening of a big ditch. Both of them entered into the ditch. Brahmin Guru found that there was a big field in the ditch. The cow Rupan, along with other cows was grazing in the field and many people were milking them in big pots.

"Rani Rupan, please come with me. The son of Dharmi Raja is starving. He wants to drink your milk only", the Brahmin Guru requested the cow Rupan.

"Go to Dharmi Raja and tell that in the evening he should stand near the entrance of his palace, taking a burning *diya* (oil lamp), a handful of rice and a little vermilion in a bronze plate wait for me. I will come. When I will reach him, he should put a *tilak* (mark with vermilion) on my head, scatter some rice on me and should take *aarti* (wave the bronze plate around my head). I will fill the small pond near the palace with my milk", the cow Rupan told the Brahmin Guru.

Wasing Cobra (snake god) removed the stone again and Brahmin Guru came out. Riding the horse fast he reached Dharmi Raja.

"What happened? Did you find the cow Rupan? Did you arrange for milk or not?" Dharmi Raja asked impatiently.

"Oh king, have some patience. I have found the cow Rupan and she is ready to come here", Brahmin Guru replied smilingly.

"When will she come? How will she come?" Dharmi Raja was losing his patience.

The Brahmin Guru said every thing to Dharmi Raja which Rupan cow had told him.

In the evening Dharmi Raja taking a diya (oil lamp), a handful of rice and a little vermilion in a bronze plate, stood near the entrance of his palace. The cow Rupan running fast came near Dharmi Raja. Dharmi Raja put the vermilion mark on the head of the cow, scattered some rice on her and waved the bronze plate with the burning *diya* (oil lamp) round and round over her head. The cow filled the pond near palace with her milk and went away.

The son of Dharmi Raja drank the milk and became healthy.

Dharmi Raja was very happy. He had taken a vow to sacrifice one goat as well as one cock near the *jhapa* (entrance) of his palace after getting success in arranging for milk for his son. He did so. Since then Bhil tribesmen, during

*Diwali* (festival of light) sacrifice goat or the cock near the entrance of their house to increase the productivity of the milk of their cattle.

1. To search the heavenly cow Rupan Dharmi Raja had to take help from Brahmin Guru. He is considered the supreme god who is responsible for the welfare of cattle. He might be aware of the whereabout of the cow. 'Possibly yes', the Bhil tribesmen say but they also say that some times god has to behave like normal human being.
2. How can a new born baby talk and why did he refuse to take even the breast milk of her mother? Bhil tribesmen believe that he was the son of a god who can talk at any age. Why did he refuse to take the breast milk of her mother? Bhil tribesmen have no idea about it. They just say that the baby did so to increase faith in the cow Rupan.
3. By believing in this tale the Bhil tribesmen get sanction to celebrate the festival *jhapa-puj* (worshipping the entrance of the house) and sacrificing animals near that while celebrating Deewali (festival of lights).

## THE HAG AND HER DAUGHTER

In a village there lived a woman with her son, daughter-in-law, and an unmarried daughter. That woman was a hag and she had trained her daughter in this act as well.

One day both the mother and the daughter hags came to know that in one of their neighbour families, one woman was alone. The family members of that woman had gone to city for some work.

"My daughter, let us eat the heart of that woman who is alone in her house", the mother hag told her daughter.

"Mother, we will go to her house in the night", the daughter hag replied to her mother.

In the evening both of them turned into pigeons and sat on the roof of that woman who was alone in her house.

When the lonely woman saw the two pigeons on the roof of her house she praised their beauty and became happy. She was unaware of the reality of the pigeons.

In night the woman went to bed.

"It seems that the woman has slept. Let us go near her and do our job", one pigeon (the mother hag) told to another pigeon (the daughter hag).

The lonely woman was not sleeping. When she found hat the pigeons were talking like human beings she sensed some danger.

"It seems these two pigeons are not ordinary birds. They have come here to do some thing wrong with me. I should remain alert and pretend to be sleeping", the lonely woman thought.

While the lonely woman was busy in thinking the two pigeons took the form of two cats and climbed on the bed of that woman. As soon as one of the cats put her paw on the stomach of the woman, she sat down and caught the cat tightly. Holding the foot she started dashing the cat on the floor repeatedly. The cat started bleeding from her mouth and nose and finally lost her sense. The woman threw the unconscious cat out from her window. The other cat ran away from there.

In the morning the lonely woman narrated the incidents of night to other women of her neighbourhood. Two women wanted to find out the mystery of the cats. They started visiting every house of the village one by one. When they came to the house of the hag they found that the mother hag was lying in the bed. Her nose and mouth were wounded and bleeding. The daughter hag was busy in performing house hold duties.

"What happened to you?" The women who visited her house asked.

"My bull has kicked me", the mother hag lied.

Though the mother hag told lie, the women understood the truth. Slowly the truth of the mother and the daughter hags spread all over the village and the villagers started keeping eye over them.

One day the daughter hag told her mother, "Mother, since long we have not eaten the heart of any human. Do some thing."

"You are true my daughter. But it has become difficult for us to kill any one. The villagers keep eyes on us and watch our every activity very carefully", the mother hag replied.

"Under these circumstances what will we do? How can we survive?" The daughter hag asked.

"There is no other way. We will have to kill the man of our own home. Tomorrow when your brother will go out in the jungle to cut woods we will follow him in the form of vultures. Whenever we will get the chance we will fulfil our desire after killing him", the mother hag said.

The mother and the daughter hags were talking in the night. However they did not notice that the daughter-in-law of the family was listening to their words.

In the morning when the son of the house was going to jungle for cutting woods his wife said, "Do not go anywhere today and stay at home."

"Are you crazy? If I will not cut and sell woods today how will I buy edibles for all of us? What will we eat?" The son replied smilingly.

When the son of the house did not agree to stay home her wife followed him. In the jungle the son climbed on a dry tree and started cutting the branches of that tree. His wife kept guarding him moving round the tree. When he finished cutting the branches he came down and started making small pieces of those branches. Unfortunately a piece of wood hit his head and he fell unconscious. At the same time two female vultures started hovering there. The wife of the man was alert with an axe in her hand. When the vultures came near the man his wife beheaded both of them with the axe. Though beheaded the bodies of the female vultures flew away from there.

When the man gained consciousness he saw two heads of female vultures near him. Ha asked from his wife about the heads of the female vultures. The wife told him every thing. When both of them returned home they found the beheaded bodies of the mother and the daughter were lying on the floor.

When the villagers came to know about the end of the mother and the daughter hags they became very happy.

## KHOKHA AND KASSUMAR DEV

Khokha and Kassumar Dev were the sons of Veerma Sethani. Their father's name was Khalun Damor who was a watchman in the house of Meegal Moti Seth, the first husband of Veerma Sethani. In the absence of Meegal Moti Seth Veerma Sethani had developed relationship with Khalun Damor and both of them had eloped from there. In the rage of taking revenge Meegal Moti Seth had gone to the king of Dhar Satra Joshi. The king, too, was not happy with the behaviour of Bhil tribesmen of his locality. The story of Meegal Moti Seth had provoked his anger. The army of the king had attacked the group of people of Damor clan (Bhil tribesmen). Every one was killed but pregnant Veerma Sethani had managed to escape and had left for a remote and hidden place.

When time came Veerma Sethani gave birth to two male children and named them as the Khokha and the Kassumar Dev. When they were born Satra Joshi came to know that some one had taken birth in the Damor clan. He sent his minister Duda to find out who was born.

Riding on a horse, taking a spear in his hand Duda was roaming in the market of Dhar. Veerma Sethani was also there. To protect her children from the enemies, she had kept them in a bamboo basket and had covered that basket with a cloth. All of a sudden a cobra came in the market and the people present in the market gathered near the snake to have a look. Seeing the crowd at one place Duda also came there to find out the reason.

"Show me what have you kept in the basket?" Duda asked Veerma.

"Today we all are going to be killed", Veerma thought.

"I have kept the young one of the snake Balu Nag (the snake named Balu) in my basket", Veerma replied.

Duda put his spear on the basket and said, "I do not believe it is so. Show mw what is here. Remove the cloth and the lid of the basket."

Frightened Veerma removed the cloth and the lid.

Kassumar Dev took the form of a snake and started hissing. He broke the spear of Duda. Horrified Duda ran away from there.

"It seems your enemy is alive", Duda told the king and described the incident how one snake had broken his spear.

For the security point of view Veerma decided to leave her children under the care of her brother Mangliser Seth. She went to her brother and described every thing what had happened with her.

"*Bhaiya* (elder brother) my children will remain safe under your protection. Please give shelter to them", Veerma requested her brother.

"Sister, do not worry. Your children are safe here", Mangliser Seth gave assurance to Veerma.

With passage of time Khokha and Kassumar reached the age of puberty. One day Khokha said to Kassumar, "Mama (mother's brother) has taken good care of us. Now the time has come when we should help him in his work."

Both of them went to their *Mama* and asked for some work. Mangliser Seth was a businessman. He also used to take contract to graze the cattle of the village. The *Mama* gave the work of grazing cattle of the village. First, they were asked to graze horses of the village.

In a jolly mood both of them went to forest with the horses. After sometime they wanted prank to play with their *Mama*. They cut the tails of the horses and chased them in the deep forest. After that they entombed the tails of the horses in an ant hills in such a way that half of the tails remained visible.

Running fast Khokha went to Mangliser Seth and said, "*Mama, Mama*, the land near the ant hills split making a big ditch and all the horses went inside."

Mangliser Seth came near the ant-hill with Khokha Damor. When, Mangliser pulled one of the tails that came into his hand.

"May be what Khokha is telling is true", Mangliser thought and returned home. Khokha and Kassumar Dev followed their *Mama* (mother's brother) carrying the tails of the horses on their shoulders.

Six months passed peacefully. One day both of them went to their *Mama* and said, "We want to do business."

Mangliser Seth gave bundles of clothes and packet of tobacco to them and said, "Go and sell these clothes and tobacco in the market."

Khokha and Kassumar Dev, carrying the clothes and the tobaccos on the back of donkeys went to the market of Ahmadabad (a city in Gujarat, India).

When they reached the market they looked at each other and smiled. Out of mischievousness they distributed all the clothes and the tobacco to the people free telling them that their *Mama* had asked them to do so. After that they returned home laughing and joking with each others.

"Did you sell every thing? How much have you earned?" Mangliser Seth asked them.

"Mama, people had borrowed everything. They have not paid us but will pay to you later on", Khokha and Kassumar Dev replied.

"Both of them are not fit for business", Mangliser Seth thought angrily but he did not say any word to them.

After a few months both of them again went to their Mama and said, "Mama we want to graze the goats of the village." Mangliser Seth forgetting their previous mischievousness allowed them to graze the goats.

The brothers went to grazing ground with all the goats. In the afternoon the goats sitting under the shadow of the tree were chewing their cuds. Khokha went home and brought breads and cooked vegetables for them. Both the brothers were having their lunch. After some times Khokha said to his brother Kassumar, "Brother, look at the goats. They are imitating us. We are chewing our breads and the goats are moving their mouths like us."

In anger both immersed all the goats in water and after burning dry woods they threw the goats in the fire. When Mangliser Seth saw them returning home alone he asked, "What have you done with the goats? Where are they?"

Kassumar said what they had done with the goats. This time Mangliser Seth could not control his anger and said, "After all you are the sons of Bhil tribesman. You can never behave properly."

After hearing the piercing remarks of Mangliser Seth Khokha and Kassumar Dev decided to leave the home of their *Mama*.

"What should we do now?" Khokha asked Kassumar.

"Let us go to Assam (one the states of India) and learn some magic there", Kassumar replied.

Khokha agreed to go to Assam. Kassumar killed a wild lizard and with the skin of that lizard made one *ektara* (one-stringed musical instrument). Then both of them killed some fish and applied the flesh of lizard and fishes in their hair. Their hair grew long and tangled like *sadhus* (saints). Both of them playing *ektara*, singing and dancing proceeded towards Assam.

Veerma Sethani was crying remembering her sons, because she had not heard about them since they had left their *Mama's* house. To entertain herself she started watching the dance of *sadhus* (saints). Those *sadhus* were none other than Khokha and Kassumar Dev. Veerma Sethani did not recognize them.

"Look Khokha, mother has not recognized us", Kassumar laughingly told Khokha and proceeded further.

Sawan Mata (the goddess of seasons) was watching them. She cooked delicious food for them and when the Khokha and Kassumar Dev came near her, she offered food to them. When they finished eating she asked, "Where are you going and from where have you come?"

Khokha and Kassumar Dev narrated their story to her said that they were going to Assam to learn some magic.

"I am like a sister to you. I also want to go to Assam with you", Sawan Mata told them.

Khokha and Kassumar Dev along with Sawan Mata left for Assam. Travelling a long they reached a hillock named Bhimoriya which was under the control of Bhima (not the one among the mythological characters of five Pandavas). There they saw that monkeys were digging the field, jackals were removing grass from there, and instead of bulls lion were ploughing the field.

When the Bhima saw the Sawan Mata he thought, "This *jogin* (female ascetic) is very beautiful. She should stay with me." Thinking bad about them Bhima wanted to give some tough tasks to Khokha and Kassumar Dev.

"Pull five bundles of grass from my field, otherwise, I will not allow this *jogin* to proceed", Bhima threatened Khokha and Kassumar Dev.

Kassumar Dev pulled one hair from his chest and gave that to Bhima. He said, "Keep this hair with you as my identity proof. On my return journey I will give gold to you. Let us proceed now. We are in hurry to reach our destination."

They all proceeded from there and reached at a place where people used to have only one leg, and they used to drink starch and throw the cooked rice. Seeing the heap of cooked rice at one place Kassumar said, "I am hungry." He ate the rice surfeit. Now he wanted to pass motion.

"Go and sit behind the tree", Khokha advised Kassumar.

When Kassumar sat behind the tree, the tree started saying loudly, "Look every body what is Kassumar going to do here." Embarrassed Kassumar got up from there and sat behind a rock. Now the rock started saying, "Look every body what is Kassumar going to do here."

Restless Kassumar passed motion in a dry pumpkin and carried that with him because he did not find suitable place to throw that.

After travelling a long they reached a place name Kalmand.

"I want to smoke tobacco", Kassumar said and sent Khokha to bring burning coal. In the market of Kalmand Khokha found that only one shop was open. The owner of that shop was an old woman named Kalman. When Khokha reached there Kalman pretending like a sick woman laid down on a cot.

"Mother, I want burning coal", Khokha Dev told Kalman.

"There are burning coals in the hearth. One tong is also there. I am sick and can not move from the bed. Go and take the coal", Kalman replied.

As soon as Khokha touched the tong he turned into a bull. Kalman tied the bull in her cattle shed.

"Oh! It is gaiting late Khokha has not returned. Let me find out the reason of this delay in bringing the burning coal", Kassumar thought.

In search of Khokha he reached the shop of Kalman. She turned Kassumar into the bull as well.

When Sawan Mata saw their brothers were not returning she started crying. In search of Khokha and Kassumar Dev she, too, reached Kalman.

"Have you seen my brothers?" Sawan Mata asked Kalman.

"No, I have not", Kalman replied.

"My Daughter, tell me what kind of medicinal plant it is? One medicine man has given it to me", Kalman said to Sawan Mata.

Sawan Mata took the plant and as soon as she tried to smell that she turned into a cat. Kalman, the old woman tied the cat with her grinding stone. She forced Khokha and the Kassumar Dev turned into bulls to plough her field and Sawan Mata turned cat to grind the wheat.

One day Kalman had to go to meet lord Indra. She left the bulls and the cat under the care of her friend who was her neighbour as well. She told her friend to take hard work from the three.

"If you people promise me to give gold to me then I will make you as you were previously", the friend of Kalman said to them.

They agreed to give gold to that lady and she returned them into their original form.

"If you will unlock the seven doors of one of the room of Kalman's house you will find a bag full of magical power and many gold ornaments as well. But, do not open the eight doors because Kalman has locked her husband there. He can kill you", the friend of Kalman said to them.

Kassumar brought the bag and all the ornaments from the house of Kalman. Now they all said good bye to the friend of Kalman and started their return journey. They all had got the magical power for which they had started their journey for Assam after leaving their *Mama's* house. Before leaving the place they did not forget to take leaves of palm, water in a metal pot, and burning coals of sacred fire with them.

In the court of lord Indra Kalman came to know that her three prisoners had escaped from her house. She started chasing them. Khokha and Kassumar Dev had become the master of magical power. They were not afraid of anybody. When they saw Kalman was behind them, Kassumar Dev threw the leaves with some magical power towards Kalman. The leaves became the forest of palm tree. Though, Kalman was facing difficulties in crossing the forest she continued chasing them. Kassumar Dev threw burning coal towards Kalman which turned into the trench of burning coals. Kalman took the form of a female vulture and started flying over the trench. Finally Kassumar threw water towards her which turned into a sea and Kalman could not cross the sea and returned from there.

Khokha and Kassumar Dev along with Sawan Mata reached the hillock where Bhima was waiting for them. Bhima stopped them and wanted to capture Sawan Mata. Khokha and Kassumar Dev were no more the weak persons; they started beating Bhima. Kassumar Dev began to press hard upon Bhima. He knocked him in to the soil up to his knees. Then he asked, "Whose property is this hillock called after you?"

Bhima replied, "Mine it is and my father's.". They continued the fight and Kassumar Dev hammered Bhima into the soil up to his middle and again he asked, "Tell me Bhima, whose hillock is this?" And again Bhima replied, "Mine and my father's."

The combat was resumed and the Kassumar Dev knocked Bhima down into earth, entirely. A last time he asked, "Bhima, whose property is this hillock?"

Bhima replied, "Yours, it is your and of your father. If you eat bull give a goat to me. If you have a goat, give a cock to me. If you have a cock, give some liquor to me. If you take a sip of liquor give some *bakla* (boiled maize corns) to me. But please forgive me."

When Bhima asked for forgiveness Kassumar Dev pulled Bhima out of the ground and said, "Look Bhima! We are cousins. Here after do not fight with other without any reason. This hillock is your and of your father. Now eat, drink and live happily." Khokha and Kassumar Dev left Bhima there and proceeded further.

They reached a hut of an old woman and spent the night there. Next morning Sawan Mata left for her home giving thanks to them. Kassumar Dev saw cocks in the courtyard of the old woman. She asked for one cock.

"Kassumar Dev is the owner of the cocks", the old woman said. She did not recognize that she was talking with Kassumar Dev. She had heard that Khokha and Kassumar Dev, after gaining the magical power, had become very powerful. Using the name of Kassumar Dev she was trying to frighten the man standing in front of her.

Kassumar Dev laughed at her. He turned into a scorpion and bit that old woman.

"Kassumar Dev, please cure me. Scorpion has bitten me", the old woman started crying with pain. When Kassumar Dev cured her she recognized him and begged for forgiveness. She gave cock to him

Khokha and Kassumar Dev asked for some wheat flour.

"I have only *mahua* (bassia latifolia) flowers with me", the old woman replied.

Khokha and Kassumar Dev ate the cooked cock only. After giving thanks to that old woman both of them left the place and reached a mountain near Dhar. That mountain was the settlement of the ghosts. Khokha and Kassumar Dev with their magical power hypnotized the ghosts and made them dance. When the ghosts got tired they threw their sticks and sat down. Their sticks turned into the forest of bamboos. Bhil tribesmen believe that at the place where the ghosts had danced, even today grass does not grow.

"During worshipping us when devotees will offer us goat, we will give you cock. If they will offer us cock, we will give you liquor and in case they will offer us liquor we will give you coconut", Khokha and Kassumar Dev promised to the ghosts and moved from there.

When they reached near the garden of the city Dhar, they erected their tent and sitting in the tent started singing *bhajans* (sacred songs).

Heermal was the only sister of the king of Dhar Satra Joshi. She was living in the palace with Satra Joshi. Kassumar Dev taking the dirt from his body made a *nagin* (female snake) Padma and asked that to bite Heermal. The *nagin* went to the palace but could not climb the wall of the palace. Then Kassumar Dev made a rat from the dirt and asked that to dig a burrow for the *nagin*. Through that burrow the *nagin* went inside the palace and bit Heermal. Heermal fell unconscious. Satra Joshi called *Barwas* (shaman) from many villages but they all could not cure Heermal.

"The person who will cure Heermal would become her husband", a worried Satra Joshi announced.

In the garden where Khokha and Kassumar Dev had erected their tent, one woman was collecting cow dung cakes.

"I can cure Heermal but for that there is condition", Kassumar Dev told that woman.

"What is the condition?" the woman asked.

"Satra Joshi will have to carry me to the palace in a palanquin and before that he will have to offer me porridge mixed with salt", Kassumar Dev replied.

That woman ran fast to Satra Joshi and repeated every word of what Kassumar Dev had told her. Satra Joshi had no other way to cure Heermal He agreed with the Kassumar Dev and went to him. Khokha and Kassumar Dev ate the porridge and sat in the palanquin. Satra Joshi and his men carrying the palanquin on their shoulders returned to the palace. Khokha and Kassumar Dev had eaten salty porridge. They started vomiting on the men who were carrying them.

"If any one of you feel nasty I will not cure Heermal", Kassumar Dev said.

They all reached the palace.

"Kassumar, cure Heermal soon and make her your wife. I am egger to eat bread prepared by her", Khokha told Kassumar.

Kassumar Dev captured the Padma *nagin* and put her mouth near the place where she had bitten to Heermal. The *nagin* sucked the poison and Heermal got cured.

When Satra Joshi found that Heermal was cured he wanted to play trick with both the brothers.

"Why should I give Heermal to marry with this *sadhu* (saint)? I ask him to bring the dangerous horse Kaliya Khet to me. That horse will kill Kassumar", Satra Joshi told his minister Duda.

Satra Joshi was not aware that the horse Kaliya Khet belonged to Bhil tribesmen and that would not harm Kassumar.

When Kassumar Dev came to Satra Joshi riding on Kaliya Khet he became aware of the power of Kassumar Dev. He agreed to marry his sister with Kassumar Dev.

Kassumar Dev married with Heermal. The people of Damor clan (Bhil tribesmen) believe that they are the descendent of Khokha and Kassumar Dev.

1. The story of Damors (see The Damors) ends mentioning pregnant Veerma Sethani escaped from being killed by the army of the king of Dhar. This story starts with the information that she gave birth to twin sons.
2. By birth Khokha and the Kassumar Dev had the power to take on any one. They changed into snakes when Duda wanted to kill them. Bhil tribesmen say that they were their gods and not ordinary children.
3. The father of Khokha and Kassumar Dev was a Bhil man and their mother was a non-tribal. Bhil tribesmen say that in earlier times this type of marriage used to happen. Now it happens rarely.
4. The maternal uncle of Khokha and Kassumar Dev had taken good care of them. Why did they not think about the loss of their uncle and left home after a scolding from him? Bhil tribesmen laugh and say that even today they play prank with their maternal uncle. They left home because a Bhil can not tolerate insult and scolding even if it is for their welfare.
5. Sawan Mata, the goddess joined Khokha and Kassumar Dev when they were going to learn magic. How was it possible? Bhil tribesmen say that they all are gods and goddesses.
6. When Kassumar Dev wanted to pass motion the tree and the stone started talking. About this incident the Bhil tribesmen say that some time the *Barwa* (shaman) tells such thing only to make people especially children laugh.

7. When Khokha, Kassumar Dev and Sawan Mata went to old woman to ask for burning coal, she made them fool. She, an ordinary human, was more powerful than them; how? Bhil tribesmen say that the old woman had a bag full of magical tricks and they had gone to learn magic.
8. About the incident when Khokha and Kassumar Dev got rid of the old woman chasing them, the Bhil tribesmen say that this incident proves that they had become more powerful than that old woman after they had taken the bag full of magical tricks.
9. Why did Khokha and Kassumar Dev become ready to share their offerings with the ghosts? Bhil tribesmen claim that they are more close to ghosts than any other tribesmen.
10. Why did Kassumar Dev marry the sister of Satra Joshi who was the enemy of Damor people? Bhil tribesmen say that marrying with the relative of enemy is one of the ways of taking revenge with their enemy.
11. Who was the king of Dhar? Satra Joshi or King Gaihlot? Bhil tribesmen say that they both were the king? How was it possible? They have no idea.
12. How many times the king of Dhar had snatched the horse Kaliya Khet from the Damor people. Bhil tribesmen say that Kaliya Khet was a powerful heavenly horse. Many times the king had taken that horse from the Damor people but he was not able to ride that horse.
13. Duda was the minister of whom? King Gaihlot or Satra Joshi? Bhil tribesmen say that they call every minister as Duda.

The *Barwa* (shaman) of Bhil village sing this story as song before going in trance. The Khokha and the Kassumar Dev are the ancestral heroes of the Bhil tribesmen.

## JAHMA MATA

Satra Joshi, the king of Dhar was the father of seven daughters, still people used to call him childless fellow.

One day he asked his minister, "Duda, why do people call me childless, when I am the father of seven daughters?"

"Yes my king, you are the father of seven daughters but you have no son. That is why people call you childless", Duda, the minister of the king replied.

"Why is it like this? Why is there difference between a son and a daughter?" The king asked.

"It is like this because a son is known by his own work whereas a daughter is gets recognition by her father's work and name", Duda replied.

"Is it true? Do my daughters know this fact? I will ask them", the king said to Duda.

In the late evening the king and his minister were standing near the entrance of the palace. When the girls returned home after playing in play-ground the king asked them one by one, "You are identified by whose name?"

Except Jahma Mata they all replied that they were known by their father's name. The answer of all the six daughters satisfied the ego of the king and made him proud.

"My father has given birth to me but he is not my fortune-maker", Jahma Mata said.

The reply of Jahma Mata hurt the ego of the king and he became angry.

"I will fix the marriage of Jahma Mata with an old and ill fellow. I will make her sit on a donkey without tail and will force her to leave the village. I will show her how can I control her destiny", the frustrated king announced in front of every one.

He got his six daughters married with healthy, wealthy, and handsome boys and ordered his servants to search for an old and ill guy for Jahma Mata.

A group of Bhil tribesmen had erected their tents in a field named Valodiya near the village of Dhar. They used to work as labourer for their livelihood. They were very poor and were hand to mouth. One day all, except Kalu and the Kadva Bhil, had gone to work. Kalu and Kadva were there to take care of and protect children and their belongings as well. Kalu was standing near the tents with a spear and Kadva was lying there on a cot. The Bhil children were playing the game of catching the snake nearby. They started piercing their spears in the ant-hill the home of a black cobra. The cobra became nervous and crept away from there.

"Save me, else these children will kill me", the cobra requested to Kadva Bhil.

"I will swallow you and you will remain safe in my stomach", Kadva Bhil said and opened his mouth. The black cobra entered into his stomach through his mouth.

Kadva Bhil saved the life of the black cobra, but his own life became hell. His whole body swelled up due to poison. His legs became like pillars, which made him unable to move on. When his family members as well as co-fellows saw him in this condition they thought that it would be better to get rid of him because he was of no use for them.

"It seems he will eat away half of our earned grains and will make our children starve", one of his co-workers said.

"I think he will die soon", his family members said.

They all decided to leave Kadva Bhil there alone and left the place after demolishing their tents.

In search of an old and ill person for Jahma Mata the servants of Satra Joshi reached the field Valodiya. They saw Kadva Bhil who was alive but lying motionless in the field.

"We have found the suitable groom for Jahma Mata. Our king would be very happy", they all shouted with joy and carried Kadva Bhil to Satra Joshi, the king.

Satra Joshi after marrying Jahma Mata with Kadva Bhil made them sit on a donkey without tail. The servants of the king chased the donkey out of the village.

Jahma Mata came to the field Valodiya. She erected her tent there and took the job of agricultural labourer in a nearby farm. She was working hard, taking good care of Kadva Bhil, and had no regrets in her life at all. One night she was not feeling sleepy and while sitting near the entrance of her tent she was planning about the next morning. She saw a snake coming out from an ant-hill and said, "If some one gives the paste of *kachari* (cucumis madrapatanus, a small fruit of the melon family) mixed with milk and salt to this man, the snake inside his stomach will die and the man would be cured."

The snake residing in the stomach of Kadva Bhil peeped through his mouth and said, "Why did you announce my secret openly? I will also tell about you. If some one pours twelve pots of hot water into the ant-hill near this tent, the snake inside the hill will die and if he/she digs the hill he/she will get lots of gold."

The words of the two snakes made Jahma Mata happy. In the morning she went in the forest and brought the fruits of *kachari* and the milk of she-goat who was grazing in the forest. She ground the fruits on a stone and mixed the paste, salt, and milk together. She gave that mixture to Kadva Bhil to drink. When Kadva Bhil drank that milk the snake inside his stomach died but he started writhing in pain and fell unconscious. After some time he got up and vomited the pieces of the dead snake. Thus Kadva Bhil was cured and turned into a handsome and healthy man.

"Where are your family members and other colleagues?" Jahma Mata asked the Kadva Bhil.

"They had gone to another place in search of job", Kadva replied.

"Go and call them here immediately", Jahma Mata Said.

"It seems this *jogin* (female ascetic) wants to get rid of me", Kadva Bhil thought.

Jahma Mata understood what was going on in the mind of Kadva Bhil.

"Do not worry, I will not move from here. Go fast and call them back", Jahma Mata said.

Kadva Bhil went in search of his family members as well as co-workers and soon reached up them. They all became very happy to see Kadva healthy and alive.

"Come with me, we will go to the field Valodiya. I have come here to take all of you", Kadva said to them.

"No, we do not want to return there", they all said unanimously.

"We have to do very important work there. That work will change our life. Your daughter-in-law (Jahma Mata) is waiting for you", Kadva Bhil tried to make them understand.

They all came to Valodiya. Jahma Mata welcomed them and offered food to them as well. She poured hot water in the ant-hill and killed the snake present there. After this she began digging the ant-hill and soon found lots of gold inside that hill. All became very happy. They put all the gold on the back of twenty donkeys and proceeded their journey for a new destination.

From Himalayan regions to western India, Jahma Mata built numerous temples at almost all the famous places and got several ponds dug near every temple. She helped poor persons to stand on their own foot and helped people in many ways. With her noble works she earned name, fame and so much money which she was unable to carry. She put half of her earned money in the various ponds. People believe that even in the village of ghosts she had arranged for liquor-kin for the ghosts. Every one became the admirer of Jahma Mata.

Jahma Mata reached Dhar, her father's village. There she found that people were suffering due to scarcity of drinking water. The village wells were completely dry due to drought.

"Duda! I have heard that a *jogin* (female ascetic) has come to our village. She has power to turn dry mud into water. Why not we go to her for help", Satra Joshi told his minister.

"Yes my king, you are right, we should go there. If she digs a pond here, too, it will solve the water- problem of our village", Duda replied.

The king sent his minister Duda to Jahma Mata. Duda did not recognize her.

"We are facing the problem of scarcity of drinking water. Please help us. Please build a temple, dig a pond near that temple so that our villagers can quench their thirst easily", Duda requested Jahma Mata.

"I will help you but for that your king should come to me in my tent", Jahma Mata said.

Satra Joshi along with Duda went to meet Jahma Mata. He, too, did not recognize his daughter. Jahma Mata laughed at them and said, "Once an ox kicked his she-calf, today the ox is standing behind that calf with his head down".

Jahma Mata built a temple and a pond there. She wanted to put a dome on the top of the temple but hundred and twenty-five men of the king could not lift the dome. Jahma Mata alone put that on the top of the temple and left for unknown place.

1. Jahma Mata was the daughter of Satra Joshi, a non-tribal man. Why did he marry his daughter with Kadua Bhil a tribal man? Bhil tribesmen say that many years ago there was no difference between Bhil tribesmen and the non-tribal people. In addition, Satra Joshi wanted to teach his daughter a lesson. He was in search of an old, sick and useless fellow for his daughter Jahma Mata.
2. Jahma Mata earned name, fame, and wealth. Where did her husband and in-laws go? Bhil tribesmen have no idea.
3. Which temples and ponds she had built? Bhil tribesmen say that from Himalayan region to Kanya Kumari she had built many temples but non-tribal people do not believe it. They said that if any one asks non-tribal people who had built the famous temple of Badrinath, they will not give the right answer. When we the tribal people say that Jahma Mata had built that, they will not accept.
4. Jahama Mata was not a Bhil woman by birth. She married a Bhil man made him wealthy. She did lots of good work for the welfare of people; that is why Bhil tribesmen consider her as their goddess.

## MEGH RAJA AND SAWAN MATA

When king Gaihlot came to know that his horse Kaliya Khet snatched from the Bhil tribesmen was missing he asked his public to search the horse out.

"Duda, come with me. We will find out where the horse has gone", the king said to his minister Duda.

When both were searching for the horse they saw the foot prints of Kaliya Khet with the foot prints of Halun Sorya (the mythological hero of Bhil tribesmen) in the garden of Megh Raja (the king of clouds). Halun Sorya had made the horse free from the captivity of the king Gaihlot and had hid that in a safe place. The king mistook the footprints of Halun Sorya with the footprints of the Megh Raja.

"Duda it seems that Megh Raja has stolen our horse", the king said.

"Yes my king I also think so", Duda replied.

Both of them decided to teach a lesson to Megh Raja. Megh Raja after getting *bowni* (seed sowing ceremony) done by the farmers and giving them good rain for that was sleeping peacefully. The king Gaihlot and his minister Duda overpowered the Megh Raja and handed him to Meegal Moti Seth, a businessman of Dhar.

"Seth, hide Megh Raja in your home", the king said to Meegal Moti Seth.

"Do not worry I will do so", the Seth replied.

Meegal Moti Seth hid Megh Raja in his godown where he had kept salts to sell. However, he did not understand what he has done. Due to Megh Raja his salt got dissolved.

"Damn it. Where have I burnt my finger", Meegal Moti Seth thought.

"My king I can not hide Megh Raja any more. There is no place in my home where I can keep him. My salt got dissolved due to him only", the Seth cried before the king.

The king Gaihlot handed over the Megh Raja to a potter named Hoja. He hid the Megh Raja in a big earthen pot. He also suffered like Meegal Moti Seth. Due to Megh Raja all his pots got dissolved and his hearth extinguished. When Hoja refused to keep Megh Raja with him any more, the king handed over Megh Raja to a gardener. The gardener, too, cried out before the king because all his plants were becoming rotten.

Megh Raja had become a nuisance for the King Gaihlot. He decided to kill him. He called the shooter Vageera.

"Kill Megh Raja and hang his eyes at the entrance of the cattle shed so that every cow can hit those eyes while going out and coming in the shed", the angry king said to Vageera.

Vageera felt pity for Megh Raja. He did not kill him but concealed in the horn of a wild he-buffalo. He hanged the eye of a doe at the entrance of the cattle shed. Megh Raja was happy in his new place. He wanted to take rest and therefore slept in the horn of that he-buffalo.

The absence of Megh Raja created havoc on the earth. It was drought every where. The ponds, the rivers and the wells dried up. Human beings, animals and birds were thirsty and were pining for a drop of water. The plants were withering away.

Dharmi Raja, the supreme god of Bhil tribesmen was also facing the problem of scarcity of water. Once the wife of Dharmi Raja had gone to fetch water from water stream-slit, where there was a long queue of the persons who had gone there to fetch water. The wife of Dharmi Raja got delayed in returning home with water. There Dharmi Raja was impatiently waiting for her.

"Where had you gone? You are coming after making fun. Bringing a bucket of water can not take so much time", Dharmi Raja asked his wife putting his trident on her head.

"Shame on you, what kind of king are you I have noticed. How much do you take care of your people I know. In your reign people are buying water after weighing counted grams. It is easier to bluster a wife rather than perform own duty perfectly", the wife of Dharmi Raja taunted on him.

Dharmi Raja bowed his head out of shame.

"My wife has passed comments on me. Let me do some thing", Dharmi Raja thought. He called his attendant the black-bee and asked him to call all the gods and the goddesses for an important meeting.

"You all know what is happening in the absence of Megh Raja. Human beings, animals and birds are thirsty. Plants are withering away. If this situation will continue no one will survive. For the welfare of all living beings we will have to search out the Megh Raja. I want to know who among you all will accept and take the responsibility? Dharmi Raja asked all present there.

Galeli, the she-elephant of Dharmi Raja started waving the betel leaf holding that with her trunk in front of every god and goddess. No one was accepting the leaf because accepting that meant to accept the challenge to find out the whereabout of Megh Raja. At last the she-elephant went near the Sawan Mata. She took the leaf and after chewing that spit into a pot.

"I will find out where Megh Raja is?" Sawan Mata announced in a confidant tone. All the gods and the goddesses returned to their abodes.

Sawan Mata came to the house of Megh Raja. Ratna Meghan, the wife of Megh Raja was sitting there in grief and her daughters were crying.

"My *Nanadi* (husband's sister), you have come here after long", Ratna Meghan greeted Sawan Mata.

"*Bhabhi* (brother's wife) tell me what has happened to Megh Raja?" Sawan Mata asked Ratna Meghan.

"Megh Raja on getting *bowni* (seed sowing ceremony) done by the farmers and giving them good rain for that was sleeping peacefully. The king Gaihlot and his minister Duda overpowered Megh Raja. What they actually did with Megh Raja, I do not know", Ratna Meghan replied.

Sawan Mata consoled all of them and said, "Bring any clothe of Megh Raja to me."

One of the daughters of Megh Raja brought one jacket of his. Sawan Mata applied her magical power on that jacket, closed her eyes and after some time said, "Megh Raja is alive but someone has concealed him at an unknown place. I will find out where is he and will bring him back. You people do not worry for them", Sawan Mata assured them.

In the kingdom of King Gaihlot, Sawan Mata came to know that the king had handed over the prisoner Megh Raja to Meegal Moti Seth and then to Hoja the potter. After that he had handed over Megh Raja to a gardener and finally to a hunter Vageera.

Sawan Mata went to Vageera and brought him to the king Gaihlot.

"Oh my king! Please pardon me. Do not give me death sentence. I had not killed Megh Raja and instead of his own eyes, the eyes of a doe were hung at the entrance of the cattle shed", Vageera implored humbly to the king.

"I had concealed Megh Raja in the horn of a he-buffalo and had chased away that buffalo in the forest", Vageera told Sawan Mata.

Sawan Mata went into the forest but it was difficult to find out one he-buffalo in a dense forest. When she was moving in search of the he-buffalo she noticed an old woman making bread of millet flour. She went to her and asked, "Mother, from where did you bring millet? Where is water and where is Megh Raja?"

"My daughter, I do not know where is Megh Raja. In this forest there is a big animal from whose horns water drips drop by drop, which flows into a ditch. That is the spot where millet plants grow", the old woman replied.

"Mother, take me to that animal", Sawan Mata requested.

Both of them went near a tree.

"Look there, that animal is sitting there under the tree. It comes here daily", the old woman told Sawan Mata.

Sawan Mata took the form of a bird and started pecking insects sitting on the head of the buffalo. She heard the gurgling sound inside the horn of the buffalo. She understood that Megh Raja was there.

"If I set Megh Raja free, what will you give me?" She asked the Dharmi Raja after going up to him.

"What do you want?" Dharmi Raja asked.

"In every village do build a temple in my name. Sacrifice one un-married girl every year in the temple and give me all the ornaments of sixteen wives", Sawan Mata asked.

"I will build temple in your name in every village but instead of un-married girl I will sacrifice a goat every year in the temple", Dharmi Raja said.

Sawan Mata agreed for this change but when Dharmi Raja refused to give ornaments, she became furious and left the place. Once due to drought when the condition went worse the wives of Dharmi Raja said to him, "What will we do with our ornaments when every one will die? It is better to hand over the ornaments to Sawan Mata for the welfare of the world."

Dharmi Raja went to Sawan Mata and said that he was ready to hand over the ornaments to her.

Sawan Mata went to the market and got a wooden mallet made. She called the man Hoda Kut Jamai with her who followed her with a rope. After going near the buffalo Hoda Kut Jamai tied that with the rope. Sawan Mata started dancing near the buffalo carrying the wooden mallet in her hand. While dancing she hit the horn of the buffalo and set Megh Raja free. It started thundering, lightening and raining. The rivers, the ponds, and the lakes were filled with water making every one happy. Sawan Mata went back to her abode.

[Halun Sorya had made foot prints of the horse Kaliya Khet in the garden of Megh Raja (see the story Halun Sorya). The king of Dhar imprisoned Megh Raja thinking he had stolen the horse. In the absence of Megh Raja (the Cloud), people suffered from drought and famine. Bhil tribesmen were not the exception. They suffered badly. Bhil tribesmen said that their forefathers suffered but they had taught Megh Raja a lesson.]

## BHOLA ISHWAR

(Bhil tribesmen believe that Bhola Ishwar (one of the name of lord Shiva) is their god whom the Hindus have accepted as their god as well).

There lived a pair of swan in a country in the north. One day the female swan hatched her egg and found that instead of a bird a male child came out of her egg.

"We are birds but our child is of the human look. May be it is a mysterious child", the female swan told the male swan.

When the male swan saw the child, he was afraid. Out of fear the pair of swan flew away to a new destination leaving the child alone. The child became an orphan. The child was none other than but Bhola Ishwar (lord Shiva) himself.

Bhola Ishwar was moving here and there in search of a shelter. He saw a deserted palace and he entered in to that. The palace was dirty. Bhola Ishwar cleaned that palace and started living there peacefully.

One day the supreme god Dharmi Raja wanted to celebrate a day with all the gods and the goddesses. He sent invitations to every one. To make that meeting a success he wanted to take the help from some other gods. He called Bhola Ishwar and gave him a heap of wheat to grind. Bhola Ishwar carried that wheat on his head to his home. He went on grinding the wheat for the whole night and the next morning he reached with flour to Dharmi Raja. Dharmi was surprised to see that Bhola Ishwar had ground the wheat in a night only.

"Who lives with you? Who has helped you in grinding the wheat? Where is your wife? Who helps you in performing household duties?" Dharmi Raja asked Bhola Ishwar.

"Oh so many questions in rapid succession", Bhola Ishwar thought.

"No one lives with me. No one has helped me in grinding the wheat. I am a bachelor. I do my work alone", Bhola Ishwar replied.

"You should get married", Dharmi Raja advised Bhola Ishwar.

Bhola Ishwar decided to get married. Brahmin Guru a helpful man to every god and goddess dreamt that Bhola Ishwar was in need of his help. Next morning wearing new *dhoti* (waist cloth), *kurta* (upper garment), and tying a new turban he proceeded to meet Bhola Ishwar. He did not forget to pick his stick.

"Search a bride for me. I want to marry. See your *potha* (sacred books) and tell me where my wife is?" Bhola Ishwar asked the Brahmin Guru. He was so eager to know about his wife that he neither did offer seat to Brahmin Guru nor did he welcome him properly.

"From north to south, from east to west, and from heaven to *patal* (hearth), I will search every where and will find a good wife for you. Give me some money for my travel expenditure", Brahmin Guru said.

Bhola Ishwar gave a gold-brick and some silver coins to Brahmin Guru.

Brahmin Guru searched every where but failed to find out a suitable bride for Bhola Ishwar. At last he returned to Bhola Ishwar and said, "I have searched every where, I am sorry, I could not find suitable bride for you."

The failure of Brahmin Guru in finding a suitable bride made Bhola Ishwar sad. One day he dreamt that a girl belonging to the Gond tribe was calling him. He called Brahmin Guru again and asked, "Did you go to the settlement of Gond tribesmen in search of bride for me".

"No that is the only place I had not gone to", the Brahmin Guru replied.

"Go there immediately and find a suitable bride for me", Bhola Ishwar said to Brahmin Guru.

Wearing a yellow *dhoti* (waist cloth), blue *kurta* (upper garment) and tying a pink turban Brahmin Guru became ready to visit the settlement of Gond tribesmen. This time, too, he did not forget to pick his stick.

"Give me some money as well as your identification mark I am going to the settlement of Gond people", the Brahmin Guru said.

Bhola Ishwar gave one gold-statue resembling him, diamond ball, coconut made of silver, and some coins as well.

Taking every thing the Brahmin Guru reached the village of Gond tribesmen and sat down under a tree. After some time some girls came there to fetch water.

"Among you all who are un-married and who are not?" Brahmin Guru asked them.

"Why do you want to know about us? You should not be concerned with us. Do not ask such questions to us", those girls replied to the Brahmin Guru. However, the Brahmin Guru came to know that only one, among them named Gaura, was un-married. Following the foot prints of Gaura, the Brahmin Guru reached her home. He came to know that Gaura was the daughter of the chieftain of Gond tribesmen. He started begging in front the house of Gaura and when the mother of Gaura wanted to give him alms he refused to accept that.

I have come here to fix up Gaura's marriage with Bhola Ishwar", Brahmin Guru said to the mother of Gaura.

Many elder men of the village came near the house of Gaura to know what was happening there.

"We should accept the offer of the marriage", one of them said.

"But we do not know how does the groom look and also we are not aware of his economic condition. How can we fix up this marriage without knowing anything", another fellow said.

The Brahmin Guru put out the statue of Bhola Ishwar from his knapsack and said, "The groom looks like this statue."

Then he put out the diamond ball, silver coconut, and coins and said, "He had given me all these items to give to his would be wife. Now you can guess about his economic condition."

The elders present there were happy and satisfied. They all agreed for this marriage. The Brahmin Guru put *tilak* (red coloured powder) mark on the forehead of Gaura and handed over all the items he had brought with him to her.

"I will come with marriage procession soon", he said to all and returned to Bhola Ishwar.

Bhola Ishwar was waiting for the Brahmin Guru. When the Brahmin Guru described about Gaura and the engagement ceremony, Bhola Ishwar became very happy. He began preparation for the marriage. He called the weaver bird and giving paddy to her said, "Remove the husk from the rice."

Singing songs the weaver bird removed the husk from the rice. Bhola Ishwar said to her, "From today you will make your nest upside down. In rainy season water can not enter into your nest and your home will remain dry."

Bhola Ishwar coloured the rice with turmeric powder and giving those rice to Kalu and Ralu Megh (cloud brothers) said, "Go and invite every one for my marriage giving a little rice to all of them as good omen."

Ralu and Kalu Megh invited all the gods, the goddesses, the kings, the queens, and the ghosts to attend the marriage of Bhola Ishwar. All were very happy.

In both the bride and the bridegroom house, the marriage preparation was in full swing. In bridegroom's house the *mandap* (marriage booth) was made of Sal wood whereas it was of black plum wood in bride's house. *Mehandi* (henna) was applied on the palms of bride as well as the bridegroom. On the selected day all the gods, goddesses, kings, queens, and ghosts came to Bhola Ishwar's house. But, the guests refused to take food because there was no arrangement for liquor. Bhola Ishwar sent his friend Hoda Dev to bring liquor from Massoori Kalal's shop. The shop owner was ready with the liquor. He put the liquor on the back of twenty donkeys; in turn Hoda Dev gave him a necklace made of gold.

When the guests of Bhola Ishwar saw Hoda Dev coming with liquor they became very happy. They drank liquor as much as they could. After drinking liquor Howan Mata started dancing while others joined her. One of the ghosts uprooted a tree and tucked that in his turban. Dancing, singing, joking, and pushing one another they all proceeded towards Gaura's house.

In Gaura's house all were waiting for the groom and his friends. The groom and the bridegroom were seated in the *mandap* (marriage booth). They started taking *phera* (moving around the fire), and after the seventh *phera* the marriage ceremony was over.

They all took food there. The parents of Gaura gave farewell to Bhola Ishwar and his friends. Bhola Ishwar returned home with Gaura. He was happy because he was not alone in his house. His wife Gaura was with him.

1. Bhil tribesmen believe that Bhola Ishwar (lord Shiva) was the son of a swan pair. Hindus also worship lord Shiva but their belief is different.
2. Bhola Ishwar called the Brahmin Guru to search a bride for him and not a *Bhanzgerio*. How and when a Brahmin actually crept into their story Bhil people are yet to explain. They say that that many a times Brahmin Guru had helped their forefathers.
3. Bhola Ishwar was a Bhil man and Gaura was a Gond woman, yet they were married. Bhil tribesmen say that possibly in the past there was no restriction in marrying with a man or a woman belonging to different tribes. They are not sure.
4. Megh Raja (the cloud king) helped Bhola Ishwar a Bhil man in his marriage. He had performed the task of inviting people for the marriage. Bhil tribesmen laugh and say that the cloud was not the enemy of their forefathers but they were his enemy. Megh Raja had done only one mistake. He had not sent the rains for twelve years.

## SAAT BHOWANI MATA (SEVEN GODDESSES)

From the eggs of female vulture named Bhada Gardan, all the babies came out one by one. At first, the king of Lanka came out and immediately after the birth he went to Lanka. After that seven goddesses came out one by one. They were Kalka Bhowani, Howan Bhowani, Sawan Bhowani, Salar Bhowani, Lal Bai Bhowani, Phool Bai Bhowani, and Pooja Bhowani. Their presence on the watch-hut where they were born made that hut crowded. Seeing her children happy and healthy Bhada Gardan flew away from there.

One day a water creeper grew fast and reached the watch-hut. All the seven goddesses came down through that creeper in the water with the help of that creeper.

"You all have come down by your own effort or you have taken help from any one?" The creeper asked them.

"We all have come down by our own effort. We have not taken help from any one", they all said unanimously.

The creeper turned into Kodiyali Mata and disappeared from there. The seven goddesses lost their way back to their watch-hut. They all came out of the water and sat under a tree.

Kana Jogi who was a watchman in the palace of the king Satra Joshi was passing from there. When he saw seven girls sitting under the tree he went near them and asked, "Who are you? You are coming from which place and where do you want to go?"

"We are orphans. Our mother threw us from the heaven. We have no place to go", they all replied.

"God has made my fortune today. I am a childless fellow and god has given me seven daughters at a time", Kana thought.

Running fast he went to meet his wife Kani and both of them went there where the seven goddesses were sitting.

"Come with us. You all are my daughters. We will live together", Kana and Kani said to them.

After reaching home Kana threw old mattress out from his house and started firing with his gun. (Even today throwing the mattress out and firing with gun are the symbolic way to inform every body that the house wife has given birth to a child).

"Duda, go and find out what is happening in Kana's house", the king Satra Joshi said to his minister Duda.

Duda went to Kana's house to find out the truth. After returning from there he said, "King, Kana's wife has given birth to seven children."

"Kana is our servant. In this happy moment we should give him some things", the king said.

The king called Kana to his palace and gave him a bag full of dry fruits. In addition, he granted Kana leave for some period to help his wife in taking care of their daughters. Kana distributed all the dry fruits among his daughters and gave coconut to his wife.

"Father, you have brought coconut for whom?" The seven goddesses asked Kana.

"It is for your mother Kani", Kana replied.

"Our mother can not eat coconut. She has no tooth", the goddesses laughed and ate the coconut as well.

After a few months the king Satra Joshi called Kana back to his work. Though not willing to join the service Kana had to go.

One day Kani along with all her daughters went to fetch water from a river. Reaching near the river Howan climbed on a tree of black-plum. She plucked a twig of the tree and started using that as her tooth brush.

"Mother do you want a twig?" Howan Bhowani asked sitting on the branch of the tree.

"Come down my child. You will fall down. I do not want any twig. I have no tooth in my mouth", worried Kani replied.

Howan Bhowani Mata came down and said, "Mother we will play in the water."

Kani did not want to enter in the water but all the Bhowani Mata forced her to play with them in the water. After returning home Kani got fever; she started writhing with pain. Kana was called immediately.

"What happened to Kani? Where you all had taken her?" Kana asked.

"Father we were playing in water and there only mother fell ill", Howan Bhowani Mata replied.

Kana, taking a few maize corns in hand waved that over the head of Kani and wanted to go to the *Barwa* (shaman) to know the cause of the illness. (The Bhil tribesmen believe that a *Barwa* can see the cause of illness in the object waved over the patient. He gives medicines accordingly to cure the patient).

"Father, you sit near the mother, we will go to *Barwa*", Howan Mata said.

Taking the maize corns they all went to *Barwa*. But, going behind a hillock Howan Mata threw the corns and brought a piece of wood of *palash* (butea fondosa) tree. She put that piece of wood near the ear of Kani and she got cured. Kani started laughing as if nothing had happened to her. Kana took a breath of relief.

"Father, *Barwa* wants sacrifice as his fee", the seven goddesses said to Kana.

"What does he want? Goat, cock, date fruits, coconut or liquor or what?" Kana asked.

"He wants goat and liquor", Howan Mata said.

"Let us call the *Barwa* here, we will hand over the goat and liquor to him", Kana said.

"No father, the *Barwa* is lame person who can not come here. We will go there and give every thing to him", Howan Mata said.

Taking a goat and liquor the seven goddesses went behind the hillock. After roasting the goat they all ate that and drank the liquor. After that they started dancing there.

"It is too late the girls have not returned. May be they are in trouble", Kana thought.

"Come with me Kani. Let us go to find out where the girls have gone", the worried Kana said to Kani.

Both of them started searching for their daughters. When they reached near the hillock they heard some sound of singing and dancing. After going behind the hillock they found that their daughters were dancing.

"What you all are doing here/" Kana asked them

"*Barwa* had given us the head of the goat. We roasted that and after eating we were dancing here to have some fun", Howan Mata replied.

"It seems they are not the ordinary girls. Let us wish them goodbye from here", Kani said to Kana.

"But my daughters, you have no good clothes and ornaments. With these old and tattered clothes how can you dance?" Kana asked.

Howan Mata took a thorn of *babool* (acacia) tree. She pierced her ear lobe and inserted the thorn in the hole. The thorn turned into gold ring.

Kana and Kani understood that the girls whom they had accepted as their daughters were not ordinary girls. With folded hands they said goodbye to their daughters and returned home.

The seven goddesses were moving in the market of Dhar. They wanted to buy clothes for them and for that they went to the shop of Meegal Moti Seth. When the Seth saw the yellow colour of the eyes of the girls standing in front him he was afraid. He gave them clothes free. Taking clothes they all reached up to a farmer and asked, "How many tailors are there in Dhar?"

"They are hundred and twenty five", the farmer replied.

"How many are good among them", Howan Mata asked.

"Only twelve", the farmer said.

"Who is the best among the twelve", Howan Mata asked again.

"His name is Nanaya-Manya", the farmer said.

All the seven goddesses went to the tailor Nanya-Manya and got their *Ghaghara* (long skirt) and *choli* (blouse) stitched.

"What will you charge for this stitching?" Howan Mata asked.

"I will not take any thing from you all. I want to marry you", Nanya-Manya said to Howan Mata.

"Oh no, he has chosen the best among us", the six goddesses cried.

"Go to Nandan-Van (the forest named Nandan), I will join you soon", Howan Mata said to her sisters.

"Heat the water and take bath", Howan Mata said to Nanya-Manya.

Howan Mata had already fixed a peg at his bathing place. When he was taking bath she hit him with a wooden hammer and killed him. She ate his heart and left for the forest named Nandan Soon she joined the group of her sisters.

"Let us beg in the market and if the alms would not be sufficient then we will earn after dancing", Howan Mata suggested to her sisters.

Howan Mata went on a mountain to bring bamboos.

"What is the price of your Bamboo?" Howan Mata asked the bamboo owner.

"One gold coin for every bamboo", the owner replied.

Khokha Dev (the mythological hero of Bhil tribesmen was passing from there. When he heard the conversation between the two he made the bamboo owner aware of the power of Howan Mata. Scared owner gave the bamboos free of cost to Howan Mata. After taking the bamboos she went to a carpenter and took a spider from there. Now she came to the market and erected four bamboos in the four corners and tying the spider with a sword she started moving the spider round the four bamboos. When a thick web was made around the four bamboos she left the spider free and decorated the web with coloured papers. Finally she erected one bamboo in the centre and climbing on that bamboo started performing aerobatic dance. All the saints of Dhar came to watch the dance of Howan Mata. The saints were very powerful but they all combined together were not able to control Howan Mata. Howan Mata took all the saints, the citizens of Dhar, animals, birds, and every good under her control but she forgot to take knife under her control. When she was dancing the knife that was not taken under control by Howan Mata cut the bamboo and she fell down. She stood up and with the help of a bamboo leaped and went to unknown place.

[In the story Bhada Gardan (The Female Vulture), had laid a chain of eggs on the watch hut and seven Bhowani Mata had come out of those eggs. The seven goddesses lived in this human world and played many pranks with the people. The *Barwa* of the Bhil village sings this story as a song with his men. The tribesmen believe that when he describes the incidents of falling of Howan Mata from the top of the erected bamboo he gets the power of her. After that he starts predicting about the future correctly].

## BAPSI DEV

In the village Rambapur there lived a *baniya* (business man). One day he went to a sculptor in Rajasthan and requested him to make a statue of Bapsi Dev. The sculptor made a beautiful statue of Bapsi Dev and handed that over to the baniya. The baniya put that statue in his bullock-cart and started his return journey to Rambapur. When he was coming home the statue fell down from the cart and the baniya put that back in his cart. But, the falling of statue continued from time to time.

"Why my other goods are not falling from the cart? Why is it happening with this statue only?" The baniya was thinking and driving the cart.

When he was crossing the mountain-pass near the village Itawa the statue fell down again and trickling down the slope of the mountain rolled ahead. He wanted to know the mystery behind the falling down of the statue and sent his men to call the *tadvi* (village chief) of that village. The *tadvi* came with the *Barwa* (shaman) accompanied by a few elders of the village.

"I, after getting this statue made, was taking it to my village home Rambapur. But, this statue continued falling down again and again and this time it has rolled down there", the baniya pointed his finger towards the statue said to the *tadvi* (village chief).

The *tadvi* (village chief), the *Barwa* (shaman), and the other elders started consulting one another.

"It seems as if this statue does not want to go out of this village", the *tadvi* (village chief) said to the *baniya*.

They all went near the statue and the *tadvi* (village chief) put that under a banyan tree. The baniya said to the tadvi (village chief), "Alright, take care of this statue. I am leaving for my own village". However, the baniya once in a year used to come to see the statue of Bapsi Dev.

When the villagers saw a deity under the tree they made a hut-cum-temple there and put the deity in that temple. Gradually they started worshipping the statue of Bapsi Dev by offering red coloured powder, coconut, and incense sticks. The villagers of other villages also started coming there.

One day a mad dog bit the *tadvi* (village chief) of the village. In those days there was no doctor in the village who could cure him. A man in Gujarat (state of India), was famous for curing the patient of dog-bite. The *tadvi* (village chief) wanted to go there but it was raining and impossible to cross the river which was in ebullition. Seeing no way to get cured the *tadvi* came in the temple of the Bapsi Dev.

"I am in your protection. If I get cured, I will offer you sweets and *churma* (bread-crumbs mixed with ghee and sugar)", the *tadvi* requested Bapsi Dev.

By the grace of god nothing happened to him and he got cured. When people came to know about this incident, they started coming to temple during illness and taking a vow for getting cured.

[Even today every year the day after the Holi (the festival of colours) a fair is organised near the temple. The main attraction of the fair is walking on burning coals by the devotees after the fulfilment of their vow of getting cured from the illness. People request god to keep them healthy. No one comes in the temple after drinking liquor. It is believed that if any one does so he would die the next morning.

This mythical tale helps people to celebrate the day after Holi (festival of colour) with full devotion.]

## BHILJI BHIL

There was a king in a village. He had engaged a Bhil tribesman as a labourer to work in his field. One day the king wanted to eat flesh of any animal.

"Go and hunt any deer, or rabbit, or pig, or partridge for me", the king ordered the Bhil man.

The labourer Bhil spent the whole day in the forest but could not succeed in hunting any animal. In the evening when the king saw him returning empty handed he became angry and shot at the Bhil man with his gun. The labourer Bhil died on the spot. The labourer Bhil had a son named Bhilji Bhil. Bhilji Bhil was a kid when his father had died. When he grew up he asked his mother about his father. His mother told him what had happened to his father.

"Mother, do not worry. I will take revenge from the king. He had killed my father without any valid reason", Bhilji Bhil said to his mother.

Bhilji Bhil went to king and asked for some work. The king engaged him in his field.

"My king, I will do exactly what is told by you. Except that I will not do any thing", Bhilji Bhil said.

"Alright, do what I ask you to do", the king replied.

Next morning Bhilji Bhil went to graze the oxen of the king. He sold all the oxen in the market. After that cutting the tails, and horns of dead animals he trusted those tails and horns in the pond.

"King, my king, all the oxen bogged down near the pond. Only the tails and horns of them are visible", Bhilji Bhil said to the king.

The king went to the pond with Bhilji Bhil. When he pulled all the tails and horns came in to his hands. Desperate and worried king returned home without saying any word to Bhilji Bhil.

One day Bhilji Bhil was working in the field. The horse of the king, standing near the field, started neighing.

"Bhilji Bhil! Go and show water to this horse", the king said to him

"Alright my king, I am going to do so", Bhilji Bhil replied.

"I have got another chance to teach a lesson to this king. He has asked me to show water to the horse and not to make him drink the water. I will do so", Bhilji Bhil thought.

He went riding the horse near the pond and returned to the field. The thirsty horse remained thirsty. His thirst was not quenched only by seeing the water. He started neighing again.

"Go and make this horse drink water after pressing him well", the irritated king said. Bhilji Bhil smiled and went with the horse. He sold the horse in the market and fixed the tail of a dead horse in the mud of the pond. After that he came to the king and said, "Like your bulls your horse, too, went inside the mud. Only his tail is visible."

The king came near the pond and when he pulled the tail that came in his hand.

"You have killed my horse", the king shouted at Bhilji Bhil.

"No, I have not killed your horse. You had told me to make the horse drink water after pressing him well. When I pressed the head of the horse he went in side the mud. It is not my fault", Bhilji Bhil replied. The king returned home.

One day the wife of the king had gone to her mother's house leaving her son under the care of the king. The king was taking his lunch and the son was sleeping in the cradle. When the son started crying the king said to

Bhilji Bhil to make him sleep. He made him sleep by swinging the cradle. However, after a few minutes he pinched the child and he started crying again.

"Go and make the child sleep by pressing him well", the king said to Bhilji Bhil

Bhilji Bhil, to press the child, sat on him and the child died due to suffocation. Bhilji Bhil covered him with a blanket and went to work in the field. In the evening when the child did not wake up the king went to see him. When he found his child dead he started crying nervously, "Bhilji Bhil, Bhilji Bhil, come here fast."

Running fast Bhilji Bhil went to the king.

"What have you done with my child? How did he die?" The king asked Bhilji Bhil.

"I have not done any thing wrong with your child. You asked me to make him sleep by pressing him well. I did exactly that. How he died I can not say", Bhilji Bhil replied.

"Hurry up. Go and call the queen here immediately. Keep one leg here and other leg there", the king said to him.

Driving a bullock-cart Bhilji Bhil reached the queen and told her that the king was calling her immediately. When the queen sat in the bullock-cart, Bhilji Bhil tied her one leg with a tree and another with the cart. He drove the cart fast and reached up to the king. Seeing the bullock cart near the palace the king came there. He found his wife wounded and dead. He started crying and blaming Bhilji Bhil for his misdeeds.

"You can not blame me. You told me to keep one leg here and another there. I did exactly that. If the queen died what can I do?" Bhilji Bhil said.

"You have killed my family members one by one. I do not want a man like you to work for me. Get out from here", the king said to him.

Bhilji Bhil returned home. He was not willing to work for the king. He had to take revenge of his father's death and he had done so.

[In this story we see that a clever and brave Bhil boy took revenge from a non-tribal king who had killed his innocent father. This story gives emotional support to Bhil tribesmen who said that during the feudal time they had suffered at the hand of the ruling Rajput kings].

## THE MOVING ROOM

In a village of Bhil tribesmen there lived a farmer with his wife and young son. The farmer got his son married with a beautiful girl named Sonali. At the time of marriage the mother of Sonali said to her, "My daughter, remember one thing. In your in-laws village if any woman gives you any thing accept that but do not use that."

"Alright my mother I will not forget your words", Sonali replied.

After marriage Sonali started living with her husband and the parents–in-law. She was not only beautiful but intelligent and obedient as well. They all were leading happy and prosperous life. The wife of the elder brother of the farmer used to live in their neighbour hood. She was a hag and she had trained two other women in this act as well. When she saw the happy family of her *devar* (husband's younger brother) she felt jealous. She wanted to kill Sonali, who was the main source of happiness of that family.

One day she gave a twig to Sonali charging that with her black magical power and said, "Sonali brush your teeth with this twig. I have brought it only for you."

"Yes aunty I will do", she replied but kept that twig in a room. She had not forgotten her mother's advice. Seven days continuously the hag gave her the twigs and Sonali kept collecting those twigs in the room. Sonali named the room as *dakin ki kothi* (the room of hag), where she had kept all the twigs. One day the hag gave her curd in a big bowl, Sonali kept that bowl of curd in the room. Next day she found numerous big insects moving in that curd.

When the hag found that nothing was happening to Sonali she doubted whether she had lost her power. She called her hag colleagues and narrated them what she had done to Sonali and what was the result.

"It seems I have lost my power. Sonali is still healthy. I have tried my best to kill her", the hag said to her friends.

"Do not worry. We will go to cremation ground and will call back the power you had used. We will find out the reason of this failure", the colleagues gave assurance to the hag.

In the night when all the villagers were sleeping they all went to cremation ground. They lit a *diya* (oil lamp) there and started dancing and moving round that. While dancing, they all three were spelling magical-spells to call hocus-pocus power of the main hag which she had applied on Sonali.

The room in which Sonali had kept all the twigs and the curd started moving towards the cremation ground. Due to the sound of the movement of the room Sonali woke up. When she saw the room was moving she called her husband. Her scared husband called her parents. Sonali told them what her mother had said to her and what she had done with the twigs and the curd. Meanwhile a few elders of the village also came there. They all saw the room moving and followed that by taking stick, sword and spear. They all reached the cremation ground and there they saw three women dancing around the oil-lamp. They understood every thing. When the three women saw the villagers and the family members of Sonali in front of them they wanted to escape from there. One brave tribesman saved the head of all the three women with his sword. They all returned home happily. There after Sonali, lived without any fear with her husband and in-laws.

[The Bhil tribesmen believe in witch craft, hag and black magic. Their belief has made this story popular. One can also say that this type of story helps in developing faith in witch craft].

## BANISER RAJA AND ONKHA KUMARI

The king Baniser had seven wives still he was childless. He was very desirous of becoming a father and had taken help from many saints and shaman.

One day he was roaming in a market. In that market a woman named Rupali was selling bamboo made baskets. The baskets were expensive and no one was buying them. When Baniser Raja saw the baskets he liked all very much.

"How beautiful baskets these are. I will buy all of them", Baniser Raja thought. He gave gold and silver coins to Rupali and took all the baskets. When Rupali reached home her husband Kaliya asked, "From where you have brought these coins?"

"Baniser Raja has purchased all my baskets", Rupali replied.

"We should not accept the money given by Baniser Raja. He is a childless fellow. It is a bad omen to keep any thing given by such a man. Go and return every thing to him", Kaliya said to her.

Rupali went to Baniser Raja to return his coins.

"Come Rupali, why did you come here? Do you want any thing more from me?" Baniser Raja asked her.

"No my king I do not want any thing. Actually I have come here to return the coins given by you. My husband says we should not accept the coins given by a childless fellow", Rupali said.

After taking a breath she continued to say, "My king! You should go for pilgrimage. You will become a father soon". She returned the coins to the king and went back.

Rupali's words made Baniser Raja grief stricken. All became very sad seeing their king in such a condition. One day Baniser Raja after having dressed like a saint went on pilgrimage and moved from place to place. After a year, the sad and defeated king in his endeavour taking blessings from god wanted to burn himself. In a forest he collected heap of dry woods and after setting fire to those woods, he wanted to jump into that. At that time Potiser Dev appeared before him and asked for his desire.

"I want children. In my village all animals and birds are unable in procreation", Baniser Raja said to god.

"Look, I am giving you this stick. Go home you will find on the mango tree laden with fruits. Pluck the fruits hitting the tree with this stick. Remember one thing, hit the tree only once. Do not be greedy else the result would be disastrous. Take the fruits home. Extract the juice and drink that with your all the wives. Throw the left out food as well as the leaf plates in which you all will have your food, out side and flush the liquid in the drain. When the animals and the birds will eat the left over and drink the water they all will also produce offspring", the god said to Baniser Raja.

Taking the sticks the King went near the tree. When he hit the tree with the stick seven fruits fell down. The king forgot the warning given by the god. In lure of getting more fruits for having more children he hit the tree again. The result was disastrous. The fallen fruits went up and stuck back to the tree again. The king realized his mistake. He started lamenting and went back to Potiser Dev again.

"Oh my god, please forgive me. I did blunder by disobeying you", Baniser Raja requested the god.

The god forgave him and said, "Go and take fruits which are still lying on the ground". Saying this he disappeared from there. Baniser Raja returned home with the fruits. He told his wives what had happened with him. All the six elder wives of the king ate the fruits secretly leaving the younger one whose name was Leela. They threw the skin of the fruits near the heap of the cow dung.

Leela had kept watchful eye on the activities of the elder queens. She collected the peels of the mango and prepared good dishes with that. She called Baniser Raja in her room and both of them took the lunch together. As said by the god Leela flushed the water in the drain and threw the left over fruits out. All the animals and birds of the village drank and ate the eatables which had a little quantity of the fruits given by the god. All the animals and birds started procreating children quite similar to them.

The seven queens became pregnant. When the time came the six elder queens gave birth to male child whereas Leela became the mother of a daughter. Baniser Raja was very happy. He had become the father of six sons and one daughter. Leela named her daughter Onkha Kumari. Slowly they all grew young.

One day Onkha Kumari went to fetch water. While returning home she came across a group of saints who were passing through her village. She stole the son of the head saint and hid him in her palace. When the saints came to know about their missing child they all went to the palace. Onkha Kumari was not ready to return the child to the saints. Finally they all decided to marry Onkha Kumari with the child. Onkha Kumari was too old to be the wife of that child; however, she married the child.

At the time of farewell Onkha Kumari asked her father's head in her *dapa* (bride price).

"Oh my god, what kind of girl is she? It seems she is a hag who is asking for her father's head", the guests present there were surprised. Onkha Kumari was firm on her decision. At last a fellow cut the head of a buffalo and put that in the lap of Onkha Kumari. She was satisfied then. She went to live in the land of saints with her husband.

In this story we find that:

1. A childless couple can not have access to things in the Bhil society.
2. Rupali, a non-tribal woman advised Baniser Raja to go on pilgrimage to get a child. Did going on pilgrimage become popular in the Bhil society after coming in contact with non-tribal people? Bhil tribesmen say, 'Possibly Yes'.
3. Who was Potiser god? The Bhil tribesmen use this name very rarely. They say there are many gods and goddesses who reside in forest. They do not know much about them.
4. Why did Onkha Kumari, a young woman agree to marry a baby? Bhil tribesmen have no idea.
5. Why did Onkha Kumari ask for the head of her father after her marriage? Bhil tribesmen are unable to answer. They just say it is a story hence any thing can happen.

## DUDI MEGH AND BHADA GARDAN

The marriage ceremony of Dudi Megh with Kanwa Kumari was over and all the guests had returned to their homes. The newly married couple was happy and ready to lead their new life.

A year after the marriage Kanwa Kumari gave birth to twelve Megh and at last one goblin child. The goblin child had big teeth and thin legs. Soon after the birth the goblin child started doing mischief. The worried father Dudi Megh went to Kaliya, the bamboo-man.

"Kaliya, make a cage which has twelve layers of bamboo. I am in a hurry, do it immediately", Dudi Megh requested Kaliya.

Kaliya made a strong cage and gave that to Dudi Megh. Dudi Megh returned home and locked the goblin child in that. Carrying the cage Dudi Megh went to cremation ground with all his twelve sons. The goblin child understood why they were going to cremation ground.

"Father do not burn me but bury me", the child requested Dudi Megh.

Dudi Megh agreed for that and buried the child on the cremation ground and put spiny bushes over that. They all returned home.

One day a storm removed the bushes and heavy rain washed the mud. Thus the cage in which the goblin was locked came out. The child had grown up and was none other than Bhada Gardan (the female vulture, one of the mythological characters of the Bhil tribesmen). Bhada Gardan cut the bamboo with her beak and made her free. She was hungry so she started pecking insects and after that reached the kingdom of Megh (the clouds). She sat near the entrance of the palace.

Ratna Meghan, the wife of Megh Raja (the cloud king and the elder among all the Megh brothers) saw a female vulture sitting near the entrance of the palace.

She went to Megh Raja and said, "One big bird is sitting near the gate."

All the Megh brothers taking their bow and arrows came to hunt the bird. When Bhada Gardan saw them she said, "You can kill me but before that you will have to fulfil my last wish." All the brothers were unable to do that so they left the idea of killing the Bhada Gardan. When the Bhada Gardan saw that the Megh brothers had put their bow and arrows down she said, "I am your sister, the child you all had buried on the cremation ground."

They all become happy and Bhada Gardan started living with them. Ratna Meghan used to take good care of Bhada Gardan.

One day Megh Raja gave their cows to Relashi, the milk man to graze them on the nearby field. Bhada Gardan wanted to do mischief with the milk man. She pecked him over the head and cried, "Save me, save me."

Running fast Ratna Meghan came to her and asked what had happened to her.

"Nothing serious, one cow had hit me", Bhada Gardan replied.

"If you want to eat some thing special and have some fun then come to me in the night", Bhada Gardan said to Relashi.

In the late evening Relashi pretending sick lied down on the bed. He refused to take food. His wife Lodan took good care of him and after finishing the house hold duties she slept. When Relashi realised that Lodan was sleeping he went to meet Bhada Gardan. They all played for the whole night and in the morning Relashi returned home. His wife was sleeping and she could not know where the husband had gone. However, in a hurry Relashi left her sickle in the house of Bhada Gardan. In the morning Lodan asked for sickle from Relashi.

"Yesterday I had gone to chew grams. May be I have left my sickle there", Relashi replied. Lodan went to the gram shop to take her sickle.

"Relashi has not turned up here for a year", the shop owner said to Lodan. She came to Relashi.

"May be I have left that in liquor-shop", Relashi said. However, from the liquor shop Lodan returned empty handed.

"Why are you not telling the truth and sending me to this shop and that shop again and again?" Lodan asked in irritated mood.

"After working in the field I had gone to the bank of river to wash my hands and legs. The cow Kajali ate up the sickle", Relashi said.

Lodan went to Kajali and the cow told her the truth.

"If you do not believe me go and see on the bank of the river Shipra. Both Bhada Gardan and Relashi are playing in water", Kajali said to Lodan.

Lodan went to the bank of the river Shipra. She saw Bhada Gardan was pouring water on Relashi with her beak and Relashi on her with wood. They were laughing and joking. Relashi saw Lodan from faraway hence could not recognize her.

"Look Bhada Gardan one beautiful woman is coming towards me", he said to Bhada Gardan. When Lodan came near Relashi recognized his wife and ran away from there. Bhada Gardan and Lodan started fighting with each other. Relashi was watching them fighting while hiding behind a tree. Bhada Gardan put Lodan down and sat on her.

"This bird is going to kill my wife. I can not live without her. Bhada Gardan is a bird I can play and enjoy with her but can not spend my life with her. I should protect my wife", Relashi uttered and ran to save Lodan. He separated both of them. Bhada Gardan flew from there. Lodan came to Ratna Meghan and complained her about Bhada garden.

"See Bhada Gardan, Relashi is the husband of Lodan and he is a human as well. If you need some body to play with then search out a male vulture for yourself", Ratna Meghan said to Bhada Gardan.

Bhada Gardan understood what her sister-in-law was telling her. She decided to find out a husband in a male vulture. She promised her sister-in-law that she would not disturb the peace of any family in future.

In this story we see that:

1. Megh Raja (the cloud king) was cloud but he had a cloud father and a human mother. This happens only in story.
2. Bhada Gardan (the female vulture) was the sister of Megh Raja. How was it possible? Bhil tribesmen say that Dudi Megh (the cloud), Kanwa Kumari, (the human), Megh Raja (the cloud), the Bhada Gardan (female vulture), they all are gods and goddesses. They can marry, understand the language of each other, and can do any thing which is not possible for ordinary human beings.

## THE BHIL BOY AND THE KING

There was a king in a village. His daughter was very beautiful. Daily early in the morning she used to go to temple to worship god. A Bhil boy watched her worshipping the god daily.

"I will also worship the god in the temple", the boy decided. The Bhil boy belonged to a fisherman family. His duty was to catch fish. In the morning he caught a fish and put that in the temple. When the princess came to temple she was surprised to see a fish in the temple. She threw the fish out and after performing her *puja* (worship) returned home. Next day she again found a fish in the temple and when this process continued she reported the matter to the king.

"Do not worry I will send my men in the mid of night. They will guard the temple till morning", the king said to the princess. When the Bhil boy came to the temple with the fish he saw army men guarding the temple. He hid himself behind the tree and kept waiting for the right time. In the morning when the army men started taking nap, the boy got a chance. He put the fish in the temple and ran away from there. When the princess came she found the fish again. She told about it to the king.

"Do not worry, this time I will myself guard the temple", the king said to the princess.

Next morning when the Bhil boy came with the fish he saw the King present there. He climbed on a tree and kept waiting. In the morning the king went behind the bushes to urinate. The boy got the chance; he put the fish in the temple and ran away.

The king said to the princess, "We can not find who keeps the fish there. You just throw the fish and worship there".

One day the boy got delayed. While he was returning from the temple the princess was going in. when the princess saw that boy she wanted to stop him. Out of fear the boy ran from there and the princess followed him. Both of them reached a forest.

"Do not run. Stop! I want to marry you", the princess shouted. The Bhil boy stopped. The princess reached near him. Both of them got married and decided to settle in the neighbouring village. The princess sold out her gold necklace in the village and brought good clothes for the Bhil boy. Both of them went to the king of that village to ask for some work. The princess had covered her face in veil. The king engaged the Bhil boy in his service.

One day one of the servants of the king saw the face of the princess. He went to the king and said, "My king! The wife of the Bhil boy to whom you have engaged in your service is more beautiful than all of our seven queens." The king felt jealous and wanted to snatch the princess from the Bhil boy. Immediately he got an idea. He called the Bhil boy and said, "My wife is suffering from eye-pain and to cure that she needs lioness-milk. Go and bring that from the forest." The king thought that the tigress would kill the Bhil boy and after that his wife could be owned.

The Bhil boy returned home sad and worried. He refused to take food and lied down on the bed.

"What is the problem with you? Why are you worried and sad?" The princess asked the Bhil boy. The Bhil boy told her what the king had demanded from him. The princess smiled and gave the solution of this problem to her husband. The Bhil boy jumped from the bed and went to forest. After reaching near the cave of the lioness he noticed that the lioness was not there in the cave. He collected heap of dry leaves near the entrance of the cave and burnt that. After that he started extinguishing the fire by hitting that with a thick bamboo. The cubs present in the cave came out and saw the Bhil boy trying to extinguish the fire. When he finished his job the cubs came near him and said, "Mama (mother's brother) has come and jumped in to his lap."

The Bhil boy started dandling the cubs. In the evening when the lioness returned the cubs told her how Bhil boy had saved their life. The lioness gave thanks to the Bhil boy and asked, "Tell me brother what do you want from me? Why did you come here?"

"I have come here to take your milk", the Bhil boy said. The tigress gave that in a pot. When the Bhil boy wanted to return one of the cubs wanted to give company to him. Both the Bhil boy and the cub started their return journey. In the mid of the forest the cub said to the Bhil boy to ride on him so that they could reach home soon. They reached near a pond and wanted to take some rest there. The cub saw a crab and advised the Bhil boy to keep the crab with him. The boy put that in his bag. The Bhil boy was tired; he slept under a tree. Near the tree there was an ant-hill. A snake came out of that hill with an intension to bite the boy. The crab saw the snake and cut that in seven pieces and this way saved the life of the Bhil boy. When the boy woke up he saw the pieces of snakes and understood every thing. He gave thanks to the crab from bottom of his heart. Riding on the cub the boy reached the palace. When the king saw him coming riding on a cub he got afraid. The Bhil boy gave lioness milk to the king. The trick of king failed, the lioness did not kill the boy. The king started thinking about another trick.

After a few days the king called the Bhil boy and said, "Bring me the tooth of a demon. To get the tooth of the demon the princess advised him to apply the same trick he had applied to get the milk of a lioness. The Bhil boy went to the palace of the demon and burnt dry leaves. When he was extinguishing the fire the daughter of demon came out and watched every thing. She said to the Bhil boy, "you are tired. Come inside and take some rest."

"No, your father is a man-eater. I can not go inside", the Bhil boy replied.

"Trust me. Nothing will happen to you. I will hide you", the demon's daughter replied. The Bhil boy went inside and the demon's daughter hid him by turning him in to a fly. When the demon came he said, "The smell of human body is coming. What is the matter?"

"Father, first listen to me, then only I will tell you what is the matter", the demon's daughter said to her father. She told how the Bhil boy had saved her life from the fire and she had decided to marry him.

"Father, if you promise me that you will not kill him then I will call him here", the demon's daughter said to her father.

"How can I kill him? He is my son-in-law", the demon replied.

The demon's daughter called the Bhil boy there.

"Tell me my son-in-law, what do you want from me?" The demon asked the Bhil boy.

"Father I want your tooth", the Bhil boy replied.

The demon not only gave his tooth but a flying-horse as well. The Bhil boy got married with the demon's daughter and both of them sitting on the flying-horse reached the terrace of the king. When the servant of the king saw the Bhil boy coming with not only the tooth of demon but a beautiful wife and a flying horse as well he ran fast to inform the king. The king had nothing to do but to accept the defeat silently.

The Bhil boy was living happily with his both the wives and the king was leading a restless life. One day he called the Bhil boy and said, "Dig a pond near the palace in one night. If you will do so I will give you half of my kingdom otherwise I will hang you till you are dead."

Digging a pond in one night was a difficult job for the Bhil boy and he was well aware of the fact; this time the trick of burning dry leaves was not going to work. He came home and slept. His two wives went to him and asked what the problem was? The Bhil told them every thing. The daughter of the demon smiled and said, "Do not worry. Take me there where the king wants the pond to be dug, and leave every thing to me."

In mid night they all three went to the place where the king wanted the pond to be dug. The daughter of the demon taking water in a bowl kept on the ground and swirled the bowl round. The water started coming out of the bowl continuously. The bowl was not becoming empty, but was moving and spreading water every where. In the morning there was a big pond near the palace. When the people saw the pond in the morning then they started shouting, "Our new king has dug the pond! Our new king has done so in one night." The king came there running fast. He gave half of his kingdom to the Bhil boy.

One day the king called the Bhil boy and said, "I am giving you the last task to perform. If you perform this successfully I will make you the king of this village otherwise I will kill you."

"What do you want me to do?" The Bhil boy asked him.

"Bring me the sour butter milk", the king said. This is the story of that period when no one had heard about sour butter milk in that village. The Bhil boy returned home in sad mood. This time, too, his wives were ready to help me. The daughter of the demon said, "An old woman lives in the middle of the forest, she knows how to prepare butter milk. But, countless poisonous snakes surround her hut and it is difficult to enter into the hut."

The princess gave an idea to the Bhil boy and he went in the jungle. Going near the hut of that old woman he climbed on a tree and started shouting, "Mother! My mother! I have come to meet you." The old woman came out and kept a pot full of milk. The snakes started drinking milk and the old woman called the Bhil boy inside the hut.

"Why did you come here? What do you want from me"? The old woman asked the Bhil boy.

"I have come to take sour butter milk", the Bhil boy replied.

The old woman asked the boy to wait and she went to prepare sour butter milk. To spend his time the Bhil boy was roaming near the hut. Since he was the guest of the old woman no snake was coming near him. The Bhil boy saw four girls were taking bath in a pond. The boy took their clothes and began to move from there. When the girls agreed to marry him, he returned their clothes. All five came to the hut of the old woman. She gave butter milk to the boy and one of the girls asked for a flying cot from the old woman. The old woman obliged that girl as well. They all sat on the cot and reached the palace.

The King gave whole kingdom to the Bhil boy and went to an unknown place with his family.

A poor Bhil boy became the king of the village and lived happily with his six beautiful and wise wives.

[A Bhil boy got impressed by a non-tribal girl and started imitating her. Both of them got married but why did they leave their own village? Bhil tribesmen have no idea about it. The intelligence of the girl and the bravery of the boy worked and thus he became the king. Bhil tribesmen claim that a Bhil boy can work as much as ten non-tribal men do but they do not apply their brain.]

## THE BHIL FARMER AND THE GOD

One day a Bhil farmer and the god quarrelled with each other. The god became angry and said, "This year I am not going to send rain to your village."

"You do what you want to do but I will do my job. I will plough the field and sow the seeds", the farmer replied in a careless tone.

The god asked *Chatak* (an Indian birds) bird and frog to keep quite. It is believed that when the *Chatak* bird and the frog speak, it rains.

During rainy season it did not rain but the Bhil farmer ploughed his field. When he was ploughing his field, by chance a frog came under the plough and in pain it started crocking. When the *Chatak* bird heard the crocking of the frog she also started chattering. Thus when the rain heard the crocks of the frog and chattering of the *Chatak* bird he thought god was telling him to rain. It rained well and the farmer became happy. The whole episode increased the anger of the god. He called the rain and asked why he rained.

"I heard the chattering of the *Chatak* bird and thought you were telling me to rain", the rain replied. The god asked the bird about the reason for its chattering.

"When I heard the crocking of the frog I thought it was the time of my singing", the bird replied innocently. Now the god called the frog and the frog said, "Out of pain my lord, out of pain I started crocking."

Now it was all finished. The god was unable to do anything. However, he got an idea to teach a lesson to the farmer. He went to him and said, "Alright by chance you got the rain but do not think that you have won. I will take half of the yields what ever you sow."

"Which portion of the crops you will take?" The farmer asked.

"I will take the upper portion of the crops", the god replied.

The Bhil farmer smiled and agreed to give the upper portion of the crop to the god. He sowed groundnuts in his field and after harvesting gave upper portion, only shoots and leaves to the god whereas he kept nuts with him as it grew under the ground. Defeated god left the field for his abode but promised to come the next year because Bhil tribesmen play any game three times and then decide about the winner.

Next year the god asked for the lower portion of the crop but the farmer sowed millet, which sprouts on the top of the plant, in his field and defeated the god again.

"This farmer is very clever; any how I will have to win the last time", the god thought and third time asked for the middle portion of the crops from him. However, the god could not assume how smart the Bhil farmer was. This time he sowed maize plants in his field in which the corns grow below the middle portion of the plant. The god was defeated again. He accepted his defeat in front of the Bhil farmer and promised not to disturb the farmer any more and left for the heaven.

Bhil tribesmen say that rarely one can find an intelligent person in their society. However they also claim that an intelligent Bhil can defeat even the god in any challenge.

This story is a good example of an intelligent Bhil who had defeated god. It gives emotional support to the Bhil tribesmen.

## SOMARA

In a village there lived a Brahmin. Other than a horse he had no one to live with him. The Brahmin was unable to perform all the household duties alone though he remained busy for the whole day. Whenever he used to go out he always met a Bhil boy. That boy was neither interested in studying nor in doing any work. He used to spend his time in rambling.

"I should engage this Bhil boy for performing my household duties. He will live with me and will help me in my work", the Brahmin thought. He went to the boy and asked, "What is your name"?

"My name is Somara", the boy replied.

"Where are you going?" The Brahmin asked.

"I am going in search of bread", the boy replied.

"Will you live with me? I will give you bread, shelter and other things as well", the Brahmin asked.

"I will live with you. However, in turn what I will have to do?" The Bhil boy asked.

"You will give grass and water to my horse, clean the house, and accompany me whenever I go out besides other small things which I ask you to do", the Brahmin replied.

Somara agreed to live with the Brahmin. Next morning the Brahmin prepared *batis* (small round breads made of thick dough) and roasted those *batis* on cow dung cake fire. Then he put *karhi* (a preparation consisting of gram-flour dressed with spices and curd) on coal fire to boil.

"Somara I am going to take bath. When I leave put the *kari* (rafter) on the door, otherwise street dogs will enter inside and will make the home dirty", the Brahmin said to Somara. The Brahmin never ate without taking bath. He was very hungry because he was on fast the earlier day.

"I should obey my master otherwise he will scold me", Somara uttered. He went inside, left the *batis* on the cow dung cake fire and brought the pot in which the *karhi* (curry) was kept for boiling. He smeared the *karhi* on the door. When the Brahmin returned home he saw the door and asked, "Who has done this? Who has smeared the *karhi* on the door"?

"I have done so", Somara replied obediently.

"Why? Why have you done so? You have wasted it", the Brahmin said.

"I have followed your instruction sir. You had told me to put karhi on the door to stop street dogs from coming inside the room", Somara replied.

The Brahmin cursed his luck and said, "You do not know the difference between the *kari* (rafter) and *karhi* (curry). I had kept fast yesterday. I am hungry. What will I eat now?"

Both of them tried to eat *batis* only but could not eat the dry breads more and gave those *batis* to dogs.

"I am going to other village follow me there", the Brahmin said to Somara. He sat on the horse and Somara was walking behind him. The Brahmin was hungry hence was feeling giddiness. After covering some distance he noticed that his towel was missing from his shoulder.

"Where is my towel? Have you seen that?" The Brahmin asked Somara.

"That has slipped away from your shoulder. I had seen that", Somara replied.

"Why you did not lift that? Why you did not tell me about that?" The Brahmin asked.

"You had not told me to do so", Somara replied.

The Brahmin controlled his anger and said, "If any thing falls take that without asking me. Go and bring the towel."

Somara ran fast and brought the towel back. They proceeded ahead. After some time the horse started excreting. Somara thought if he would not collect the horse dung the Brahmin would make him run back again. He collected the horse dung in the towel of the Brahmin which was still with him. When they reached near the bank of a river the Brahmin wanted to take rest. He sat down under the shadow of a tree. To wipe up his sweat he asked for his towel from Somara. Seeing horse dung in his towel he became angry and scolded Somara badly. Somara said innocently that it was the Brahmin who had ordered him to collect every thing which had fallen.

"Throw out the dung and wash the towel", the Brahmin said to Somara. It was out of Somara's ken why the Brahmin was angry when he had followed every instruction of him honestly.

The Brahmin was hungry and tired, too. Though he had rice and lentils with him he had no strength to cook. He gave some money to Somara and said, "Go and bring some ting to eat from the nearby village."

Somara ran fast as he too was hungry as well. He purchased four *pethas* (sweet meat preparation of gourd) from a shop. In his return journey he thought that out of four *pethas* the Brahmin would give him two so he ate two immediately. He had not reached the Brahmin. In the mean time he thought that the Brahmin would not eat any thing alone and would give half of his food to him so he ate away another one *petha* again. He reached up to the tree under which the Brahmin was sitting. He gave only one *petha* to him.

"You got only one *petha* for the amount I gave to you", the Brahmin was surprised.

"No I got four but ate three", Somara replied and told what he thought and how he ate the three *pethas*.

"Why and how did you eat my *pethas* simply by imagining the situation?" The angry Brahmin asked.

Somara took the last *petha* from the hand of the Brahmin and keeping that in his mouth he said, "I ate like this."

The Brahmin could not control his anger. He slapped Somara twice and sacked him from his service. Somara ran away from there.

[Bhil tribesmen claim that in general a Bhil boy is just like the boy Somara. They make fun of themselves and laugh. They say that the boy Somara had made a Brahmin fool.]

## THE RABBIT AND THE GIRL

In a village there lived a brother and a sister. Both were laborious and after the death of their parents they had taken good care of their home and field. The brother used to work in the field in the day and in the night the sister used to watch the crops sitting in the watch-hut. Daily while climbing on the stairs of the watch-hut the sister used to sing:

*"Nanhe nanhe pairo wale khargosh aaja*
*Aakar meri god me soja".*
(Small footed rabbit come and sleep in my lap)

A rabbit after listening to the song, used to come and sleep in her lap. One night a boy saw the rabbit and told the brother about the whole incident. The brother wanted to eat the mutton of the rabbit. One night he asked his sister to stay home and went to guard the crops. While climbing the stairs of the watch-hut he, too, sang the song:

*"Nanhe nanhe pairo wale khargosh aaja*
*Aakar meri god me soja".*
(Small footed rabbit come and sleep in my lap)

The rabbit came and slept in the lap of the boy. The boy killed the rabbit with his sickle. He hanged the head of the rabbit against the beam of the ceiling of the watch-hut and after roasting the remaining body of the rabbit relished the mutton. Next night the sister went to watch the crops. She sang the song many times but the rabbit did not come. In the morning she noticed drops of blood in her lap. When she looked up she saw the head of the rabbit hanging from the ceiling of the watch-hut. She understood every thing. By that time shepherds had started grazing their sheeps in the nearby field. She went to them and said, "Brother please collect some dry wood for me."

In minutes the shepherd collected heap of dry woods there. The sister lit the fire and jumped in to that with the head of the rabbit. The farmers and the shepherds present there started shouting, "Look *Holika* is burning." Holika burning (Burning of piles of dry woods) is a part of the celebration of Holi (festival of colour) , celebrated by the Hindus.

The villagers of that village took the whole incident as a mark of the indication to celebrate Holi in their village. They started ever since, celebrating *Holika Dahan* and Holi festival every year.

About this story:

1. Bhil tribesmen claim that it is a simple story. They also say that the myth behind the celebration of festival Holi (Festival of colour) is different. That the villagers of the place where this incident took place, started celebrating Holi after the death of the girl gives emotional satisfaction to the listeners: that the girl received some recognition after all.
2. Why did the boy kill the rabbit so dear to his sister? The Bhil tribesmen say that a Bhil boy first fulfils his own wish and then thinks about others.

## THE CUNNING STEP MOTHER

Bhilba was a farmer. His wife died when his daughter Sumangli was only two years old. Bhilba married again and his second wife Lila became the mother of two daughters namely Budhani and Sanichari. Budhani was one eyed girl and Sanichari was deaf whereas Sumangli was a good looking and soft spoken girl. The behaviour of Lila was not good with Sumangli. She used to give her only half-a-bread to eat. Though the step sisters of Sumangli were in good terms with her, occasionally they did not hesitate in insulting Sumangli.

When the girls grew up Lila sent Sumangli to the forest to graze the cattle. Budhani and Sanichari remained at home and helped their mother in performing household duties. One day Sumangli met a saint. The saint asked her why she was so lean and thin.

"My step mother gives me only half bread to eat", Sumangli replied. The saint gave her one seed of papaya and asked her to sow that on the grave of her real mother. Next day when Sumangli went to her mother's grave she found a papaya tree standing on the grave full of fruits. She ate well and returned home after grazing the cattle. Everyday she was going near the grave and eating the fruits. Slowly her health improved and she looked more beautiful in comparison to her step sisters. Lila noticed the changes taking place in Sumangli. She wanted to know the reason.

Next day she sent Budhani and Sanichari with Sumangli to find out the reason. In the forest Sumangli gave papaya fruits to both of her sisters and requested them not to tell anything to mother. Budhani and Sanichari promised Sumangli that they would not tell anything to their mother; however Budhani put one seed of the papaya in her hair. Next morning when Lila was combing the hair of Budhani she found the seed and asked about that. Budhani told her everything. Lila gave substantial beating to Sumangli. They all went near the tree. Lila put all the fruits in her bullock-cart to sell in the market and after uprooting the tree threw that in a pond.

Except the half bread Sumangli had nothing to eat. She became thin again. One day she met the same saint. The saint wanted to know from her why she had become thin again. Sumangli told him what had happened with the tree. This time the saint had nothing which he could give to Sumangli. When they were talking a snake came to Sumangli and requested her to hide it some where. Sumangli hid that snake in her mantle. After some time the snake charmers came near her and asked about the snake. She told a lie that she had not seen any snake. When the snake charmers left the place the snake came out.

"Sumangli, why are you so thin?" The snake asked Sumangli. She told about her problem to the snake. The snake asked her to close her fist. When Sumangli closed her fist the snake asked her to open the right fist first.

When she opened the right fist one pond appeared there and when she opened her left fist a market itself appeared there.

"When you will close the fist again the pond and the market would disappear from here. Right now I am making you expert in this art. Soon some body will come to you riding a horse. After that you will be happy for ever", the snake said to her and went away from there.

One day Sumangli while taking rest under the tree in the forest slept with her fist opened. A pond and a market appeared there. Meanwhile a prince of nearby village came there riding a horse. Seeing a pond in the forest he quenched his thirst and he roamed in the market. Suddenly Sumangli woke up and closed her fist. Both the pond and the market disappeared. The prince was surprised to see every thing. He had seen Sumangli sleeping under the tree. He wanted to ask her but by then she had returned home. Searching Sumangli the prince reached her home. He found Budhani and Sanichari playing there. When he asked them about the pond and the market they played their ignorance. The prince asked about Sumangli and they said that she was her elder sister. The prince understood what he had seen was the wonder of the elder daughter of the family. He returned from there.

One month later the prince sent marriage proposal to Bhilba indicating that he was interested in marrying his elder daughter. Lila out of jealousy was not able to accept this proposal.

"Sumangli will marry a prince and my daughters will lead an ordinary life, I will not let it happen", Lila uttered in great frustration. She wanted to play a trick. In the marriage proposal she turned 'his' into 'her' and convinced Bhilba that the prince was interested in marrying Budhani and not Sumangli.

After the marriage Budhani went to live with the prince. Soon the prince understood that he was cheated and Budhani was not the girl he wanted to marry. He sent her back to her parents' house. Finally he married Sumangli and both lived happily there after.

[This is a typical story to show the wickedness of the step mother. The happy ending of the story gives satisfaction to the Bhil tribesmen.]

## IN SEARCH OF FORTUNE

Somara and Mangla were two brothers. The elder brother Somara was a poor farmer whereas his brother Mangla was rich. The houses and the fields of Somara and Mangla were adjacent to each other. Both were working hard in their field, yet nothing was growing in the field of Somara whereas Mangla was yielding good crops. The children of Somara were starving and the children of Mangla were leading a happy and prosperous life.

Mangla used to wear silver ornaments and the one out of those ornaments was a heavy bangle. One day Mangla went to the gram-field. After removing his bangle he put that on the ridge of the field. He roasted the gram and after eating that returned home without taking his bangle.

"I am going to take my bangle which I have left on the ridge of the gram-field", Mangla said to his wife.

"Who will take your bangle in the night? We will go and take that early in the morning", his wife replied to him.

As the house of Somara was adjacent to Mangla's house, he and his wife also listened about the bangle.

"Go and take the bangle right now. After selling that we will be able to provide food to our children who are starving", the wife of Somara advised her husband. When Somara went to gram field he saw a man in white clothes guarding the bangle taking a thick stick in his hand.

"Who are you?" Somara asked him.

"I am the fortune of your brother Mangla", the man replied.

"Where is my fortune? I am hungry. My children are starving", Somara asked.

"Your fortune is hidden in between the four seas", the man said to him.

Next morning Somara went in search of his fortune. On the way he saw a mango tree. To take rest he sat down under the tree. The tree asked Somara, "Where are you going?"

"I am going in search of my fortune, a man in white", Somara replied.

"If you find the man in white ask him about my fortune as well. I wear fruits but they fall down from the tree before ripening. No one eats my fruits. Why is it happening with me? Please ask him", the tree said.

"Alright I will ask about you", Somara replied and proceeded ahead.

After covering some distance he met a horse that was running round and round. When the horse saw him he asked, "Where are you going?"

"I am going in search of my fortune, a man in white", Somara replied.

"If you find the man in white ask him about my fortune as well. I am unable to stop. Ask the man how I can stop", the horse said.

"Alright I will ask about you also", Somara replied and proceeded ahead. Finally he reached near the shore of the sea but he was unable to find the meeting point of four seas. He saw a crocodile in the sea. He asked crocodile to help him.

"Why do you want to go there?" The crocodile asked.

"I am going in search of my fortune, a man in white", Somara replied.

"If you find the man in white ask him about my fortune also. How can I get rid of my stomach pain?" The crocodile said to him.

"Alright I will ask about you", Somara replied, "but take me to the meeting point of the four seas first."

Somara sat on the back of the crocodile and that carried him to his destination. Somara found a big palace there. When he entered the palace he found the man in white. He was swinging on the swing.

"Come with me. I have come here to take you. I am hungry and so is my wife. My children are starving", Somara said to that man.

"You go home I will follow you", the man in white said to him.

"Alright I am going but before that tell me about the crocodile, the horse, and the mango-tree", Somara asked the man.

The man in white told him as to how the crocodile, the horse, and the tree would get rid of their problems. Somara gave thanks to him and returned from there. When he came out of the palace he found the crocodile was waiting for him.

"Did you ask about me?" The crocodile asked.

"Yes I did but first take me to the shore of the sea", Somara said.

Again the crocodile carried him at the sea-shore.

"Now tell me what did the man in white say about me?" The crocodile was eager to know.

"You have eaten many diamonds and gold. If you vomit those diamonds and gold your stomach pain will be suppressed", Somara said.

"Alright, I am vomiting. You take all the diamonds and gold with you because those are of no use to me", the crocodile said. He vomited and Somara taking diamonds and gold moved away from there. He reached near the horse. When the horse saw him he asked, "Did you ask about me?"

"Yes I asked about you. If some one jumps and sits on you back, you will stop", Somara said.

"No one comes here. Please sit on my back. I will live with you", the horse requested.

Somara jumped and sat on the horse. Riding the horse he reached near the mango tree.

"Did you ask about me?" The tree asked.

"Yes I did. If some one digs near your root and take all the ornaments buried there you will get rid of your problem" Somara said to the tree.

"No one comes here. Please dig out the ornaments and take those with you", the tree requested.

Somara did so and returned home riding on the horse with all the wealth. His fortune followed him. Now he was a rich farmer. He lived happily with his family.

[This is a simple story for entertainment. However the Bhil tribesmen claim that they do not believe in fortune but hard work.]

## THE CLEVER GIRL

There was a mason named Liba. His wife was Liban. He wanted to make his only son a good mason and gave good training to him. It was his cherished desire that his son would live only with wise persons, so that he could learn only good things. He wanted to marry his son with a clever girl but unfortunately she proved to be a fool. One day Liba asked his son, "How are you? What is going on".

"Nothing is going on", his son replied and started digging the ground uselessly. Liba understood that by living with a dolt wife his son had become a dolt as well. Next morning he went to take a round of the village in search of a clever girl for his son. He did not find any girl of his liking and at last sat under a berry tree. He saw a girl was eating berry fruits sitting in the courtyard of her house.

"Give me some fruits to eat", Liba said to that girl

"Would you like to have hot fruits or cold fruits?" The girl asked Liba.

"Oh my god, what is happening with me? I am on a look out for a clever girl but coming across only fools. This girl seems to be a moron. How can berry fruits would be hot or cold? Any way I want to eat the fruits so I should reply", Liba thought.

"I want hot fruits", Liba said. The girl gave him the fruits which were kept in hot sun. Indeed the fruits were hot and Liba did not enjoy eating those.

"I want cold fruits", Liba said again. The girl went inside her home and brought the fruits kept in the room. Liba ate those fruits with pleasure.

"Where is your father?" Liba asked the girl.

"After tying a knot he has gone to eat the dung of vulture", the girl replied.

"What does it mean? I could not understand", Liba asked.

"My father has gone to meet one of his relatives. He has tied one coin in the corner of his *dhoti* (waist cloth). It means he has tied a knot. While coming back he will drink liquor and will fall in drainage. He will eat all short of dirty things there. That is why I said he will eat the dung of vulture", the girl replied.

Liba liked her word and thought that the girl was not a moron. He asked, "Where is your mother?"

"She has gone to mill for grinding the wheat. If mother will come, mother will not return and if mother will not come, mother will return", the girl said.

"Again I could not understand the meaning of your words", Liba said.

The girl said smilingly, "One has to cross the river to go to the grinding-mill. My mother has gone there after crossing the river. If it starts raining the Mother River will overflow and my mother can not return. That is why I said if mother comes, mother will not return. If it will not rain the river will not overflow and my mother will return. It means if Mother River will not come my mother will return."

Liba understood that his search was over. He married his son with that clever girl. One day he asked his son, "How are you? What is going on?"

"Father I am going to build a palace which will have only one pillar", the son replied. Liba noticed the changes which had taken place in his son. He was satisfied thinking that the clever girl had made his son clever. The son of Liba built a beautiful palace for the king which had only one pillar. Now he has to put one dome on the top of the palace. It was a dangerous job and the son of Liba was reluctant to do it.

"You will have to put the dome on the top of the palace otherwise I will hang you. However, if you come out successful in doing this job I will give you hundred thousand coins", the king said to the son of Liba. Now he had no choice other than to put the dome on the top. He wanted to take help from his clever wife in coming out of this problem.

"My king I am ready to put the dome on the top but for that I need special thread which has been kept at my home. Send your servant to my home he will bring that thread from there", Liba's son said to the king. The king sent one of his servants to bring the thread. When the servant of the king reached the house of Liba's son he met the first wife of the Liba's son. She gave raw thread to the servant. When the son of Liba saw the thread he understood what had happened in his house.

"Who has given this thread to you?" Liba's son asked the servant.

"Your first wife has given this thread to me", the son replied.

"Go and ask for the thread from my second wife", Liba's son said to the servant. When the servant went to bring the thread the second wife of the son of Liba asked why he was in need of thread. The servant described to her everything. The second wife realized that her husband was in danger. She said, "I will not give the thread till the son of the king himself does come to take it from me."

The king sent his son to the second wife of Liba's son. She locked the prince in a room. Giving finished thread to the servant she said, "If while putting the dome my husband falls and breaks his leg I will break the leg of the prince. Whatever will happen to my husband I will do exactly to the prince."

The servant returned to the king and told what had happened with the prince and what did the second wife of Liba's son say. The king took special precaution for the safety of the son of Liba. When the servant gave finished thread to the Liba's son he understood that his wife would have taken right steps for his safety. The king's servants were standing around the palace taking net and other things to make sure that the son of Liba would not fall down on the ground. He put the dome on the top of the palace. The king gave him hundred thousand coins. He went home and his wife made the prince free.

Liba was happy with the achievements of his son. They all lived happily.

[A clever girl saved the life of her husband and made him prosperous. Bhil tribesmen claim that a clever wife makes the family happy because Bhil man does not use his brain.]

## THE BOON OF JALMATA

In a Bhil village there lived a farmer couple. The couple was childless and it was the main reason of their sorrows. One day the wife of the farmer had gone to fetch water at the bank of the river. There she saw a number of baby frogs jumping around their mother. She said, "Jalmata (the goddess of water) if you make me the mother of daughter, I will offer that girl to you." The Jalmata heard the words of the farmer's wife. She appeared before her and said, "Alright, I will give you a daughter but you will have to fulfil your promise."

"Yes, I will remember my words", the farmer's wife replied. She returned home but did not say anything to her husband about her commitment to Jalmata. After ten months she gave birth to a baby girl. The farmer couple was happy after becoming parents of a child. When their daughter was two months old the farmer's wife told her husband about her promise to the Jalmata. The farmer was shocked but he did not say any thing to his wife. After the birth of the daughter the farmer's wife gave birth to two sons. They all were living happily. Gradually the children of the farmer grew up. One day when the farmer's wife had gone to fetch water with her daughter, Jalmata appeared before her and said, "Your daughter has grown up. Recall your promise and give this girl to me." The farmer's wife returned home in a pensive mood. However, she was ready to fulfil her promise.

Next morning she went to river with her daughter. She had not forgotten to take a flower with her. Coming near the bank of the river she told her daughter, "My daughter, throw this flower in the water." The girl threw that flower in the water. The flower started flowing with the current of water. Now the farmer's wife said to her daughter, "My daughter, bring that flower back." When the girl went near the flower, the flower flew away from her. Like this she was going to the flower but that was flowing away from her. The girl started singing:

My mother, my foot has drowned but the flower is away
My mother, my knee has drowned but the flower is away
My mother, my waist has drowned but the flower is away
My mother, my chin has drowned but the flower is away
My mother, my nose has drowned but the flower is away

Singing like this the girl kept informing her mother about her status in the water and about the distance of the flower from her. Every time her mother kept saying, "Move forward and bring the flower." At last the girl drowned in the water and the farmer's wife returned home. She informed about her daughter to her husband.

The Jalmata took that girl home. Both were living together. After some time the Jalmata got that girl married with a frog. One day the girl said to her husband, "I want to meet my mother. Tomorrow I am going to meet her. If you want to come with me, you are most welcome."

"Crock, crock", the frog husband agreed to go with her. Next morning the girl with her frog husband and children went to meet her mother. When the farmer's wife saw her daughter she came running to her and hugged her. The girl felt happy meeting her parents and brothers. Her frog husband was also showing his happiness saying, "Crock, crock." In the night they all slept well. Early morning the farmer's wife asked her frog son-in-law, "Would you like to take bath in hot water or in cold water." When the farmer's wife said hot water, the frog said, "Crock, crock." This way the frog said that he was willing to take bath in hot water.

The farmer's wife kept boiling water in a big bronze plate. The frog jumped in to that and died. The farmer's wife put all the baby frogs in a basket and left that basket near the bank of the river. Here after the girl live happily with her parents and brothers.

[This story is only for entertainment. Bhil tribesmen say that in a story any thing can happen. A girl can marry a frog and have frog children.]

## HURA AND PURA

Many years ago, in a village there lived two brothers. The name of the elder one was Hura Bhil and Pura Bhil was the younger one. They were notorious thieves and had made all the villagers scared with their misdeeds.

One day a group of milkmen came to their village with their cattle. At the centre of the place where they had erected their tents, they put a stone as a symbolic form of their god. After that they cleared the area around the stone and smeared the area with cow dung. Some of them made small idols of mud and put those idols in the name of various gods and goddesses near the stone. They used to take good care of their gods and goddesses and used to worship them daily.

One day Hura and Pura, with their group men, were crossing near the settlement of the milkmen. When the milkmen saw a group of people coming to them they thought they were coming to ruin their gods and goddesses. They all went near the stone and the idols and requested, "My god, the group of people coming towards us may never reach us and die out there itself where they are." All the men of Hura and Pura died immediately. Hura and Pura were surprised when they saw their men dead. They went near the milkmen and said, "You have killed our men. Tell me why you people did so? Make them alive otherwise we the brothers will kill you all."

The milkmen replied, "We have erected one stone and had kept some idols there. We consider that stone and those idols as our gods and goddesses. When you all were coming to us we thought that you all were approaching to ruin our gods and goddesses. We requested our gods to kill them and what happened you have already seen."

"If your god is so powerful better ask him to make our men alive. If it happens we will start believing in the power of god", Hura and Pura said to them.

"Yes, we will do that but first make a promise. You will not do any harm to our idols", the milkmen said.

"Alright we promise we will not harm your gods and goddesses", Hura and Pura said.

The milkmen requested their gods to make the dead men alive and it did happen in no time. They all were happy and surprised. They asked the milkmen, "What is god? Who is god?"

"The creator of this world is god. He has made me, you and every body", the milkmen said. The thieves developed faith in god. They left their bad habits and started living with the milkmen. But, the police were after Hura and Pura. When they came to know about the new settlement of Hura and Pura they covered the whole area.

Hura and Pura said to the police, "It is true that we were thieves and had stolen many things but now we have left our bad habits. We work as labourers and are leading a peaceful life."

The police men spread spiny bushes, swords, and spears on the ground and said to Hura and Pura, "If you are telling truth, walk on these bushes, swords, and spears bare footed. Nothing will happen to you. If you are telling a lie you will get hurt and we will arrest you."

Taking the name of god Hura and Pura walked on those bushes, swords, and spears bare footed and nothing happened to them. The police men left them free and went away. Hura and Pura lived peacefully worshipping gods and goddesses.

Even today the Bhil tribesmen pour some liquor in the name of Hura and Pura at the time of celebration of any festivals.

[Bhil tribesmen claim that this story is based on a real incidence. May be some imaginary things, such as death of a group of thieves as well as their gaining lives again, have been added in it to make it impressive, the Bhil tribesmen believe in it. This story also shows that how one man can change completely when he comes in contact with any body different from him and is impressed by him.]

## THE TRICK OF A WOMAN

In a village a poor farmer lived with his wife. His wife was very clever. Before the rainy season every villager was preparing his field for sowing the seeds after the first rain. The poor farmer had no bull so he was unable to plough his field. One day his wife said to him, "If it starts raining how we can sow seeds in our field? Go and bring the bull from any one known to you. After ploughing the field we will return the bull."

The farmer went every where, met every person but none was ready to lend his bull to him because they all were busy in their own field. The poor fellow went from door to door in search of bull and returned home in the evening disappointed. Seeing him returning without the bull his wife said, "Do not worry. The one who is up will give us the bull."

One day when the farmer went out in search of bull his wife also went out pretending she was collecting cow dung cakes. She was beautiful and every man wanted either to spend some time with her or to talk to her. When she was collecting the cow dung cakes one man saw her. He was happy to see her alone. He went near her and asked, "*Bhabhi* (elder brother's wife, but some times people call friend's wife as *Bhabhi* as well), where the farmer brother has gone?"

"He has gone out in search of bull and will return late in night. If you want to talk to me come to my house in the evening. At present I am in a hurry", the farmer's wife replied. Like this she invited five men to her house.

In the evening when she was preparing bread all the five men came to her house one by one. She hid four men in the four corners of her room and made the fifth one sit on the beam of the ceiling of the room. She was preparing breads and was throwing towards all the five men. The men who were sitting in the corners of the room could not see one another but that who was sitting on the beam saw every one. Meanwhile the farmer returned home empty handed. His wife as usual said, "Do not worry. The one who is up will give us the bull."

The man who was sitting on the beam jumped down and said, "Why I alone will give the bull? The other four who are sitting in the corners will also have to give bulls." The farmer caught all of them and started shouting. The villagers living nearby came to him running fast. They all started beating these five men. At last each of them gave one bull to the farmer and asked for forgiveness. The farmer left them but he had become the owner of five bulls.

[Bhil tribesmen say that such things never happen in reality. This story is only for the sake of entertainment. At the same time they also claim that a woman can fool all the villagers, because the men are innocent beings.]

## AFTER THE CATACLYSM

The population on the earth was growing fast and it became difficult to accommodate all in the land. The heavenly cow Rupan pulled up one of her feet and was not ready to put that down.

All the gods and goddesses held a meeting at the palace of the supreme god Dharmiraja. The supreme god asked the others, "The population on the earth is growing fast. The cow Rupan is not ready to put her foot down. What should we do now?"

They all thought and came to the conclusion that the entire population should be drowned in the water. They selected the dark moon day of the coming month for this purpose. Rohit, the fish was also present there where the gods and goddesses had gathered and were deciding about the cataclysm.

The fish wanted to save two children, one boy and one girl, from the consequence of this cataclysm. The children used to feed the fish their food when they came to the bank of the sea. The next day when the children came to the sea-shore Rohit said them, "Listen to my words carefully. The entire earth is going to be drowned by the god on the dark moon day of the coming month. All will die. If you both want to save yourself do some thing needful."

The worried children asked, "What should we do now?"

"Build a cage cum boat. Load the food and water for twelve months in that cage. Before a day of cataclysm lock yourself in that cage. I will help in floating that cage for twelve months", the fish said.

The children built a cage and loaded food and water in that. A day before the cataclysm they entered the cage with their cock and locked themselves. Before they locked themselves a fly also entered the cage. It rained continuously for several days and the entire world was flooded with water. Pushing the cage Rohit the fish kept that floating on the water.

Although all the gods and goddesses had given there consent for this cataclysm, the lord Mahadeva and the lord Rama were sad. After twelve months they heard the crocking of a cock. The Mahadeva said, "It seems some one is alive on the earth."

Mahadeva, Gaura and Rama came to earth to find out who was alive. When they were having their lunch sitting on their flying cot the fly came out of the cage and started roving over the food. Following that fly the gods reached near the cage. They pulled the cage nearer to them and when opened the door two children came out.

"Who told you about the cataclysm?" Mahadeva asked the children. When the children did not reply Lord Rama started beating them. The children told them the name of Rohit. Rama cut down the tongue of the fish. From that day onwards fish lost the power of speaking. Rama asked the children who were they. The children replied that they were brother and sister and were the offsprings of a washer man. Rama made them lose their relationship and made them husband and wife.

Taking some mud from his own body the lord Mahadeva put that over the head of heavenly snake Baniser Nag. Lord Rama blowing the mud spread that. The level of water came down. Baniser Nag promised that he will not let the earth drown in the water.

From the children of the washer man the Bhil, Bhilala, Rajput, Brahmin, and many other tribesmen and caste people originated and the earth was populated again.

# 3 Folktales of Barela

## BARELA: AN INTRODUCTION

The Barela tribesmen inhabit the western as well as central part of India, particularly the states of Gujarat and Madhya Pradesh. The tribe Barela is one of the sections among the two sections of Bhilala tribe, as the Bhilala is divided into two sections, the Greater (Bara) and the Lesser (Barela) Bhilala (Stiglmayr 1970, Kapp 1986, Tribhuman 2003).

The Barela-Bhilala ranks just above the Bhil tribe, since they are the direct descendents of the Rajput (Considered higher caste in Hindu caste system) chiefs who married the daughters of the Bhil chieftains (Russell 1916, Nath 1960, Haekel 1963, Deliege 1985).

Although Barela-Bhilala tribesmen are slightly better off than Bhil tribesmen, basically they are very similar to them in culture, language, and social organisation (Venketachar 1933, Aurora 1972, Fuchus 1973, Malhotra 1992). They celebrate all the fairs and festivals with the Bhil tribesmen living in the same village. Their mythological stories related with festivals are almost the same. However, at the same time we may notice the impact of dominant Bhil culture in their other folktales.

### RINGIYA AND JINGIYA

There were a king and a queen. They had two sons named Ringiya and Jingiya. One day a sparrow pair built their nest in the bed room of the queen. The female sparrow hatched the eggs and two sparrow chicks came out. Although the male and the female sparrow used to take good care of their young ones, it was the female sparrow who took more care of her babies. One day the female sparrow died in an accident and the male sparrow made a new female sparrow his mate. In the beginning every thing went well but one day the new female sparrow fed poisonous spine to the sparrow chicks eating which they died and fell down on the bed of the queen.

The queen was watching every activity of the sparrow pair very minutely. When she saw the dead sparrow chicks, she got scared.

"What will happen to my sons Ringiya and Jingiya if I die? Will the new queen kill my sons?" She started thinking. She told about her fear to the king.

"Nothing will happen to you and your sons. Do not worry and live happily", the king assured the queen. After a few months the queen died after a short illness and the king married again. In the beginning the new queen took good care of Ringiya and Jingiya but when she became mother of her own daughter she wanted to get rid of Ringiya and Jingiya.

One day the king had gone to forest for hunting the prey. Ringiya and Jingiya were playing with their friends near the palace. The new queen was watching their game. One of the friends of Ringiya and Jingiya kicked the ball and that reached near the new queen. One by one all the boys went to take their ball from the new queen but she refused to return that. At last Ringiya and Jingiya went to take the ball and when the new queen refused to give ball to them they got irritated. They tried to take the ball forcefully. The new queen got a chance to get rid of both of them. She started shouting, "Look every body, Ringiya and Jingiya are misbehaving with me."

Gradually this rumour went all over the village and the king also came to know about it. He burst out in anger. Taking a sword in the hand he started his return journey to palace. He was also singing a song which meant he was going to cut the heads of Ringiya and Jingiya. When both the boys heard the saying of the king they replied that the new queen was their mother and they had not done any thing wrong with her. However, when they found that the king was not ready to hear any thing and was firm with his decision to cut their heads they fled away in the forest. The new queen was happy because her trick to get rid of Ringiya and Jingiya was successfully executed.

Ringiya and Jingiya were wandering in the forest hungry. The failure to feed themselves and find any shelter for comfort made them exhausted and finally they fell down unconscious. By chance an old woman was passing through the forest. When she saw two kids weak, tired and unconscious she felt pity for them. She prayed to god, "My god, make these two boys healthy, wealthy, and arrange for their shelter as well."

The god heard the prayer of that kind hearted woman and made Ringiya and Jingiya healthy and wealthy. He also provided a good castle to them. The old woman asked Ringiya and Jingiya who were they and what had happened to them. They told their story to that woman.

"Live happily in this castle which god has provided to you. One room of this castle is filled with gold coins. You are wealthy as well", the old woman said to them. Ringiya and Jingiya lived happily in the castle and with times they grew up into handsome young men. On the other hand time took a turn and the parents of Ringiya and Jingiya lost their wealth and power.

They were living like ordinary persons. The old woman who had made Ringiya and Jingiya healthy fixed the marriage of Ringiya with the daughter of the new queen. When Ringiya and Jingiya went to see the girl they recognized their parents and understood that the girl was their sister. They did not say any thing to their parents and returned home saying that the girl was not of their liking.

Slowly the king and the queen lost their remaining wealth and they started begging. One day they reached the castle of Ringiya and Jingiya to beg. After seeing the big and beautiful castle of Ringiya and Jingiya the new queen said, "Once we had a big palace, wealth and every thing. We had two sons like you but they left us after a small rift."

"You are telling lie. There was no rift between you and your sons. Your sons did not leave you but you forced them to leave the palace by playing a dirty game with them", Ringiya and Jingiya said. Then they described the whole incident that had happened with them in past and due to which they had left the palace.

"How do you know all about it?" The king asked.

"Because we are Ringiya and Jingiya", they replied.

The queen bowed her head out of shame. She asked them to forgive her. Ringiya and Jingiya forgave their parents. They built a good palace for them near their own castle. After some time they married their sister with a good boy and both of them also got married with good girls. They all lived happy after that.

[This is a typical story to show that seldom does a step mother remain good. Barela tribesmen say that for the sake of welfare of the children one should not marry again. However they also admit that if a man does not marry who will take care of home? They say that if a woman becomes mother she should not die early.]

## THE BOY NAMED RAJU

In a village a potter lived with his wife and two sons. His elder son Rakesh was a laborious potter whereas the younger Rajesh, called as Raju was not interested in doing work. He used to spend his time in playing the game of tip-cat.

"I will make Raju a laborious labourer", the potter uttered. He told his wife, "Today I am going to take an important decision. Cook festive food for all of us."

The potter's wife cooked delicious food and Raju was served with his favourite dishes. The potter had two donkeys, two spades, and two shovels. When Raju finished eating, the potter distributed his belongings among his two sons. Giving one donkey, one spade, and one shovel to Raju he said, "Raju, from today you will have to earn your living."

Raju took the spade and the shovel and riding on the donkey proceeded towards the unknown destination. He reached near the bank of a river. Tired Raju wanted to take some rest. He tied his donkey with a tree and slept under that tree. He dreamt that his donkey was grazing green grass. Meanwhile his donkey cut loose his rope and made him free. He started grazing grass in the nearby field. When Raju woke up from his sleep he saw that his donkey was grazing grass.

"It seems that the sleep has made my donkey free and fed him the grass. I should do justice with the sleep and hand over this donkey to him", Raju thought.

He shouted, "Sleep, I am giving my donkey to you." He left his donkey there and started his journey forward. After covering some distance he saw a rat was making burrow for him by removing mud by his mouth and legs. He felt pity for the rat and to make his work easy he decided to give his spade to him. He left the spade near the rat and moved from there. On the way he saw a cockroach pushing the cow dung with his head and was giving that a round shape. Again he took pity on the cockroach and gave his shovel to him.

Now he reached another village. The king of that village had announced that the person who would make his daughter laugh would become his son-in-law. In addition the king was ready to give half of the kingdom to his would be son-in-law. Many people had tried their luck by telling jokes to the princess. They had tried to make her laugh. Raju also wanted to try his luck. He decided that he would not tell jokes to the princess but would tell what had happened with him after he left his home.

Raju reached the court of the king in time. All the king's men were present there. The princess was sitting near the seat of the king. Raju started telling his story to them. When he said that he had given his donkey to sleep, they all started laughing. The princess was also among them. When Raju told that he had given his spade to the rat and shovel to the cockroach the princess could not control her laughter.

In accordance with the announcement the king married his daughter with Raju and gave half of his kingdom to him. When Raju was taking rest in his palace with his wife, the minister of the king came to him and said that the princess was his wife. He kicked Raju out and told the princess, "Go and heat water for me and cook delicious food."

Unable to do any thing to the minister, Raju sat at the entrance of the palace. Just then the sleep, the rat, and the cockroach came to him and said, "Raju you do not worry we will help you."

"I will make the minster sleep", the sleep said.

"I will make a hole in the wall of the palace", the rat said.

"I will kill the minister", the cockroach said.

The sleep made the minister sleep. The rat made a hole in the wall and with the cockroach reached near the minster.

"Put your tail in the nostril of the minister", the cockroach said to the rat. When the rat did so the minister started sneezing. When he opened his mouth to sneeze the cockroach entered into his mouth and reached inside his stomach. He cut the intestine of the minister into pieces and broke his heart. This way he killed the minister.

The enemy of Raju was dead. He called his parents and elder brother to live with him and lived happily with them and his wife ruling half of the kingdom.

[This is a simple story for entertainment. Barela tribesmen say that if any one does well to others, the others will also do well to him.]

## THE FARMER, THE BULL, AND THE JUSTICE

In a village there lived a farmer. He was in need of a bull but he had no money to buy that. He went to the man who was selling bulls.

"What is the coast of a bull?" The farmer asked the bull owner.

"Thirty coins only", the bull owner replied.

"Give me a bull. I will pay you tomorrow in the afternoon", the farmer requested him.

"If you will not pay the money in time then what will I do?" The bull owner asked.

"You can take your bull back and in addition you can cut half kilo flesh from my body", the farmer replied.

The bull owner agreed for this condition and gave a bull to him. The farmer tried hard but could not arrange thirty coins. The bull owner reached farmer in time. He took his bull back but could not cut flesh from the body of the farmer. The farmer was very thin and weak and cutting the flesh from his body meant making him dead.

"Let us go to the king. He will do justice", the bull owner said to the farmer.

When they both were going to meet the king a woman was sitting under the tree with her new born baby. Unfortunately the farmer's leg slipped and he fell down on the baby. The baby died and the woman started crying. The husband of the woman wanted to kill the farmer. The bull owner stopped him from killing the farmer and told what had happened with him and they both were going to meet the king for justice. The husband of the woman also joined them. They all proceeded forward to meet the king for justice. On the way the farmer was uselessly throwing pebbles here and there and by chance one of the pebbles hit the eye of a horse and the horse became one eyed. The owner of the horse became angry and he wanted to make the farmer one eyed man. This time the bull owner and the husband of the woman stopped him from doing so telling him what had happened with them and they were going to the king for justice. The horse owner, too, joined the group.

Near the palace of the king a man was digging water well and his father was testing whether the mud was wet or not by going inside the ditch. The farmer did not noticed the well and fell down into that. He fell on the father of the man who was digging the well. The old man died on the spot. His angry son wanted to kill the farmer. The bull owner, the husband of the woman, and the horse owner all stopped that man telling him what had happened with them and that they all were going to the king for justice. The man also joined the group and they all reached the king for justice.

"He has taken the bull but could not give the money in time", the bull owner said.

"He has killed my son", the husband of the woman said.

"He has made my horse one-eyed", the horse owner said.

"He has killed my father", the man who was digging the well said.

The king heard the story of every one and did justice but he left the farmer free.

Why the king left the farmer free? What was his judgement? The person who is reading this story or listening it, decide him/herself.

[Barela tribesmen find it necessary to tell such story to their children. They think that by doing so they will involve their children in discussion and will increase the power of imagination of them.]

## ABBA KULCHI

In a village there lived a woman named Abba Kulchi. She was in need of labourers who could plough her field. In search of men she went to the neighbouring village. That village was facing the problems of drought and almost all the villagers had gone to other place in search of work. Two brothers Hiru and Bhiru were also planning to go out with their mother in search of work. Abba Kulchi went to them and said, "You all three come to my village. I will give job to both of you and your mother will live with you."

Hiru, Bhiru and their mother went with Abba Kulchi to her village.

"You two brothers will plough my field", Abba Kulchi said to them. The two brothers worked hard and after ploughing the field they saw the seeds of millet in that. Abba Kulchi paid them for their work and they returned to their own village. When the millet plants grew up to knee height, Abba Kulchi went to call Hiru, Bhiru, and their mother to weed the field.

"Stay one night with us. Tomorrow we will go with you", Hiru and Bhiru said to Abba Kulchi. In the night Hiru dreamt that millet plants were saying to him that they two did not welcome the new plants when they came out from the earth. Similarly, Bhiru dreamt that their home-hearth was telling him that they did not give importance to him. They should give rest to their hearth at least once in a year. In the morning Hiru and Bhiru exchanged their stories of dream with each other. Both the brothers decided to welcome the new plants and give rest to the home-hearth.

"We are ready to weed your field but you will have to give an earthen pot to me", Hiru and Bhiru told Abba Kulchi. Abba Kulchi agreed for this. After going to the village of Abba Kulchi they fixed a bamboo pole in the middle of their field. Then they put the earthen pot upside-down on this pole. This is physically possible because the pot was filled with mango leaves and hay and the leaves were tightly compacted in the pot. This way they protected the crops from the evil eyes. They burnt perfumed saw dust on the burning coal near the field and also broke one coconut there. This way they gave warm welcome to new crop. They cooked outside the home and gave rest and importance to home-hearth.

Even today the tribesmen give welcome to their new crop and cook outside the home to give rest to their home-hearth.

[To protect their crop from the evil eyes the Barela tribesmen fix an earthen pot in their field when the crop grows up to knee height and cook out side home. This way they welcome their crop and give rest to their home-stove. This story gives sanction to their celebration.]

## THE BULL AND THE TIGER

Once upon a time in a forest there lived a cow and a tigress. They were good friends. Daily they used to drink water together in a waterfall. The tigress used to drink water after climbing on a stone whereas the cow drank standing on the ground level.

One day both of them ate *avla* (fruits of emblic myrobalan tree). If any one drinks water after eating *avla* the water tastes sweet. When the tigress drank water it tasted sweet. By chance that day the cow had climbed on the stone to drink water whereas the tigress was standing on the ground. The tigress thought that the water tasted sweet because she had drunk that after the cow. That day the cow was standing up, and the saliva of the cow had made the water sweet.

"Oh, if the saliva of the cow is so sweet then the whole cow must be the sweetest", the tigress uttered and in greed killed the cow and ate the flesh. However, this incident did not affect the friendship of their young ones, the tiger cub and the he-calf. After a year the cub became a healthy tiger and the he-calf became a bull. Both were good friends and used to spend time, as much as possible, together. The bull used to go out to graze the grass in the morning and the tiger to hunt in the night.

One day a group of hunters saw the bull and wanted to eat the flesh of that. They killed the bull. When the bull did not return in the evening the tiger started searching for him. In the forest a vulture was singing song describing how the hunters killed the bull. The tiger went there, where the hunter were distributing the flesh of the bull among them. The tiger turned into a dog and went closer to the hunters. When the hunters saw a healthy dog near them they started fighting to decide as to who would become the master of the dog.

"We will throw one piece of flesh of the bull of our part to the dog. The person whose thrown piece the dog would accept first, will become his master", one of the hunters said. They all threw pieces of flesh towards the dog. When the tiger saw the flesh of his friend he turned into his original form. Seeing a tiger close to them the hunters ran away. The tiger chanting some *mantras* (Religious spells) made his friend alive. Both of them returned home and lived together for ever.

[This imaginary story is meant for entertainment. The happy ending of the story makes it popular among the Barela tribesmen especially among the children.]

## SEVEN BROTHERS

In a village an old Barela man lived with his wife and seven sons. After some time the old man died and all the brothers started living separately. The youngest among them was Vilash who lived with his mother. All the elder brothers of Vilash were wicked in nature and they did not care for their mother. They also wanted to keep Vilash away from them because he was very good and helpful in nature. He had respect for his mother and he used to take good care of her.

One day the elder brothers of Vilash planned to go to forest for hunting the prey.

"We will go early in the morning leaving Vilash here. Even Vilash should not know where we are going", they all talked with each others. However, Vilash came to know about their plan and he followed his brothers secretly. In the forest the six brothers killed a bird whereas Vilash killed a partridge. While they all were returning home the elder brothers met Vilash.

"Brothers, what did you hunt in the forest?" Vilash asked his brothers.

With great pride the elder brothers of Vilash said to him that they had killed a bird but they were not going to share that bird with Vilash because he was not with them.

Vilash smiled and said, "I do not want any share in your bird because I have killed a partridge for me and my mother."

All the six brothers of Vilash were surprised to see a dead partridge with Vilash. They said to him, "Look Vilash, we are six and you are two. Give this partridge to us and take this bird". The kind hearted Vilash agreed for it and gave his partridge to his elder brothers. When he reached home he told every thing that happened to his mother and asked, "Have I done right mother?"

"Yes my son what you did was right", the mother said to Vilash.

Next day the elder brothers of Vilash again planned to go to forest. Vilash requested his mother to prepare bread for him before sun rise. Taking bread Vilash followed his brothers. But, this time the brothers saw Vilash and scolded him, "Do not follow us. You are a kid. There are numerous wild animals in the forest." They all proceeded forward leaving Vilash there. Vilash kept following them secretly. This time the elder brothers killed a rabbit and Vilash killed a deer. The brothers again exchanged their rabbit with the deer of Vilash. Vilash's mother said what he did was right.

Third day the brothers killed a deer whereas Vilash hunted a *nilgai* (a species of deer bigger in size) and exchanged his *nilgai* with the deer of his elder brothers.

"This Vilash does not stop following us. Let us stop going to forest for some time", the elder brothers talked with each other.

One day the brothers of Vilash planned to rob a rich business man. Vilash came to know about their plan. He said to his brothers, "Take me with you otherwise I will inform mother where you all are going." The brothers had no choice but to take Vilash with them. However they did not stop themselves playing trick with Vilash. They all sat on a healthy horse but gave an old mare to Vilash. They robbed a bag full of coins from a businessman. While returning they gave some coins to Vilash. Vilash fed those coins to the old mare and said, "Give me some more coins otherwise I will inform mother where you all had gone." His brothers gave some more coins to him. Again, he fed those coins to the old mare.

After returning home Vilash tied the old mare with a tree and started beating that. The mare started excreting and the coins came out with her dung but the mare died. Vilash took all the coins. He cut the mare into pieces and sold in the market earning good money. In the market he told that he was selling the meat of *nilgai*.

The elder brothers were watching the activity of Vilash. They also started beating their horses. The horses excreted but no coin came out with the dung. The horses died. The brothers cut the horses in pieces.

"How did you sell the meat in the market?" They all asked Vilash.

"In the market I started shouting come and take the meat of donkey. People came to me and purchased all the meat", Vilash said smilingly.

The brothers went to market and started shouting, "Come and take the meat of donkey."

People came to them and asked, "What did you say? Whose meat you all are selling?"

"We are selling the meat of donkey", the said.

People gave substantial beating to them and threw their meat into a ditch. After receiving beating the brothers returned home. Leaving the village they went for unknown place with their wives and children.

## THE MONKEY

One day a monkey came into city area. He saw a man who was wearing goggles and a wrist watch. He was also hanging a transistor from his shoulder.

"These human beings move how smartly when they wear goggles, wrist watch and hang a transistor. In the forest when I will move like this I will impress other animals", he thought.

In the forest he brought gum from a gum tree and made goggles. Taking a white stone he made a hole in that and inserting a grass leaf in that hole he made a wrist watch. After that he hanged a water-melon from his shoulder like the man was hanging transistor. He started moving in the forest on two legs. But, in scorching sun the gum made goggles dried up and made him unable to open his eyes. The monkey got nervous. He prayed to lord Hanuman (the entellus god), "Hey Hanumanji, make my eyes open. I will offer you the tooth of pig and ribs of a lion. I will come to you sitting on an elephant." The monkey had seen an old temple of lord Hanuman in the forest. When he was praying to god his leg slipped and he fell down in water. In water the gum got dissolved and the monkey started seeing again.

"It seems lord Hanuman had heard my prayer and he has cured me", the monkey thought.

"Now I will have to offer tooth of pig and ribs of lion to lord", the monkey uttered.

He decided to worship lord Hanuman as early as possible and started searching for a pig. When he was moving in the forest he saw a pig. Going near the pig the monkey asked, "Pig brother I am thirsty. Is there any source of water in nearby area?" The pig was thirsty, too.

"Let us find out where some water is", the pig said. In fact the monkey was not as thirsty as he was pretending to be. Both of them started moving here and there in search of water. Meanwhile the monkey was also thinking about how to kill the pig. He got an idea and brought the pig near a well.

"Sit on the curb of the well and hold my tail tightly. I will be hung upside down. Drink water and come out", the monkey said to the pig.

After drinking water the monkey sat on the curb of the well and said to the pig, "Hold my tail tightly, go down in the well and drink water after that I will pull you up."

When the pig went inside the well the monkey started shouting, "You are heavy. You will uproot my tail." With a jerk he made his tail free from the clutches of the pig and left the pig inside the well. The pig was drowned in the water and died. It was not possible for the monkey to pull out the dead pig from the well. However, he got an idea to do this work easily. He went to lion. At that time the lion was chewing the dry bone of an animal.

"My king, why are you chewing this dry bone?" The monkey asked the lion.

"I am hungry for eight days and I have nothing to eat", the lion replied.

"My king I have killed a pig but that is lying inside a well", the monkey said.

Both of them went near the well and together they pulled the pig out of the well.

"My king let us drink water before eating this pig", the monkey said to the lion.

Both of them went to drink water near a river. While coming back the monkey ran and reached near the pig first. He hid the tooth of the pig. They ate the flesh of the pig. By now the lion had become a friend of the monkey but the monkey was thinking about how to kill him. Both had overeaten so they wanted to take a round of the forest running fast. While taking round of the forest the monkey was running ahead of the lion. He went inside the hollow of a tree and came out from the other side. When the lion wanted to do that he got stuck in the hollow. The monkey started beating the lion and killed him. Now he had the tooth of the pig and the ribs of the lion. He was in search of an elephant. He soon met an elephant.

"My brother it seems you are hungry and thirsty. I know a place where there is plenty of grass and water as well", the monkey said to the elephant.

"Take me there", the elephant requested.

"I will take you there but there is a condition. I will go there sitting on your back", the monkey said. The elephant agreed for that. The monkey jumped and sat on the back of the elephant. The monkey guided the elephant towards the Hanuman temple. When they reached near the temple the monkey said, "I am fulfilling the vow I had taken. I have come here riding on an elephant and I have the tooth of the pig and the ribs of the lion." The monkey jumped down from the back of the elephant. He offered the tooth and the ribs to lord Hanuman and leaving the elephant ran away from there.

## THE OLD COUPLE AND SEVEN CHILDREN

Many years ago there was an old couple in a village. The couple was childless and used to spend time playing with the children of the village. Daily in the morning after finishing the house-hold chores they used to lock the door of their house and go out to play. In the same village there was a saint who used to roam in the village for alms. When he saw the house of the old couple always locked he wanted to know the reason. One day he came early, before the couple locked the door.

"Where do you go daily?" The saint asked the old man.

"We have no children. We go out to play with other children of the village", the old man replied.

"Next morning after taking seven fruits from the pond which is near the temple give those fruits to your wife. You will have your own children", the saint said to that old man. Next day the woman ate the fruits and after ten months gave birth to six sons and one daughter. Though the couple became parents, they did not stop going out to play with the children of the village.

One day all the seven children talked with each other, "Our parents do not take proper care of us and remain busy in playing with other children of the village. It would be better if we leave this house and this village as well."

Next morning when the couple went out their own children left the home. Each of them took new route to go to new destination. The girl reached a village where a rich family adopted her as their daughter. Similarly the one among the six brothers reached another village and chief of that village adopted him as his son. Time passed and they all grew up.

One day the village chief, who had adopted the son of the old couple, went to the village where the daughter of the old couple was living. When the village chief saw the daughter of the couple he wanted to fix marriage of his adopted son with the girl. He talked with the foster father of the girl in this regard.

"Send your son here. We will see him first then only I will say 'yes' or 'no' for this marriage", the foster father of the girl said to him.

The boy came to meet his would be wife and her family members. When the girl saw the boy she recognized her brother who had a cut mark over his left eye. She refused to marry the boy but her foster father taking a good amount as bride price from the father of the boy married his daughter with him. When the marriage was over the girl was not ready to go with the boy but her family members forced her to sit in the bullock-cart. Two red coloured bulls were ready to drive the cart. Seeing the bulls the girl started singing:

"Red bull, my red bull,
My husband is my brother,
Do not proceed, my red bull"

The bulls understood the plea of the girl and refused to move even after receiving substantial beating from the hands of the father of the girl. The father of the girl replaced the red bulls with the golden bulls. Seeing the bulls the girl started singing:

"Golden bull, my golden bull,
My husband is my brother,
Do not proceed, my golden bull"

When the golden bull refused to move, the father of the girl replaced the golden bulls with the ordinary white coloured bulls. The ordinary bulls could not understand what the girl was saying and the father of the girl driving the cart reached her in-law's house. Leaving the girl there he returned home.

In the in-law's house the girl refused to keep any relation with her husband who was her brother. The boy became angry and decided to kill the girl in the field at the time when she would bring bread for him. Next day when the girl reached the field taking bread she saw that her brother was not there and the birds were eating the grains. She started singing:

"My brother, my dear brother, birds are eating the grains,

Where are you my brother, where are you".

The boy did not reply and remained lying on the heap of hey, covering his face. When the girl reached near her the boy jumped and wanted to cut her head with a sickle.

"Do not kill me. We are brother and sister. I can not live with you as your wife", the girl said to the boy.

"How do I believe you?" The boy asked.

"Remember we were seven brothers and sister. Our parents did not take proper care of us when we were young. We had left our home for new destination", the girl said.

The boy recalled every thing and said, "You can not be my wife because you are my own sister. But we are married. What should we do now?"

Both of them decided to leave the village secretly. They went to another village. The girl married another boy and her brother got married with some other girl. They all lived happy here after.

[Barela tribesmen tell this story to their children for entertainment. This story raises some questions.

1. Why did the old couple not take proper care of their own children? The Barela tribesmen say that possibly they were emotionally attached with the children of the village.
2. Why the girl did not make it clear to her foster father that why she was not ready to marry with the boy? She could have told the boy that he was her brother. The Barela tribesmen laugh and say that in a story such things happen.]

## GAPPA AND SAPPA

One day Gappa Barela went to a tailor to get his shirt stitched. He said to tailor, "Brother, stitch my shirt quickly. I have to go to attend a marriage ceremony." The tailor was busy stitching the shirt of another man who had come first.

"I am busy stitching the shirt of another person. If you want me to work fast, tell me a story. I can work fast listening to a story."

Gappa had no time to tell story to him. He had to perform lots of work at home. Above all, he did not know story telling.

"It would be better to come to take my shirt tomorrow rather than tell story to you", Gappa said to the tailor and returned home.

Next day Sappa Barela, the younger brother of Gappa went to tailor to take the shirt but the shirt was not ready. Sappa wanted to teach a lesson to the tailor.

"Tailor brother, please stitches the shirt quickly I have to go to buy fish which is available at a very low price in the market. One woman in selling it only 25 paisa kilo", Sappa told the tailor.

"If fish is available so cheap then I will buy it first. You take care of my shop while I go to market and return soon after buying the fish", the tailor said to Sappa. Sappa agreed for it. The tailor went to market and started asking from the people about the woman who was selling fish at the rate of 25 paisa kilo. People started laughing at him.

After some time the wife of the tailor came to the shop and asked about the tailor from Sappa.

"The tailor has gone to market with a woman who had winked her eye when she saw your husband", Sappa replied.

The wife of the tailor became angry and taking a bamboo stick she went to search her husband. In the market she found that her husband was searching for a woman. Both of them started quarrelling and while quarrelling they fell down into a drainage. They went to the river to take bath. Meanwhile, the parents-in-law of the tailor came to the shop and asked for the tailor from Sappa.

"The son of the tailor expired and the tailor and his wife have gone to river to burry the child at the bank of that", Sappa replied.

The parents-in-law of the tailor started crying and ran towards the river. When the tailor saw his parents-in-law coming crying to him he thought some thing wrong had happened. He as well as his wife started crying in anticipation. Now they all four were crying. After some time the father-in-law of the tailor asked him what had happened to his son.

"To my son? Nothing has happened to him? He is alright and is playing at home", the tailor replied.

"But the man sitting in the shop told me some thing different", the father-in-law said. After this they all narrated what Sappa had told them.

The tailor understood that it would be better to stitch the shirt as soon as possible and get rid of Sappa. He ran towards his shop.

[This story is only for entertainment. At the same time the Barela tribesmen also say that do not take on a Barela man.]

## GANGA TELI AND BHLAT DEV

In Nangal Wadi village, there lived a woman named Moyala Gobali. She gave birth to Bhilat Dev, a snake. Moyala was a human and Bhilat Dev was a snake and this made his father suspicious towards his birth. He put the baby in an open field of the village and said, "If you are my son then ask your mother to feed you living in the home."

"Mother feed me, I am here", Bhilat Dev told his mother. A flow of breast milk came from the home and Bhilat Dev satisfied his need.

Lord Shiva made Bhilat Dev his pupil and trained him in every art. He put Bhilat Dev around his neck. One day lord Shiva sent Bhilat Dev to village Kahud for some work. Bhilat Dev took human form and proceeded towards Kahud with his nephew. After performing the assigned job Bhilat dev started his return journey. On the way they reached near a well. Bhilat Dev wanted to prepare bread to eat. He collected dry wood, prepared dough, and sent his nephew to bring burning coal from any villager. The nephew reached the house of Ganga Teli.

"Brother I have to burn dry woods to prepare breads. Please give me burning coal for that", the nephew told Ganga Teli.

Ganga Teli was crushing oil. He did not give coal to him but made him his galley slave. Bhilat Dev came to know what had happened with his nephew. He put the crusher of Ganga Teli on fire while sitting near the well. When Ganga Teli saw the fire he started shouting and calling his daughters-in-law.

"My daughters come fast and bring water, the crusher is burning", he said to his daughters-in-law. His daughters-in-law poured all the water of home in the crusher but the fire could not be extinguished. Ganga Teli sent them to bring more water from the well. When they reached near the well, Bhilat Dev turned them into female vultures and said to lay eggs sitting on a banyan tree.

When Ganga Teli noticed that his daughters-in-law were not returning he went to well to see what the reason of delay was. Bhilat Dev was sitting near the well.

"Have you seen my daughters-in-law?" Ganga Teli asked Bhilat Dev.

"I had sent my nephew to you to bring burning coal but you made him your galley slave. I have turned your daughters-in-law into female vulture. Now they will come down after one year and one month", Bhilat Dev replied.

Ganga Teli requested Bhilat Dev to return the human form of his daughters-in-law. Bhilat Dev agreed for that and said, "You will have to send my nephew with the burning coal."

Ganga Teli sent the nephew of Bhilat Dev with burning coal. Bhilat Dev prepared breads and both of them ate and returned to lord Shiva. But, they got delayed in returning. Lord Shiva told them to live there where they stayed for a while and got delayed.

Barela tribesmen believe that Bhilat Dev lives in Onkareshwar at the bank of Narmada River.

[When Bhilat Dev was able to burn the crusher sitting near the well why he did not burn his wood for preparing breads? The Barela tribesmen say that he had taken human form and was behaving like a human. When he suffered he had to show his power.]

## CLEVER SABLU

Sablu was a carpenter who was very clever. One day two messengers of the god of death came to take him. Sablu was not ready to die so early. When he saw the messengers of the god of death he started thinking about the way to escape from the clutches of death.

"Please allow me to live in this world one week more, come after seven days", Sablu requested the messengers. The messengers agreed and went back telling that they would be back after one week. Within one week the carpenter Sablu constructed a house on a banyan tree which had twelve rooms one above another. After seven days the two messengers came again to Sablu.

"I am ready to go with you but before going I request you to see my new house which I have constructed on a tree", Sablu said to them. The messengers agreed to see the house. When they were observing the rooms, Sablu very cleverly locked them in the twelve room house and locked the door of every room one by one. Now he was free to live on the earth without any fear.

When the messengers of the god did not return, the god decided to search for them. Taking the dust from his foot the god made a seed and sowed that on the earth. A plant came out from that seed and grew into a big tree. Slowly that tree started bearing flowers. The villagers got surprised to see that the flowers of that tree started growing up in the sky. They called the *Barwa* (shaman). The *Barwa* burnt five spines near the tree and sprinkled the ashes over the tree. All the flowers of the tree dropped down. The *Barwa* after collecting those flowers in an earthen pot went to the bank of the river. He burnt dry woods there and put the pot on the fire and collected the steam in another pot. When the steam cooled down that became liquor. The villagers started drinking the liquor.

The carpenter Sablu also went there to drink liquor with his friend who was a blacksmith. Both of them got drunk there and lost there sense.

"It is true that you are a good carpenter but if I do not make tools you can not work", the blacksmith told the carpenter.

"What you are telling is absolutely correct but I had constructed a house twenty years ago and had locked the messengers of the god of death there. For twenty years they are locked there", Sablu told his friend.

God came to know about his messengers. He made them free and taking Sablu with them they all returned to their abode.

Giving the example of this story:

1. The Barela tribesmen believe that the tree grew from the seed sown by the god. It was the first tree of *mahua* (*bassia latifolia*) on the earth and the preparation of liquor from *mahua* flowers started.
2. Bhil tribesmen feel proud thinking that a clever Barela man can fool anybody.

## DHINCHIRI

In a village a boy used to live with his sister. The boy used to work in the field whereas his sister took care of home.

One year the brother got a good crop in his field. After harvesting he collected all the grains in the field.

"I am going to take food. In my absence take care of the grains", the boy said to his sister and went home. But, the sister indulged in playing with her friends and forgot to take care of grains. When the boy returned from home he saw birds were eating the grains and his sister was playing with her friends. He became angry and in anger he slapped his sister. His sister fell down and died. The intention of the boy was not to kill his sister but she died. The depressed boy buried his sister in the home. After the death of his sister the boy lost his interest in every thing and remained busy remembering her. One night he saw his sister in his dream.

"Bring a piece of teak wood and erect that in the corner of the room. Making a garland of black bangles and red thread put that on the erected wood. Worship that wood daily. You will get mental peace and will prosper", the sister told the boy in his dream.

Next morning the boy erected a piece of teak wood in the kitchen of his house and put the garland of black bangles and red thread on that. He worshiped that wood daily. Gradually he started taking interest in his work and became prosperous.

Even today the Barela tribesmen erect a piece of teak wood or put a piece of stone in one corner of one of the rooms of their home and worship that daily. They call that wood or the stone their *Kul Devi* (clan goddess). It is called *Dhinchiri* in local language.

[This story gives ratification to the Barela tribesmen to erect a wood, the symbolic form of *Kul Devi,* in their house and worship that for their prosperity and happiness.]

## THE DEATH OF A DEMON

There were a king and a queen. One day the king said to queen, "I am going to forest for hunting the prey."

"Okay, but take care of yourself", the queen replied.

Taking a gun and riding on a horse the king went to forest. He saw a deer. He fired on the deer but missed the target. Though the deer did not die, he fell unconscious. Tying the legs of the deer the king brought that to his palace.

"My queen, I have brought a deer that is alive. Cut it into pieces and cook. I am coming after drinking liquor", the king said to the queen. The queen chained the deer and went to perform some other work. Meanwhile the prince came to see the deer and made that free. The deer ran away to forest. The queen was afraid.

"When your father will come to know that you have freed the deer, he will kill you. It would be better if you run away from here", she told the prince. She cooked one cock and served that to the king. The king understood that the queen had not cooked the deer. He said to queen, "Do not try to fool me. Tell me the truth otherwise I will kill you."

The queen told the truth to the king. Angry king taking a sword searched for the prince but could not succeed.

The hungry prince was wandering in the forest. He met a Barela girl who was the daughter of a village chief. She, too, had left her house because her father was forcing her to marry a boy who was not of her choice. Both of them got married and started living in the forest. The prince used to hunt prey in the forest and the princess used to collect the fruits. One day the girl told the prince to kill a wicked demon that was living in a palace and was very wealthy. She also told the trick involved in killing the demon to the prince. The prince killed the demon and occupied his palace and took all his wealth. Both of them spent whole life there without any fear.

## THE FLYING COT

Once upon a time a village was ruled by a young king who was a bachelor as well. Two Barela tribesmen were his fast friends. One among them was a carpenter whereas the other was a blacksmith. The carpenter and the blacksmith used to spend time sitting in the court of the king. Daily morning they used to go to the court and return in the evening empty handed.

One day the wife of the blacksmith said to him, "Daily you go out in the morning and return in the evening empty handed. How long working as a labourer I will earn and feed you as well as your children? If it will continue I will go to my mother's house with my children. Your friend is a king. He can spend time sitting and chatting in the court but you can not do so. You should think about your wife and children."

The blacksmith said, "What you are telling is absolutely true. Till now I had not thought about you and our children, but you do not worry. I will make such a thing which will surprise people. I will earn good amount from that item."

The blacksmith started making a chair. He worked whole night on that chair. It was morning when he finished his work. The speciality of that chair was peculiar. The chair used to turn in the direction in which the person sitting on that, used to turn his face. Taking the chair he reached the court of the king. Seeing the chair the people present in the court were surprised.

"Give this chair to me. I will pay you as much as you ask for it", the king said.

"King you are my friend. I will not ask any thing from you. But, if you want to give some thing to me, give me any thing you think I deserve", the blacksmith replied.

The king gave him hundred thousand coins. The blacksmith gave all the coins to his wife. Now she was happy. All the hardship of the family had gone.

When the wife of the carpenter came to know about the chair she encouraged her husband to make a peculiar thing. The carpenter worked whole night and made the legendry flying cot. Next morning he reached the court of the king with his legendry flying cot. The king took that paying hundred and fifty thousand coins.

The king said his men to take care of every thing and sitting on that flying cot flew away. But, he forgot to ask from his friend how to stop that cot from flying. He tried to stop the cot but could not succeed and covered a long distance. After some time by chance he pulled a lever and the flying cot started coming down but by then he had reached another village. He hid his flying cot in the bushes and went to a nearby hut. The owner of that hut was an old woman. The king started living with that woman as her son. The woman had numerous goats and the king used to graze those goats. The king of that village, where the young king had reached, had kept a peculiar condition for the marriage of his daughter. He had announced that any young person equal to the weight of the princes would be considered illegible for marrying her. He had put one balance in his court. The princess used to sit on one pan of the balance and the young man on the other. If the man's weight was found either less or more than that of the princess the king used to kill him. Many young men had lost their lives in this process. The king's army men were forcefully bringing young men to the court and were forcing them to sit on the pan of the balance.

One day some villagers came to the court of the old king and said, "The son of the old woman who lives near the forest is young and handsome. He is grazing goats in the morning and returns to his hut in the evening. Call that man and take his weight."

The old king sent his men to the hut of that old woman. The king's men made the young king sit on the pan of the balance. His weight was equal to the weight of the princess. The old king married his daughter with the young king and gave half of his kingdom to him. The young king was leading happy life with his wife. The princess was pregnant and when the time of delivery came near the young king said to his wife, "I am not the son of that old woman. I am a king and our baby will be born in our kingdom. Let us go there."

People gave tearfull farewell to them and the young king and his wife flew away sitting on the flying cot. When they were flying over the sea the princess started crying with labour pain. The young king landed the flying cot on an island. He left the princess there and went in search of a nurse. He reached a village and asked a nurse to come with him. The nurse, with her other belongings also put some burning cow dung cakes in the flying cot. Due to burning cakes the flying cot got burnt and both of them fell down in the sea. They swung for hours and came out from the water. They reached the same village which was the habitant of the nurse. The nurse went to her home and the young king started working in the palace of the king of that village.

On the island the princess gave birth to a male child. She was living there in great difficulties. One day she was washing clothes sitting on a piece of wood. She had tied her baby over her back. All of a sudden due to a strong wave the piece of wood moved from the island and started floating with the waves of the sea. After three days that wood reached the sea shore and got stuck in the sand. After three days the princess had seen the land. She reached the same village where her husband was working. She was moving in the market of that village. Seeing a new woman in her village roaming uselessly the army men of the king got alert. They reached near the princess and asked, "Who are you? You are coming from where?"

"I am tired and disturbed. Do not irritate me asking such questions from me. Leave me alone", the princess replied. The army men brought the princess to the king. When the king saw a beautiful woman he wanted to marry her.

"Will you marry me"? The king asked from the princess. The princess understood that saying 'no' to king was dangerous for her as well as her child's life. She said, "Give me six months time after that I will tell you whether I will marry you or not", the princess replied. The king agreed for that and arranged for her living in the palace. The princess used to cry remembering her husband. One day, while peeping through the window of her room, she saw her husband working in the garden. She threw her finger ring near her husband. The young king recognized the ring and looked upward. He saw his wife and son there. Hiding from the eyes of every one he climbed on a tree and reached inside the room of his wife. Both of them cried after meeting with each other and told what had happened with them.

"The king wants to marry me and he will not allow us to go easily", the princess said to her husband.

"Do not worry we will run away from here in the night", the young king said to his wife.

Both of them taking there child ran away from there and reached their kingdom. The villagers saw their king with beautiful queen and a baby prince. They all became very happy and gave a warm welcome to them. The young king lived happily with his family. His two friends the carpenter and the blacksmith were also with him.

[This story entertains the people. At the same time gives emotional satisfaction to the Barela tribesmen when they find that two Barela tribesmen had made unique things for the king.]

## THE PARROT AND THE SPARROW

One day an old man went to a hillock to collect dry wood. He found two eggs there. After returning home he handed over the eggs to his wife.

"Boil these eggs. We will eat boiled eggs today", the old man said to his wife.

"I am going to keep these eggs in the chicken coop. We will not eat these eggs", the old woman replied.

She kept those eggs in the chicken coop and after a few days a parrot chick came out from one of the eggs and a sparrow chick came out from the other egg.

One day the old man sent the parrot and the sparrow to bring dry wood. The parrot brought only one piece of wood whereas the bird brought a bundle of wood.

"You brought only one wood and this bird has brought a bundle. You are a useless fellow. Get out from my home", the old man scolded the parrot. In anger the parrot left the home and sitting on a mango tree started singing:

"Gulai gulai aam khaya,
Thanda thanda pani piya".
(I ate ripe mango and drank cold water).

Some milkmen heard the song of the parrot. They liked the song. After capturing the parrot they brought that to the king. The king liked the song as well. He decided to keep that parrot with him.

"Where would you like to live? In the godown of grains or in the box of coins?" The king asked the parrot.

"I would like to live in the box of coins", the parrot replied.

The servant of the king put the parrot in the box of coins. After some time the king thought that the parrot would die in the box. He sent his servant to see whether the parrot was alive or dead. The servant opened the box to see the condition of the parrot and the parrot flew away. But, before flying he did not forget to take coins in his beak, claws, as well as in feathers. He reached home and said to the old woman, "Mother, clean the mortar and put that in the courtyard."

The old woman put the mortar in the courtyard. The parrot put all the coins into that and the mortar was filled with the coins. The old couple became very happy to see the coins. The old man said to the sparrow, "See the parrot has earned so much and you spend time sitting idle. Get out from my home."

The bird went to parrot and asked, "Brother, from where did you earn so many coins?"

"If you eat the thorns of *babool* (acacia tree) and plum, coins will start coming from your body", the parrot replied.

The innocent bird did exactly that and died. The old couple cooked the bird and enjoyed the flesh.

[This story is just for entertainment. The tragic end of the story makes it less popular. Barela tribesmen say that it was not necessary to kill the bird at the end.]

## THE RAT AND THE FEMALE MOUSE

There were a rat and a female mouse. Both were living together in a hole. One morning, while getting up the rat's foot touched the female mouse. The female mouse got a chance to get sulky and harass the rat. She remained lying on the bed covering her body with a sheet. When the rat saw that the female mouse was not getting up he said to her, "It is getting late, get up."

"I will not. Why did you kick me?" The female mouse said.

The rat fetched water and said, "I have fetched water now get up and prepare bread."

"I will not. Why did you kick me?" The female mouse said.

The poor rat prepared bread as well. Now he told the female mouse, "Look, we should not make a mountain out of a mole. I have finished all the house hold chores and have prepared breads as well. Now get up. It is the time for taking lunch."

The female mouse said, "Yes you are right. We should not make a mountain out of a mole and live together with better understanding."

She jumped from the bed and sat to eat with the rat.

This story entertains the Barela tribesmen especially the children.

## THE PEWIT AND THE THIEVES

There were an old man and an old woman. The old man was in search of a labourer who could guard his crop in night living in the field. One day he told his wife, "I am going to search a labourer and will return in the evening. Be careful and take care of every thing."

The old man left his home and went away. On the way he saw a bird pewit.

"Where are you going?" The pewit asked.

"I am going in search of a labourer who can guard my crop in the field", the old man replied.

"Take me with you. I will guard your field and crop in night", the pewit said.

"You are a small bird how can you take care of my field? Do not waste my time and let me go", the old man said and moved from there.

The pewit flew away and sat on a mango tree. When the old man reached near the tree the pewit repeated his request, "Take me with you I will take care of your field and crop as well."

The old man did not say any thing and kept walking. The pewit flew away and sat on the roof of a hut. When the old man reached there that pewit said again, "Take me with you I will guard your field and the crop as well."

At last the old man returned home with that pewit bird.

"I have brought a labourer with me. This pewit will guard our field and crop", the old man said to his wife. Seeing the bird the old woman said, "How can this small bird guard our field and crop?"

"This pewit was not leaving me. Where ever I was going it was coming in front of me", the old man replied.

There was a watch hut in the field of the old man. In evening he made pewit sit on the stairs of the watch hut and returned home. In the mid night some thieves came to steal the crop of the old man. When they started cutting the crop the pewit started singing:

*"Mat kaat re! Mat kaat re! Khet ki phasal,*
*Machan par baitha so raha hai Aishram"!!*

(Do not cut the crop. In the watch hut Aishram is sleeping)

The thieves coming near the watch hut broke that and started cutting the crop. The pewit started singing again:

*"Mat kaat re! Mat kaat re! Khet ki phasal,*
*Machan par baitha so raha hai Aishram"!!*

(Do not cut the crop. In the watch hut Aishram is sleeping)

The thieves came near the stairs broke that and they baked the pewit and ate. They thought that they were free to cut the crop peacefully. However when they started cutting the crop, each piece of the pewit in the stomach of the thieves started singing:

*"Mat kaat re! Mat kaat re! Khet ki phasal,*
*Machan par baitha so raha hai Aishram"!!*

(Do not cut the crop. In the watch hut Aishram is sleeping)

The thieves cut their belly with the sickle and died. In the morning when the old man came to the field he saw his darling pewit was sitting among the dead bodies of the thieves. He was happy thinking that he had not done wrong keeping the pewit to guard his field and crop.

[Even today the Barela tribesmen do not kill pewit. They become emotional when they listen or tell this story to any body.]

## BHOLA AND BHUNDA

Bhola and Bhunda were two brothers. They used to graze goats of a man. One day in the afternoon Bhola said to Bhunda, "I am going home to bring bread, till then make the goats drink water."

When Bhola went, Bhunda went to the middle of the pond with the goats. He left the goats there and after returning sat under a tree. By then Bhola came with bread and asked about the goats.

"I have left them in the pond to drink water", Bhunda replied.

Bhola went to see the goats. He found all the goats were drowned and their bodies were floating over the water.

"Oh, our master will give substantial beating to us. Let us run away from here", he said to Bhunda.

Both of them ran away from there and reached another village. They were tired and hungry and were roaming in the village in search of job. They saw one hut in a remote area.

"You stay here. I am going to bring some thing to eat from that hut", Bhunda said to Bhola. Bhunda went inside the hut but found no one there. He saw a pot full of curd. He took that pot and returned to Bhola. Bhola said to him, "You have taken the curd without permission from the owner. When he will return, he will beat us. Let us run away from here." Taking the curd they ran away from there and reached a field where a farmer was ploughing.

"You stay here, I am going to bring *bidi* (crude form of cigarette) from that farmer", Bhunda said to Bhola.

"Brother do you have *bidi* with you?" Bhunda asked the farmer.

"No, but if you take care of my field I will bring that from my home", the farmer replied.

Bhunda agreed to take care of the field and the farmer went to bring *bidi*. In the absence of the farmer Bhunda took the yoke of the plough and returned to Bhola.

"Oh, Bhunda what have you done? The farmer will not leave us without beating", Bhola said, and both the brothers ran away from there as well and reached near a hut adjacent to a forest. Bhunda stole a drum from that hut and fearing the consequence they climbed on a mountain. On the mountain Bhunda saw a wild buffalo. He killed that buffalo and uprooted his horns.

When the brothers were taking rest sitting under the shadow of a tree, Bhunda saw a honeycomb. He filled the horns with the bees and covered the opening of the horns with leaves. Both the brothers ate honey and after that they started taking a round of the mountain. They saw a cave. The owner of that cave was a demon, but at that time the demon was not there. They entered the cave and slept on the bed of the demon.

When the demon returned he saw the foot prints of Bhola and Bhunda. He understood that two persons had entered his cave and were still present there because the foot prints were not indicative of their coming out.

"Who is inside the cave?" The demon asked.

"First you tell who are you?" Bhola and Bhunda asked together.

"I am the demon. I am the owner of this cave", the demon replied.

"We are two brothers. We are the great demons and more powerful than you", Bhola and Bhunda said.

"It is not possible. In nearby area no one is more powerful than me", the demon replied.

"Okay, let us test who is more powerful. Throw your tooth inside the cave", Bhola and Bhunda said.

The demon threw his tooth which was not visible to in that big cave. Bhola and Bhunda threw the yoke of the plough. When the demon saw that he got scared.

Now the two brothers asked the demon to beat his stomach. When the demon did so, nothing happened. Bhola and Bhunda started beating the drum. Hearing the sound of the drum the demon thought that in reality Bhola and Bhunda were more powerful than him.

"Hey you demon spit near the opening of the cave", Bhola and Bhunda shouted.

The demon spitted and Bhunda threw the curd.

"Yes you are telling right. You two are more powerful than me. I am ready to leave the place", the demon said.

"Not right now. We are giving you the last chance to prove your superiority. Throw your louse to us", Bhola and Bhunda said to the demon.

The demon threw his louse and Bhola and Bhunda threw the bees towards the demon. The bees started biting the demon and made him half dead. The demon ran away from there shouting that he would not return again.

Bhola and Bhunda became the owner of not only the cave but all the treasury of the demon. They worked for any one after that and lived there peacefully.

[Barela tribesmen claim that they are just like Bhunda of this story. This story is only for entertainment.]

## BHONDU BARELA AND HIS SON

Bhondu Barela was a farmer and a great devotee of lord Hanuman (the entellus god). He used to worship the statue of Hanuman daily by offering him a flower and used to ask for a child from him. His neighbour Tutiya Barela was a fisherman. He too was a devotee of lord Hanuman.

One day in the presence of Bhondu Barela, Tutiya Barela entreated in front of the statue of Hanuman, "Oh god, make me able to catch one kilo fish today. I will offer one fish to you."

He caught one kilo fish that day and in the morning put one fish near the statue of Hanuman. He kept increasing the weight of fish day by day and putting the number of fish in front of the statue. His success made Bhondu Barela irritated.

"I also worship this god whole heartedly but he does not hear my request. He fulfils the desire of Tutiya but not mine. Today I am going to give substantial beating to this lord", Bhondu Barela uttered in anger.

Taking a shoe in hand he went to beat the statue of Hanuman. When he was about to beat the statue lord Ram appeared in front of him and asked, "Why do you want to beat Hanuman?"

"He does not hear my request and fulfils all the desires of my neighbour Tutiya", Bhondu Barela replied in irritated tone.

"Possibly fulfilling your desire is not in the hand of Hanuman. Let us go to lord Shiva. May be he will fulfil your desire", lord Ram said to Bhondu Barela.

Bhondu Barela took the statue of lord Hanuman in his hand and went to lord Shiva with lord Hanuman.

"I have watched the religious book of mine. In my book nothing is written about your child. I can not fulfil your wish. However, I can advise you to go to seven sisters who live in a corner of the world. May be they can give you a child", lord Shiva told them.

Bhondu Barela went to seven sisters Likhari, Jukhari, Vinyari, Duniyari, Vaan, Bijashni and Vayu along with lord Ram and lord Shiva.

The elder six sisters after watching their books said that they were unable to fulfil the desire of Bhondu Barela. Now the last hope for the Bhondu Barela was Vayu Mata. They watched the book of Vayu Mata and found a ray of hope. They all said to her, "You have two sons. Give one son to Bhondu. We will bring back your son after three years."

Vayu Mata agreed to give her one of the sons to Bhondu Barela and after ten months he became father of a child. Gradually three years passed. All three years Bhondu Barela kept thinking about ways to protect his son from death. He had not said any thing to his wife who was very happy after becoming a mother. He got his son married with a three year old girl.

Today was the third birthday of the son of Bhondu and all were happy except Bhondu. He was aware of what was going to happen in the night.

In the night he made his child sleep on a white sheet and put burning coals in a censer near the child. At mid night, Hanuman, Ram and Shiva came to child to take him back.

"Are you sleeping Bhondu? We have come to take the child back", all the three gods asked.

"No I am not sleeping. You can take the child back but look, Agani Dev (god of fire) is guarding the child. If you will do any harm to him he will become angry. Do you want to make him angry? What will happen to you all if he will become angry and will not come to you? How will you all cook?" Bhondu Barela asked them.

All the three gods thought for a while and went back leaving the child there.

Next night he put a pot of water near the child and when the six elder sisters of Vayu Mata came to take the child he said, "Look Jal Mata (goddess of water) is guarding the child. What will happen if she becomes angry with you? What will you drink? How will you cook?"

All the six goddesses thought for a while and went back without taking the child.

Third night he made his son sit on the sheet with his three years old wife. That day at mid night Vayu Mata came to take her son back along with her six elder sisters, lord Hanuman, lord Ram and lord Shiva.

"Look at my son and my daughter-in-law. How innocent and happy are they. Do you want to break the pair? Do you want to make my daughter-in-law a lonely child?" Bhondu Barela asked Vayu Mata.

Vayu Mata thought for a while and said smilingly, "You are very clever. I will not make your daughter-in-law a lonely child."

They all went back leaving the child to live with Bhondu Barela. Vayu Mata did not forget to bless the couple to lead a long and happy married life.

[This story shows the impact of dominant culture in the story of Barela tribesmen. They have used the names of the Hindu gods and the tribal goddesses in this story. Barela tribesmen claim that without threatening even the god does not listen to anybody. If Bhondu had not taken his shoe to beat hanuman he would have not become the father of a child. At the same time they also claim: one should use his brain to force the super power to do some thing they do not want to do. Bhondu had put Vayu Mata in dilemma and at last she had to leave her child with him.]

## RAMIYA AND SHAYMIYA

Ramiya and Shyamiya were two brothers. They were farmers and owner of two shops. After the death of their father they divided their paternal property among them and started living separately. Ramiya was a devotee of god. He used to work hard in his field and sell goods honestly in his shop. He was happy with what so ever he was earning. His brother Shyamiya was just the opposite. He was a *nastik* (an atheist) and a dishonest man. He used to sell his rice and lentils after mixing pebbles into that. He became rich by resorting to dishonest practices. He purchased cattle and sold milk after adding water. His wealth kept increasing. His wealth had made him as well as his family members proud. Shyamiya used to make fun of Ramiya because he was a god fearing honest man and he was not rich.

One night Ramiya dreamt about god. In his dream the god said to him, "Ramiya I am always with you. Your brother is a dishonest man but he has earned which is given by me. His prosperity has fleeting existence. One day he will realize his mistake."

In the morning Ramiya was very happy thinking the god was with him. He started putting more efforts in his work. Although his earning was not enough, he was not ready to use dishonest practices to increase that. Soon the villagers recognized the honesty of Ramiya and started buying grains and other goods from Ramiya's shop only. Ramiya, his wife and children worked hard and took care of their field, shop and cattle. Their hard work and honesty worked and they became rich. Even after becoming rich Ramiya remained a humble and honest man. He never made fun of any body in his family.

The wealth of Shyamiya had changed the mentality of his entire family members. His children started drinking liquor and gambling. They were not ready to work in the field and left that under the care of servants. The villagers started neglecting Shyamiya and his family members. They stopped buying goods from his shop. The servants did not take proper care of the field and the cattle. His cattle died and field became barren. Since people had stopped purchasing goods from his shop he suffered loss in his business as well. Gradually he became poor. Ramiya tried to make him understand the power of god but he did not hear his brother's advice.

One day some one killed Shyamiya's son and he became a ghost. His ghost started living on a banyan tree near his house and created havoc for every one in the village. Some times he used to cry telling he was not happy and wanted to get rid of this ghost living. The death and restlessness of the soul of his son made Shyamiya perturbed. He came to his brother Ramiya for help.

"Brother, I am sorry I did not hear your advice earlier. I have come to you for help. Please do some thing so that my son's soul can rest in heaven", Shyamiya said to his brother.

Ramiya hugged his brother and both of them went to temple with their family members. In front of the statue of the god Shyamiya said, "My god, please excuse me. Here after I will not indulge in dishonest practice. I will not make fun of any body and work hard to earn for my livelihood. Please excuse my son as well and make his soul rest in peace."

After worshipping the god they all returned home. Shyamiya started working hard in his field and became an honest man. The soul of his son never gave trouble to any one and never cried in night. Both the brothers lived together happily here after.

[Through this story Barela tribesmen give lesson to their children that a dishonest person always suffers and an honest person lives happily. Ramiya was an honest man and though in the beginning he was poor, he was happy with his family members. His brother Shyamiya got success over night but lost every thing in the same way. His dishonesty did not work for long. Barela tribesmen believe that after the death a dishonest person becomes a ghost and noble person goes to heaven.]

## THE TEACHING OF A BRAHMIN

One day Surya Barela was going to city to buy some things for his house. On the way he saw a Brahmin. That Brahmin was returning to his own village after performing some religious work in another village.

"Brother tell me some thing good", Surya said to the Brahmin.

"I take one coin to give one good advice", the Brahmin replied.

Surya without saying any thing put one coin on the palm of the Brahmin.

"Wherever you go keep one living creature with you", the Brahmin said to Surya.

After covering some distance Surya put another coin on the palm of the Brahmin.

"Do not take bath with the crowd in the river but going away from that", the Brahmin said to Surya. By then the Brahmin reached his home and saying good-bye to Surya he went away.

When Surya was going towards the city he saw a crab. He recalled the first teaching of the Brahmin and put that crab in his bag. After some time he reached near a banyan tree. He was tired so he slept under the shadow of that tree. The crab kept in the bag of Surya came out and started moving near the tree. There was a hole of a snake in the root of that tree. The snake came out from his hole and moved towards Surya. The crab saw the snake. Pouncing on the hood of the snake the crab started biting in his eyes and killed that. When Surya got up he saw the dead snake and the crab sitting over that. He understood every thing and giving thanks to the Brahmin said, "Oh, unknown Brahmin you have saved my life today. Spending only one coin for the advice and saving the life was a good deal."

Leaving the crab there he proceeded further. He reached near a river. It was hot and many persons were taking bath in the river. Surya also wanted to take bath. He recalled the second teaching of the Brahmin and decided to take bath after going away from the crowd. After taking bath he moved from there. He was going while thinking about what he had to buy in the city. Suddenly he realized that he had left the bag full with coins at the bank of river where he had taken bath. He ran towards the river and found his bag was safe. No one had taken that. If he had taken bath with the crowds and had left his bag possibly he would not have found that safe. Once again he gave thanks to that Brahmin. He was happy that he had learnt two good things.

[After telling this story Barela tribesmen say that it is always good to live in good company. Good man always tells good thing. They also say that it is worth spending money for good cause.]

## THE GIRL NAMED SONBAI

'Sonbai was the only sister of her seven brothers. She was the youngest among them. One day when she was making butter-milk a cat came to her and said, "If you will give some butter-milk to me I will tell you a secret."

Sonbai gave some butter-milk to her and said, "Now tell me what the secret you have."

"The demon Kirun wants to marry you", the cat replied.

To save herself from the demon, Sonbai left her home with her seventh brother. Both were roaming in the forest. However, the demon Kirun came to know the whereabout of Sonbai. He reached the forest and forcefully made Sonbai sit on his horse. After that he ran away from there. The brother of Sonbai was unable to save her. He started crying remembering his sister. An old woman was crossing from there. When she saw a young boy crying she hanged a drum from the neck and shoulder of him and said, "Play this drum and search for your sister. Nothing will happen if you cry only."

The boy started playing drum and searching for his sister singing:

"Oye meri piyari bahena
Tu kaha hai kahena
Tere bina mai bechara
Phirta hu mara mara"

(My sister where are you? Inform me. In your absence I am maundering)

The demon Kirun had locked Sonbai on the top floor of his palace. When she heard the song she recognized the voice of her brother. She peeped through the window and called her brother in the palace. When the demon Kirun came to know about the brother of Sonbai he wanted to kill him.

He called the brother of Sonbai and said, "If you will do my job I will make your sister free". The brother agreed for that.

The demon asked him to cross the river with his men and to bring some fruits from the neighbouring village. For crossing the river the demon gave healthy horses to his men and gave an old mare to the brother of Sonbai. However, while crossing the river all the men of the demon drowned and died. The brother of Sonbai crossed the river successfully but he understood the planning of the demon.

One day he got a chance to escape from there. He made his sister sit on a horse and flew away from there. He had taken one broom, one bamboo, and one pot of water with him. Soon the demon Kirun came to know that both the brother and the sister had escaped from there. He chased them with his men. Hearing the taps of the foot of the horses of the demon and his men, Sonbai started singing:

"Tap-tap ghodwa aabe re bhai'
Kirun sabko daurawe re bhai.
Mera jiya ghabraye re bhai"

(I am hearing the sound of foot steps of the horses of demon and his men. I am in fear).

To give courage to her sister he sung:

"Pichhe mat dekh, dekh aage re bahin,
Ghar ke bagiya ke mahak aaye re bahin,
ghar me roti khayab re bahin"

(Do not look behind but look forward. The smell of our garden is coming. Soon we will reach home and eat bread there)

When the demon Kirun and his men came near them the brother of Sonbai threw the broom towards them which turned in to forest. It took time to cross the forest by the demon and his men and Sonbai and her brother went far away from them. Again when the demon and his men came near them the brother of Sonbai threw the bamboo towards them. The bamboo turned into the forest of bamboos and again it took time for the demon and his men to cross the forest. By then Sonbai and his brother reached far away from them.

The demon and his men did not stop chasing them. Finally the brother of Sonbai threw pot of water towards them and that turned into a river. The demon kirun and his men died drowning in the water.

Sonbai and her brother were very happy. They reached home safe. When the family members saw both of them alive and healthy they were overwhelmed with joy. They all celebrated the day by eating, singing and dancing together. Hereafter Sonbai lived without any fear.

[Barela tribesmen have no idea how did the broom and the bamboo turned in to forest and the pot of water in to the river. The brother of Sonbai was not a magician. They just say that it is a story and a story goes like this.]

## THE GOLDEN HAIRED BOY

Many years ago, in a village there was a boy whose hair was golden in colour. That boy was very unlucky. His mother had died when he was only four years old. His father got married again and the step mother of that boy was very wicked in nature. The boy lived a terrified life due to the atrocities of his step mother. He had a step sister as well who was a flatterer of her mother and used to tease her brother frequently. The step-mother of that boy used to keep him hungry or gave him stale and stinking food. In the day time the boy used to graze cattle in the forest.

One day, in the forest the boy was crying out of hunger. By chance a saint was crossing the forest from that way. He saw the boy crying and felt pity for him. That saint came near the boy and asked, "Why are you crying?"

The boy told about his sufferings to the saint. Taking a teak leaf and chanting some mantras (religious spells) the saint touched the horn of the bull named Puwadiya. Cooked rice started coming out from the horns of Puwadiya bull. After that the saint touched the tail of the cow Kupan and liquid butter started coming out from that. Now the boy had no worry for his food. The saint had taught him the art of taking cooked rice from the horn of the bull and liquid butter from the tail of the cow. Soon the boy became healthy.

When the step mother of that boy noticed the changes taking place in the health of the boy she wanted to know the reason. One day she gave some wheat flour to her daughter and said, "Go and find out what the boy eats in the forest."

The girl went with her bother. However, the boy did not eat any thing that day and slept hungry under a tree in the afternoon. The girl put some flour on the mouth of the boy and when he woke up the girl asked him, "Brother what did you eat? Give that to me too, otherwise I am going to complain to my mother and she will give substantial beating to you."

The boy said, "I am always with you and you have seen I have not eaten any thing."

The girl said that there was something stuck in his mouth. She was not ready to leave her brother easily. At last the brother told the truth to his sister and the girl informed every thing to her mother.

In the night the step mother of that boy said to her husband, "We should sell the Puwadiya bull and the Kupan cow. They are of no use to us."

"Okay I will sell them but wait for some days", the husband replied.

The boy heard the conversation between the two and became very sad. The next morning he was taking bath in the river and it was his luck that the princess of neighbouring village was also taking bath down in that river with her friends. She saw the lock of golden hair in the river and vowed to marry the boy who had golden hair. She returned home and said to her parents, "I will marry the boy whose hair is golden in colour. Otherwise I will not eat." She slept hungry.

The king was worried to see the condition of his only child. He ordered his men to search for the boy who had golden hair. An old woman who was the attendant of the princess used to collect cow dung cakes in the forest. She had seen that boy. She said to the king, "I can bring that boy here but for that you should give me a bullock cart."

The king gave the cart and she went to the forest. When the boy was sleeping in the afternoon she put his flute in the cart. After waking up the boy searched for his flute and the old woman told him to search in the cart. As soon as the boy climbed the cart the driver of the cart drove that. The scared boy started shouting:

"Puwadiya sand kit.. kit.. kit,
Kupan cow kit.. kit...kit"
(Puwadiya bull and Kupan cow come fast)

The bull and the ox came running fast and started dashing their heads against the wheel of the cart. They broke the cart and made the boy free.

The old woman went to the king and said, "The boy is very clever. He has broken the cart."

Now the king gave her a cart made of iron. This time the bull and the cow could not save the boy. The driver of the cart and the old woman brought the boy to the king.

"Do not be scared. I am not going to give any trouble to you", the king said to the boy. He married his daughter with that boy and gave half of his kingdom to him. The boy brought his favourite bull and the cow to live with him. After the death of his father-in-law he became the king of the entire village. He ruled the kingdom for long and lived happily.

(There are several version of this story and it has its counterparts in Bhil stories as well).

# Folktales of Korku

## KORKU: AN INTRODUCTION

The Korku tribesmen inhabit mainly the Indian states Madhya Pradesh and Maharashtra. They also reside in significant numbers in Arunachal Pradesh, Assam, Bihar, Chhattisgarh, Nagaland and Orissa. They speak 'Korku', which belongs to Austro-Asiatic language family. However, they also speak the language of the region they reside in such as Hindi, Bhili, Assamese, Marathi, Malvi and so on.

The word Korku is coined by joining of two words; 'koro' means man and 'ku' makes it a plural meaning of tribesmen (Russell and Hiralal 1976). According to another interpretation 'koro' means road and 'ku' means a man, a street man or a wanderer. Korku tribe is a branch of the Munda tribe and in Madhya Pradesh the tribesmen live in the vicinity of the Gond tribe (Deogaonkar and Deogaonkar (1990).

Initially they were a hunting gathering community dwelling in the forest of Satpura range on either side of the river Tapti. They have become cultivators. Whilst they share the love of the forest with the Gond tribesmen, they are excellent agriculturists and have pioneered the cultivation of potato and coffee in Betul (Madhya Pradesh). Though agriculture is their primary source of livelihood, many of them earn their livelihood seasonally employed as agricultural labourers (Fuchus 1988).

Korku tribesmen of Madhya Pradesh trace their origin to the great mythological snake Karkotaka. They worship snake, hinting at their origin as Naga tribe. They also claim their origin to the Kurus or Kauravas of the Mahabharata period. Some of them consider themselves as Ravanvanshi, having their ethnic origin from the king Ravana. They also worship Ravana. Some of them claim their origin from the Chauhan clan of Rajput (an upper caste according of Hindu caste system). They also claim that they ran away from the battle field and were chased by the Mohammedans. When asked as to who were they, one of them said 'Korku'. Believing that they were not Rajput, they were allowed to remain free. They used to move like nomads in early years but later settled down.

Korku tribesmen believe in clan system. There is a myth about the creation of clans among them. They believe that many years ago their forefathers used to live like brothers and sisters. Tired and bored of their life they went to Bhola Ishwar and asked him how they could become happy. Bhola Ishwar thought for a while and all of a sudden took the form of a furious tiger. Scared by this form of Bhola Ishwar all of then ran for shelter in the forest. Every one tried to hide himself behind whatever could be found by him. After the things calmed down, Bhola Ishwar appeared again in his normal form. All the Korku tribesmen came out of their hide-outs. They gathered around Bhola Ishwar. He told them the object which was used as shelter by each one would be his clan. Thus particular trees, grass, soil, stone and other animate or inanimate objects became the names of their clans. Bhola Ishwar also asked them to marry outside the clan and thus made the clan exogamous.

The present condition of the Koru tribesmen is not good. The literacy rate among them is very poor. They live in huts made up of grass and wood. In the last few decades research studies have showed that Korku tribesmen are in the grip of severe malnutrition (Das 2010).

## THE SEVEN FRUITS

A king had two wives. He had every object of comfort but he was not happy. The reason of his sadness was his being issueless. His cherished desire to become a father was pestering him day by day.

One day he left home and went into a dense forest. He did hard penance to please the god. After six years lord Shiva appeared before him and asked, "King, I am happy with your penance. What do you want from me?"

"My lord, you have given me every thing except a child. I want to become a father", the king replied.

"Look, I am giving you this stick. Go home and you will find a mango tree on your way back home. On hitting the tree with this stick some fruits will fall down from the tree. Give those fruits to your wives to eat. Soon your desire would be fulfilled", lord Shiva said to the king and gave him a stick. The happy king was eager to go home soon. The lord Shiva stopped him and said, "Remember one thing. Hit the tree only once. If you are greedy at all, the result would be disastrous." Lord Shiva disappeared from there and the king started his return journey.

On the way home the king saw the mango tree and hit that with the stick. Seven fruits fell down from the tree. Due to greed the king forgot the warning of lord Shiva and in desire for more children he hit the tree again. He got the result of his greed. The seven fruits and the sticks disappeared from there. Soon, the king realized his mistake. He cried and asked for forgiveness from lord Shiva but nothing happened. Once again he went for penance and after six years lord Shiva appeared before him again.

"My lord, forgive me. I had done a blunder by disobeying you", the king yearned and knelt down before the lord.

"King, seeing your greed I became angry with you. Since now you have accepted your mistake and have paid for that, I forgive you. Go home; the seven fruits are lying there. Give three fruits to each of your wife and eat the remaining one", the lord Shiva said and disappeared from there.

The king went to the tree and taking the fruits he returned home. In the palace all the courtiers accorded a warm welcome to their king. The king narrated his wives what had happened with him and where he was for twelve years. He distributed six fruits between his wives equally and ate the remaining one. After ten months both the queen gave birth to sons. All became very happy and celebrated the day by decorating their houses and distributing sweets to all.

"If the god is with you, any thing can happen", the first queen said.

"And if you become greedy, he (god) can snatch every thing", the second queen said.

"There is no vice like avarice", both of them pronounced together.

## THE GAME OF LUCK

Once upon a time there lived an imperious king. His adulators used to please him with their flattering statements as it was his weakness. He was the father of seven daughters and he always wished that his daughters eulogize him.

One day he called his eldest daughter and said, "Whose luck provides you food?"

The girl thought for a while and said, "Father, you have provided me every thing. I eat by your luck." The king became very happy and he increased the expenses used for her comfort. He called all his daughters one by one and asked them the same question that he had asked his eldest daughter. They all, except the youngest one, gave the same reply that they ate by their father's luck and the king increased the expenses made for the comfort of the princess.

The youngest daughter said, "Father like all other living beings I, too, eat of my own luck. I am here in this palace because of my own luck." Hearing the words of the youngest princess, the king rose in fury. He said, "You are here in this palace because of your luck. Let me see how your luck helps you in making you a queen. If you were with me I would have married you with a king and made you a queen."

The king banished his youngest daughter in the forest. In the dense forest the princess was walking here and there in search of proper shelter. The king, after all being the father of his daughter was following her secretly with four of his attendants. However, he did not know that his daughter was aware of the fact that her father was behind her. The princess saw an abandoned house. When she opened the door she found the house very spacious and was full of all necessary items needed for a comfortable living. She called her father and said, "O father, come here and see my luck."

"I have seen the beginning of your luck but you do prove yourself to become a queen. However, I am happy that you are safe. Now I am returning from here", the king said and went back home. The princess was surprised to see that though the house was just like a palace from inside, no one was there to live in. Finally, she opened the door of the last room and found a handsome man lying unconscious there on a bed. Taking care of that unconscious man, the princess spent twelve long years there.

Once a group of nomad tribesmen came in the forest and spent night near the house where the princess was living. They slept there and went away in the morning. A girl among the group had gone to wash her mouth in the morning and the group of tribesmen did not notice her absence. When she returned, she found no one there. She started crying. Hearing her cry the princess went up to her and asked, "Who are you? Why you are crying?"

"I had come here with the group of nomad tribesmen. We all spent night here. In the morning I had gone to wash my mouth in the mean time the group left the place. I do not know where they all have gone", the girl replied.

The princess felt pity for her and brought her home. The princess told every thing about herself to that nomad girl and pointing towards the unconscious man she said that she was taking care of that man for the last twelve years.

The next morning the princess said to the girl. "I am going to bring some fruits and water. In my absence take care of this man."

While the princess was away the man returned to his sense and seeing the nomad girl near him he said, "Who are you? What are you doing here?"

The devil inside the girl became active. She said, "I am taking care of you for twelve years." The prince became very happy. The grateful prince said, "I will marry you. It would be the best reward for your service. I am the king of neighbouring village. We will marry on any auspicious day."

When the princess returned with the fruits and water the nomad girl said to the man (king) that she was her maid. The princess understood every thing but did not utter a word in her defence as she had full faith in her destiny.

One day the king was going to the village market to buy something. He asked both the ladies, "What do you want from the market?"

"Bring good clothes and ornaments for me", the nomad girl said.

"Alright, I will bring things for you", the king said. Then he asked the princess, "And, what do you want?"

"Bring two puppets for me", the princess replied. In the market the king got the clothes and ornaments for the nomad girls easily but he had to search out the puppets. In the evening when he returned home he gave the two ladies their desired things. The princess put the puppets in the bed room of the man. In the night the puppet started talking. The king was not sleeping. One puppet told the story of the princess to the other puppet, as to how she had taken care of the king for twelve years and how the nomad girl cheated her and made the king a fool. The kind hearted king heard their talk and started recalling the behaviours of both the ladies. He realized that the princess could not be a maid. She was a sober lady like a princess.

In the morning he slapped the nomad girl and asked her to tell the truth. The girl told the truth to him that it was the princess, but not she, who had taken care of him for twelve years. The king wanted to kill the nomad girl but the kind hearted princess stopped him from doing so. The king apologised to princess and married her. She became a queen. The nomad girl served them as long as she remained alive.

## THE BRAVE PRINCE

A king had four sons. His three of the elder sons were liars and were cunning and wicked fellows. Just opposite to them the youngest prince was a brave as well as humble person.

One day the gardener of the palace came and said to the king, "O king, in the night some animals trampled down the plants of the garden."

The king posted the guards in the garden but the guards failed to find out the culprits. Even a short sleep of the guards was enough to provide chance to the culprits to do their jobs. The condition of the garden had made the king worried and restless.

One day the youngest prince went to the king and said, "O father, what has made you worried and perturbed?" The king said about the condition of the garden to him.

"Do not worry, I will guard the garden tonight and I assure you that I will soon find out the culprits creating nuisance for us", the youngest prince said to the king.

In the night the youngest prince after cutting one of his fingers put some salt on the wound. He did so thinking that the pain would not let him sleep in the night. At midnight four horses after coming down from the heaven started grazing the grass, leaves and flowers of the garden. The horses were red, black, white, and variegated in colour. The youngest prince was not sleeping. He saw the horses and caught them by their tail. He tied them with a rope and said, "I will take you all to my father. He would be very happy to see you and will punish you for your deeds."

"Do not take me to your father. We will not come here from tomorrow and will not trample your plants. At the time of need, we will come to help you. We all are giving our hair to you. That colour of horse will appear before you on the hair of which, you will put vermilion mark and burn incense sticks in front of that", the horses said and gave their hair to him. The prince set them free and let them return to heaven.

The next morning he went to his father and said, "Father, I have chased the animals that used to trample the plants. They will not come again."

The king was happy. The plants in the garden were bearing beautiful flowers and were making the atmosphere pleasant.

One day the youngest prince had gone to meet his maternal grandmother. In his absence his elder brothers committed some serious crime and the king kicked them out of his palace. For their livelihood they took the job of grazing cattle of a moneylender and started living in a small house. When the youngest prince returned he missed his brothers. He went to his father and asked about them.

"I have kicked those cunning and wicked fellows out of my palace", the king replied.

"Father, you have not done the right thing. I am going in search of them and will call them back", the youngest prince said and went in search of his brothers.

He found his brothers were grazing cattle in a field. The brothers also saw their younger brother coming towards them. One of them said, "Look, the darling of father is coming."

"We will kill him when he will come to us", the second brother said. The third brother said, "It would not be wise to kill him. We will invite him to live with us and force him to do all the household works."

The youngest brother happily agreed to live with them and to perform all the household chores.

The daughter of the neighbouring country was very beautiful. She had put a unique condition for her marriage. According to the condition the young person willing to marry her will have to put one garland around her neck while she remained standing in the balcony of the ninth floor of her palace. Above all, according to the condition the person will have to do this in one jump from the ground riding a horse. No one of the country was capable of fulfilling this condition and the king remained worried. One day the elder brothers of the youngest prince were talking about the beauty of the princess and about the condition for her marriage. They were planning to go to neighbouring country to test their luck.

"We will go to neighbouring country but will not tell any thing to the youngest prince about the reason of this visit. We will take him with us because he is serving us well. In his absence we will have to cook, clean utensils and wash clothes. We will tell him that the moneylender of that country is paying us more for grazing his cattle. Pretending to be going to graze cattle we will go to palace and will try to put garland around the neck of the princess", the elder brothers talked with each other. The youngest son heard every thing. He decided to put garland around the neck of the princes.

They all went to the neighbouring country. In the morning the elder brothers said to the youngest prince, "We are going to graze cattle. Clean the house and cook. We will return in the afternoon to have our lunch." When the elder brothers of the prince left the home the youngest prince put vermilion mark on the hair of red horse and burnt incense sticks in front of that. Soon the red horse appeared in front of him.

Riding fast on that horse he went to the palace. In the presence of every one he jumped with his horse and put the garland around the neck of the princess and returned home soon. Giving thanks to the horse he sent him off. He cleaned the house and cooked for every one. In the afternoon his brothers returned. While taking lunch they were talking secretly about the princess and about one fool who even after fulfilling the condition did not make a claim for the marriage with her. The youngest prince while washing clothes heard them talking and smiled. The youngest son repeated his action continuously for four days riding on different coloured horses such as black, white, and variegated.

In the morning of the fifth day the neighbouring king announced that he was going to solemnize the marriage of his daughter with the person who had put garland around the neck of the princess for four days continuously. However, there was one difficulty in doing so. No one had seen the face of the man and no one knows about the whereabouts of that person.

In the evening thousands of people gathered in the campus of the palace. The youngest prince was also there. While his elder brothers were standing in front row he was standing in the last. He was supposed to prepare dinner for his elder brothers but he was there. He was hiding his face from his brothers.

Now the neighbouring king had to find out as to who had put the garland around the neck of the princess. The king had a faithful she-elephant. He gave a garland to his she-elephant and the she-elephant holding the garland by her trunk, searched here and there. When she saw the youngest prince, she put the garland around his neck. All present there got surprised. They did not believe that a young boy in tattered clothes could do so. They all started talking, "How can a boy in rags fulfil the condition of the princess."

For the satisfaction of every one the neighbouring king once again gave a garland to the she-elephant and once again she put the garland around the neck of the youngest prince. The king solemnized the marriage of his daughter with the youngest prince and gave him lots of goods and wealth. The youngest prince returned home with all the goods and his wife. Out of jealousy his elder brother decided to kill him. The eldest among them said, "In mid night we will kill our brother and will take all his wealth. We will capture his wife as well."

In night before going to bed the youngest prince told his wife that he was also a prince of neighbouring country and they all were brothers. In mid night the three elder brothers of the youngest prince threw their brother into a well white he was in sleep. Taking all the wealth of his younger brother and his wife they all went to their father.

"Who is the woman with you? From where do you get so much wealth?" Their father, the king asked them.

"Father we have won every thing after fulfilling the condition of the king of our neighbouring country", they all replied.

The king did not believe and he kept mum. Meanwhile the youngest prince also came there. Some shepherds had pulled him out from the well. The king became very happy to see him.

"My son, where were you? What happened with you?" The king asked.

The youngest prince did not want to tell anything to his father about what his elder brothers had done to him. He was well aware what his father would have done to his brothers after knowing the truth. He kept mum but his wife told every thing to his father.

The king burst out in anger and banished his three elder sons from the country. He lived happily with his son and the daughter-in-law.

## REALIZATION OF THE MISTAKE

The king of a country, named Dharma was a religious minded and munificent person. He used to give one gold coin as well as a cow to the first visitor of his palace. In the same country there was a poor farmer who lived with his wife and a grown up daughter. The daughter of the farmer was beautiful and intelligent. One day she told her father, "Father, go to the king. The gold coin given to you by the king will help us in coming out of poverty and the cow will not let us face the shortage of milk."

"Daughter, I also want to go to the king but I do not know what I will tell the king", the farmer replied.

"Oh father, this is not a problem. Just tell him to be happy always", the girl said. The farmer agreed to go to the king. The next morning he went to the king and said, "Be happy always." The king was happy with the blessings of the farmer. He said, "Man, I am happy with you but today I have already donated the coin and the cow to a Brahmin who had arrived here before you came." The farmer returned home sadly.

The next morning the daughter of the farmer woke her father up early and sent him to the king. The farmer said to the king, "Be happy always." the king gave him the coin and the cow. The farmer went to the king continuously for four days and took the cows and the coins from him. The fourth day after donating the coin and the cow to the farmer the king went out to take a round of his city to know the welfare of his citizens. He saw four Brahmins sitting and chatting under a tree. These Brahmins, in the hope of receiving donation from the king, were going to the king's palace for four days but returning empty handed as the farmer was going there earlier than them. They were annoyed with the farmer. The king sat with the Brahmins to take some rest. One of the Brahmins said to the king, "My king, the daughter of the farmer who used to come to you daily, is beautiful and intelligent. You should marry that girl."

"If you want me to do so, why should I object? The next morning when the farmer will come, I will ask him." The king said.

The next day, once again, the farmer went to the king. The king called him and said, "I want to marry your daughter. Are you ready for it?" The farmer got nervous. He was not able to say any thing. The king was a middle aged married man. He had grown up children as well. He replied, "My king, I will tell you after two days after consulting my wife and my daughter." The farmer returned home and sat on the bed in a gloomy mood.

When his daughter found him in this state of mind she went to him and asked, "What is the matter? Why are you so sad and depressed?" The farmer told her every thing said by the king. The girl smiled and said, "Father, tomorrow when you will meet the king, ask him to visit the heaven for two days continuously. For going to heaven and coming back he will find a black horse in his garden. After spending two days in heaven, if he will again say to you that he is ready to marry me, I will agree to that."

The next morning the farmer went to the king and the king repeated his own question: does he accept the marriage proposal or not? The farmer told him every thing which his daughter had told him. The king ran to his garden. A black horse was standing there. Riding on the horse the king went to the heaven. The heaven was very pretty and beautiful. Every means of comfort was available there. The king was very happy. He started taking a round of the heaven. He saw some men were building a gorgeous palace.

"You all are building this palace for whom?" The king asked. They replied, "On the earth there lives a king Dharam. He is noble and munificent. We are building this palace for him. After his death, he will live here." The king was happy thinking that after the death he will lead a comfortable life in a huge palace. Again he saw many cows were grazing in a field. He questioned about the owner from the grazer. He replied that those cows belonged to the king Dharam. He moved towards another direction and found his parents were taking rest on a comfortable bed. They were happy and satisfied. They said to the king, "It is the result of your good work that we are living comfortably here. Continue your noble work like this and be happy always." It was late evening and the king returned home riding that black horse.

He was willing to go to heaven once again. He spent his night restlessly and in the morning ran fast to the garden. The black horse was waiting for him. Riding on the horse he reached the heaven. He saw his palace was demolished and cows were dead. His parents were suffering and lying amidst the insects, mosquitoes, and flies. When they saw the king they said, "My son due to you only we have reached up to this state. You have made your future dark. Why did you agree to go to the wrong path? You are already married and a father of grown up children. Why did you agree to marry the daughter of the farmer? Why did you agree to follow those jealous Brahmins?" The king realized his mistake soon. He said, "You are right parents. I was on a wrong path. Now tell me what to do? What should I do to repair my mistake?"

"Ask for forgiveness from the family members of the farmer. Make the daughter of the farmer your sister and feed the entire citizens of your kingdom", the parents said.

The king returned to the earth. He did exactly what his parents had told him to do. Touching the feet of the daughter of the farmer, in front of every one, he asked for forgiveness from her and made her his sister. The farmer was not a poor man now. Thereafter he lived happily with his family members.

## TO SOLVE A RIDDLE

In a village there was a king. He used to spend most of his time with his childhood friend, a barber by profession. Both of them got married on the same day and their marriages did not bring any change in their habit of spending time with each other. The wife of the king was not a good woman. When the barber saw her, he fell in love with her. Both of them developed their relationship and started conspiring to kill the king. Somehow the king came to know about the relationship of his wife with his friend and also about their planning. He became sad and angry, too. He wanted to teach a lesson to his childhood friend who was no more faithful to him.

One day, both of them went to the forest for hunting. The king got an opportunity to take revenge from the barber. He killed him and returned home. When the queen saw the king returning alone she guessed that something wrong had happened with the barber.

In the night when the king slept, the queen called her faithful servant. She sent him to the forest to find out the barber. In the forest the servant saw the dead body of the barber and informed the queen that the barber was dead. The queen gave five coins to the servant and told him to bring the skin of the barber. The servant did so. Now the queen gave him ten coins and said that get the skin washed by a washer man and the servant followed her words. Once again the queen gave him fifteen coins and sent him to a dyer to dye the skin and once again the servant followed her instruction. Finally giving twenty coins to the servant the queen got a *kurta* (tunic) stitched of that skin by a tailor.

In the morning she cooked good foods and invited the king to lunch. When the king was about to eat she stooped him and said, "First solve the riddle then only you can eat. If you will not solve the riddle you will have to die by hanging yourself in front of every body. You can accept the defeat right now in the presence of all."

The king was not ready to accept his defeat. He said, "Ask what you want to ask me? I am accepting your challenge."

The queen said, "For five coins got the skin. For ten coins got it washed. For fifteen coins got coloured and for twenty coins got it stitched. Tell me what it means?" The king could not understand the meaning of the queen's words. The queen asked him to solve the riddle by evening. The king tried his best to solve the riddle. He asked his friends, however he failed in solving it. In the evening the queen said, "King, you have failed to answer me. Tomorrow morning you will have to hang yourself in front of every one. Fulfil your last wish."

The king said, "My sister lives in another village. I would like to die in front of her. I am going to call her." The king left for his sister's place. In her sister's house all gave warm welcome to the king. They all were surprised when they came to know about the wife of the king who had put him in trouble. They all said, "No wife can do this. Your wife is unique in this respect."

"Brother, it seems to me that your wife wants to kill you", the sister of the king said. The king was thinking that his sister and her in-laws were right but he kept mum. The mother-in-law of the sister of the king said, "My son, you can go home with your sister but remember one thing, spend the night there where it becomes dark." The king replied, "Okay mother, I will not forget your words."

The king and his sister left for the king's village. They had to go through a forest. In the middle of the forest it became dark and both of them wanted to spend their night there. They wanted to sleep under a tree. They were lying under the tree but not sleeping. A pair of birds was sitting on the branch of the tree. The female bird said to the male bird, "It is difficult to spend the night sitting like this. Tell me a story."

The male bird said, "I will tell you a real happening which is not less than any story." The male bird repeated the story of the king, the queen and the barber. That bird described how the queen giving the coins to her servant got the skin, washed and coloured and at last got a tunic stitched of that. The king and his sister understood the meaning of the queen's riddle.

The next morning the queen had arranged to hang the king in front of every one. The sister of the king solved the riddle in front of every one. The servant, the washer man, the dyer and the tailor were called. They all agreed with the sister of the king and accepted what they had done at that night. The villager decided to hang the queen because she was a characterless and deceitful woman. The king and his sister were happy and so were the villagers.

## KALUA THE BARBER

Kalua, the barber was a hard working man. One day he said to his wife, "My friend has called me to his village. The king of that village is going to solemnize the marriage of his son and he wants one more barber for his guests." His wife was happy in view of anticipation of good rewards from the king. A washer man was the neighbour of Kalua. He was greedy and his wife was wicked. When the wife of washer man came to know about the invitation received by Kalua she said to her husband, "Follow Kalua to another village and wherever he goes. The guests of the king will also need a washer man." The washer man liked the idea of his wife and requested Kalua to take him to another village so that he could earn as well. Kalua agreed for it.

On the way the washer man thought that if he and Kalua would earn equal amount how could he prove his superiority over him. He wanted to earn more than Kalua but did not know how to do that. They came near a river. They halted there to take some rest and decided to take bath. He said to Kalua, "We will take bath here again on our return journey." Kalua agreed for it. Actually the washer man had planned to steal some of the wealth of Kalua on their return journey while sending him to take bath. They decided that one would watch their belongings while the other would go to take bath. Kalua sat under a tree and the washer man went to take bath. The tree was the abode of the ghosts. One of the ghosts saw his image in the mirror of Kalua. He thought that Kalua had made him prisoner. He went to Kalua and pointing towards the mirror said, "Please free me. I will give you lots of wealth." Intelligent Kalua understood that the ghost had seen his own image in the mirror for the first time. He said, "Alright I will come here after two days till then arrange to give money to me. I am making you free." He put the mirror up side down and the ghost was happy thinking he was free. The washer man returned after taking bath and they resumed their journey.

The marriage was over and Kalua had earned much. There was no need of extra washer man and to the contrary the washer man was not interested in his work. He always kept watching Kalua and his activities. On their return journey both of them reached the river and the washer man went to take bath first. The ghost and his friends were waiting for Kalua. They all came near him together and they saw their images in the mirror. They all got frightened and gave Kalua lots of wealth for making them free. Kalua made them friends and promised them that he would come to meet them once in a while. When the washer man came Kalua went to take bath. As planned he tried to steal the wealth of Kalua. The ghosts were watching his activity. When they saw that the washer man was going to steal the wealth of their friend they gave him substantial beating. The washer man did not wait for Kalua and ran away from there. After taking bath when Kalua returned he did not find the washer man there. He started searching for him. The ghost told him every thing and after giving thanks to them, Kalua returned home.

The wife and children of Kalua were happy to see him healthy because they were worried to see the washer man returning alone. Kalua was a rich barber now whereas the washer man remained poor.

## THE ILL-BEGOTTEN EARNINGS

In a village there lived a poor farmer. He had a very small piece of land and the crop grown on that was not up to the satisfaction level for the farmer and his family. He had four sons. The three elders were married and were agricultural labourers. The youngest son was too young to work. He used to take foods for his father and brothers in the afternoon while they remained busy in their work in the field. Though they were poor, they had no regrets for their life. They used to live together and loved one another. The four brothers used to take full care of their father.

One day the younger brother was taking food for his elder brothers who were engaged in their work in a far away field. On the way he found some people gambling' sitting on a platform under the tree. He stopped there and started watching their game. They said to him, "What are you doing here. Go and give foods to your brothers. They must be hungry."

The young boy could not control his temptation and started playing with them. The lady luck was with him and he won land, home and money in the play. The poor boy became a rich boy within hours. His brothers waited for him long and when the young boy did not bring food for them they became worried. Searching their brother they reached the place where their younger brother indulged in the game of gambling. They were pleased to see that their brother had become a wealthy man.

They stopped going for work and started living lavishly. The neo-rich men lost their sense and soon got addicted to bad habits. They all became drunkard and gamblers. The peace and harmony of their house had vanished. They started abusing and quarrelling with each other. They even started neglecting the needs of their father. The farmer was not happy but he was not able to control his sons. He worked hard in his land and what ever he was growing and earning, he was saving from that for the future.

In gambling the sons of the farmer lost all their wealth and once again they became poor. Their situation was worse than it was in the past because they had earned bad name in the village. One day the farmer called them and said, "Look sons, you have not only lost your ill-begotten money but the peace and harmony of life as well. You would have not spent your hard earned money the way you did with your easily obtained money. It is not late, plan about your future and work hard. I have saved some money, take it and go to another village to work. Today no one in this village will give you any work but in future they will forgive you if you will behave properly with them."

The sons of the farmer understood the importance of hard work and hard earned money. They started working as hard as they used to do in the past. The youngest son got married. All the four brothers and their wives lived together happily, taking good care of their father.

## THE CONCEITED

In a village there was an archer. He was expert in shooting arrows and never missed the mark. The villagers used to call him Phannekhan. The love and respect received from the villagers made him a bit conceited. He started making fun of others and stopped giving respect to elders. One day a man said to him, "You think you are a great archer. There are many archers in the world like you and even better than you. Go out of the village and find out. Then only you can understand where you stand."

Phannekhan flew in anger. He said, "Alright, I am going to visit many other villages. If I will find you wrong, I will kill you."

After covering some distance Phannekhan saw a man who was looking up in the sky keeping a betel nut in front of him on a stone.

"Who are you? Why you are looking up in the sky?" Phannekhan asked that man.

"Are you looking at that betel-nut kept on the stone? I eat nut after breaking it with an arrow head. Yesterday, I had shot an arrow towards the sky. Possibly it is coming down now."

While the man was saying like this an arrow came down and shot the nut. The nut broke down. The man ate the pieces and gave one to Phannekhan. Phannekhan was very much impressed with the art of that man. He thought, "I can only shoot the mark but this man can shoot at a far distance as well."

"Friend you are a good shooter. What is your name?" Phannekhan asked that man.

"My name is Teeshmarkhan." That man replied. Both of them became good friends. Phannekhan resumed his journey in search of another artist.

This time Teeshmarkhan was with him. After they covered some distance, they saw a man shouting, "Good very good. Kick him. Put him down. I liked it."

"Who are you? Why you are shouting like this?" They asked that man.

"My name is Neegahser. I am watching the wrestling match going on in New Delhi." That man said.

"New Delhi is far and far away from here. We are in west Nimad (Madhya Pradesh). How can you see there?" They asked.

"My eye-sight is good and unique. I can see any where." Neegahser replied. Phannekhan and Teeshmarkhan were impressed with the unique quality of Neegahser. While they were talking with one another, a man came there running fast. The three men stopped him and asked. "Who are you? Why you are running so fast?"

"My name is Vayuser. A girl of this village is very sick. The *vaidya* (village doctor) has said that if the water of the river Ganga is not given to her by evening she will not survive. I am going to bring water." The man said.

"Are you crazy? It is afternoon. The river Ganga does not flow in Madhya Pradesh. How can you bring water before evening?" The three men asked him.

"I can bring the water within an hour. I can run at the speed of air." Vayuser replied. "Wait for me. I will be back soon. After that we all will go to see that girl." Vayuser said again and ran away from there.

The three men sat under a tree. Vayuser came there within an hour and they all went to the house of that sick girl. The *vaidya* poured the water in to the mouth of the girl and she got up. They all four became good friends and decided to go to the king and ask for suitable jobs for them.

The king asked them, "What special things you all can do?"

"My king, the work which no other man can do, we can do that easily", Teeshmarkhan said. The king appointed them in service.

One day the daughter of the king fell ill. She was unconscious. The physician of the palace asked for the *Gangajal* (Water of the River Ganga) before evening. The king was sad and nervous. It was impossible for him to bring water from the river Ganga in a short period of time. Vayuser came to know about the illness of the princes. He went to the king and said, "My king, do not worry. I will bring the water within an hour."

"If you will do so I will give my daughter to you in marriage", the king said. Taking a pot Vayuser ran towards the river Ganga. While coming back he noticed that he had enough time. With an idea to take rest, he sat under a tree and slept. When one hour passed and Vayuser did not return, Phannekhan said to Neegahser, "Friend, find where is Vayuser?"

Neegahser looked at the direction of river Ganga and said, "Friends, let us be alert. Vayuser is sleeping under a tree where a big snake is going to swallow him". Phannekhan putting his finger straight said to Teeshmarkhan to shoot the arrow soon. Teeshmarkhan shot the arrow and his arrow hit the hood of the snake which was going to swallow Vayuser. The snake died. Vayuser woke up and when he saw the arrow and the dead snake he understood that his friends had saved his life. He ran fast and reached the palace. The physician poured a little water into the mouth of the princess and she got up. All were happy.

The king started preparing for the marriage of the princess. Since the three friends of Vayuser had helped him in bringing the water the king decided to marry his daughter with all the four. When the princess came to know that the four men were going to become her husbands she felt dejected. She wanted to commit suicide and jumped into a well. Phannekhan and Teeshmarkhan also jumped into the well to save her. By the time the attendants of the palace pulled them out of the water they all three were dead. To give them life the extract of medicinal plants available on the Himalaya was needed. Once again Vayuser ran towards Himalaya to bring the plant and Neegahser sat for making penances to cure them.

Vayuser brought the plant in an hour and the physician put the extracts of the plants into the mouths of the three dead persons. They all got life. The king had understood that the princess would not marry all the four. Now he had to choose any one among the four friends as her husband. He was confused. He went to a sage for help.

The sage said, "The man who brought the plant and gave life to the princess is her father. The persons who jumped into the well to save her are her brothers and the person who did penances to save her is her husband."

The king solemnized the marriage of his daughter with Neegahser. Phannekhan had understood that one should not become conceited even if he has some unique quality.

## THE FIGHT

One day the Fire, the Air and the Water started quarrelling among themselves. They all were trying to prove their superiority over others.

The Water said, "I am superior to you both. I give rains which keep the earth green. All the living beings need water to drink. They all are alive due to me."

The words of the water made the Air angry. He said, "Do not be a fool. A person can survive with out water for two days but without air he would die within minutes. How can he breathe without the air?"

The Fire was not ready to accept their supremacy and said, "Both of you have given your arguments but think what will happen in my absence.

In this world every one and every thing needs heat. Even you both will become solid in my absence. Why do not you accept me over you both?"

Like this they all were busy arguing with one another but were not reaching any conclusion. While they were busy in arguments a goddess appeared before them and asked, "What is the matter? Why you all three are quarrelling like this?" They all three put their pleas in front of her.

The goddess said to the Water, "You claim you have the power to set afloat big rocks in your stream. Are you seeing the grass in between the slit of that stone? If you will make that grass flow from there, I will accept your superiority over the two."

The Water tried his best. The current of the Water kept dashing against the rock but nothing happened to that grass. That remained there stand still. At last the Water accepted his defeat and sat down calmly.

Now the goddess turned towards the Air and said, "You can uproot big tree. What the Water can not do, hence go and do that. Blow the grass from there." The Air also tried, started blowing fast but nothing happened to the grass and that remained there. The Air, too, accepted its defeat.

After this the goddess looked towards the Fire and said, "They two had accepted their defeat now it is your turn to prove your superiority. Go and burn the grass." The Fire could not burn the wet grass. They all were defeated and were ashamed.

The goddess said to them, "God has given strength to all of you. Every one is supposed to perform different kinds of work. However, it is the god who works and not you. He keeps a watchful eye on all of you. It was the god who was protecting the grass. No work can be considered less important than the other. You all are equal. You should not fight like the way you were." The goddess disappeared from there.

The Fire, the Water and the Air had realized their mistake.

## THE CURSING OF A COW

In a village there lived a poor labourer with his wife and son Radhe. Both the husband and the wife used to work hard to earn their livelihood. When their son Radhe grew up he also became a labourer.

One day the labourer told his wife, "Our son has grown up. Let us do something for his marriage."

"Yes you are right. I will start saving for his marriage and you start searching for his wife." The wife replied.

The labourer went from village to village in search of a suitable wife for his son and at last selected a girl for him. The poor labourer could give only betel-leaf and nut to the girl and fixed the marriage. He and his wife worked harder and collected some grains and money for the marriage. On the selected day the marriage was solemnized in presence of relatives and a few friends. The new bride came home and after a week went back to her father's home.

The labourer worked hard neglecting his food and comfort hence he fell ill. Radhe served him well but could not save his father's life. After the death of his father Radhe lost his mother as well. He was unable to inform his wife about the loss because he had no means to send the message any where. After the death of his mother Radhe left for his in-laws' house.

On the way he saw a cow grazing the crop in a field. He shouted, "Brother farmer, come fast one cow is grazing your crop." The farmer came fast and hit the cow with a big stone. She became lame by one of her legs. When the farmer went from there cow said to Radhe, "Due to you only I am suffering. My calf is hungry in the shed. However, tell me first where are you going?" Radhe told the cow about himself and about his visit. The cow said, "Meet me on your return journey." Radhe promised to the cow that he would meet her and moved from there.

The in-laws of Radhe greeted him well. They all were sad to learn about the death of the parents of Radhe. After two days Radhe started his return journey with his wife. He met the cow who was waiting for him. The cow was about to die and so was her calf. She said to Radhe, "I and my calf are going to die. Stand turning your back towards me till I ask you to look towards me."

Radhe stood in front of the cow turning his back towards her. The cow said, "I am cursing you to become a donkey. Now look towards me." As soon as Radhe turned towards the cow he was already a donkey. When the wife of Radhe saw her husband turned a donkey she started crying. However, thinking it was her destiny she returned home with that donkey. The villagers were surprised to see the lady taking good care of that donkey but they did not ask her the reason.

One day, a group of people were going to Omkareshwar (one of the religious places in Madhya Pradesh), to take bath in the river Narmada. The wife of Radhe was also with them. An uprooted *peepal* tree had blocked the way and the people were trying to remove that tree. When they saw the wife of Radhe with a donkey they asked her to help. She was not ready to put the donkey for this work. She went near the tree and said, "O *Peepal Dev* please give us the way so we can resume our journey." The tree moved by its own and gave way to all. The people were surprised and happy, too.

In Omkareshwar they all took bath in the river and worshipped the deity in the temple. The wife of Radhe, too, took bath in the river and standing on the bank of the river she said, "O Mother River, you are aware of every thing. Make my husband free from the curse of the cow."

The donkey jumped into the river and Radhe came out from there. Radhe and his wife were happy. Giving thanks to the River Narmada, the couple returned home.

## THE GREEDY BROTHERS

One day four brothers went into a forest for hunting. They spent hours in the forest but could not kill any animal. While the tired brothers were thinking what to do they saw a gold-deer. The brothers chasing that deer killed that.

They were hungry. The elder brother said, "Among us two will sit near the deer and two will go to village to bring some edibles. After that we will go home carrying this deer and will distribute it among us equally." They all liked this idea.

Two among them went to a village while two sat near the deer. In the village the two brothers decided to eat first. They said to the owner of the *dhaba* (road side hotel) to pack the food for two and they started eating. One brother said, "If we will mix poison in the food of our brothers they will die. We two will distribute the deer between us." The second brother agreed for it. They mixed poison in the food they were carrying for their brothers.

In the forest the two brothers who were guarding the deer conspired to kill their brothers who had gone to bring food for them. They also wanted to distribute the deer between both of themselves. They all were lured by their ill intention.

When the two brothers returned with the food the two that were in the forest attacked them. They were not prepared for this attack and were killed. The remaining two brothers started eating food and died after eating the poisonous food.

All four were dead only due to the greed.

## THE CLEVER FARMER

A farmer was very happy to see the crop of his field. He was hoping to earn good amount from his crop. There was a forest near the field of the farmer. A fox used to come daily in the night and eat some of the vegetables of the farmer. When the farmer noticed that some one was stealing his crop he became worried and sad. He wanted to know who was doing the mischief. One day he saw the foot prints of the fox in his field. He understood every thing.

"Wicked fox I will teach you a lesson. You are stealing my vegetables. I have worked hard to grow them." The farmer said to himself.

The farmer was very clever. He got an idea to teach a lesson to the fox. He went to the market and brought lots of gum. He gave the shape of an old woman to the gum and put that in his field.

The fox came in the night and saw an old woman sitting in the field. "No problem, today I will eat some peas on requesting that old woman", the fox thought. She went near the old woman and said, "Mother, can I eat some peas from your field?" the dummy did not reply and the fox kept on repeating her question again and again. At last the fox lost her temper and said, "Mother, give me some peas to eat otherwise I will slap you." The dummy did not say any thing. The fox was angry. She slapped the dummy and her paw got stuck in the gum.

"Do not prank with me. Leave my hand immediately. Otherwise I will slap you again", the fox said. She slapped the dummy again and her second paw got stuck in the gum and like this her whole body got stuck in the gum.

In the morning when the farmer came to the field he saw the fox. He gave severe beating to the fox. The fox fled away from there never to return. In this way the clever farmer protected his crop from a wild animal.

## FOUR FOOLS

There were four friends in a village. They all were big dolts. They lived together and used to do all their works together. They were famous in their village for their foolish acts and no one was ready to give them any work.

"We should go to another village and work there. Here we will die of hunger", they all decided and proceeded towards another village. They had to cross a river to go to another village. They all jumped together and swam towards another end. After crossing the river they thought that one of them had drowned in the river. As a matter of fact they started counting them but the man among them who would actually start counting did not include himself. Thus, the number always came to three instead of four. They all started crying. A farmer was watching them and their activities for sometime. He went to them and asked, "Friends, what is wrong with you? Why are you all crying?"

"We were four friends but one was drowned in the river", they replied sobbing. The farmer smiled and said, "If I will call your friend here and will make you four again, what will you pay me for that?"

"We will give our services to you free for one year", they said. Taking a stick the farmer said, "I will hit on the palms of you all one by one. You all should count one, two three and four." After saying like this the farmer hit on the palm of the first fool and he shouted, "One." Like this they all shouted, "Two, three and four." They all were happy thinking once again they were four. Now according to the term, they all had to serve the farmer for one year. They came with the farmer in his house to stay and work.

The next morning the farmer said to them, "Go in the forest and bring wood from there. Take my bullock cart with you." Driving the cart they all reached the forest and loaded lots of wood on the cart. On their way home the cart started making the sound of "*machad*, "*machad*."

The first fool said, "When we were going to the forest the cart was not making this sound."

The second fool said, "It seems some ghost has entered the cart."

The third fool said, "Let us do something to get rid of this ghost soon."

The fourth fool said, "Let us burn the cart. The ghost will be burnt along with the cart and will die."

They all burnt the cart loaded with wood to ash. The scared bulls ran towards the forest. They all returned home empty handed.

When the farmer saw them coming without the cart and wood he asked, "What happened with the cart? Where are the bulls? Did you bring wood?" They all narrated the incidents of ghost, burning of cart and wood, running of bulls towards the forest in details. The angry farmer beat them till he was tired.

One day the farmer said to them, "Go and bring some oil from the city market. I will sell them in the village and will earn profit." Taking the oil containers they all went towards the city. On their return journey they wanted to take some rest and put their containers under a tree. They saw their vague images on the containers and thought that some ghosts had entered in the container. They started kicking the containers. They crushed the containers into sheet. The oil spilled out. Once again they received severe beating by the farmer.

"Let me not send these fools out and should engage them in some work at home only." The farmer said to himself. The old mother of the farmer was sick. The farmer told them to take care of his mother. One of them started flying the flies sitting on the body of that lady. The second started waving a leaf made fan over her face. The third and the fourth started massaging her legs and hands respectively. The one that was flying the flies said, "These flies are disturbing the mother in her sleep." The second fool put some sweets on the mouth of that old lady thinking all the flies would sit together. The third brought some sticks. When the flies sat on the sweets they all started hitting the flies with their sticks. The flies flew away but the old lady died. Her tongue and tooth came out. They all thought that the mother was laughing. The fourth fool went to the farmer and said, "Your mother has been cured. She is laughing." The farmer came to see her and found his mother dead. He kicked those fools out of his house.

The fools were not ready to leave the farmer. According to term they had to serve the farmer for one year. They asked for some work from the farmer. The irritated farmer said to them, "Go and burn the dead body of my mother." They all went to cremation ground carrying the dead body of the mother of the farmer on their heads. There was a berry tree on the way and the corpse got stuck on the tree. They left the dead body hanging there and burnt some other old lady on the pyre. After returning home they said the framer, "Your mother started eating berry fruits. We left her there and burnt some one else." After giving substantial beating to them the farmer said, "Go and drown the dead body in the river."

The fools threw the body in the water but that got stuck with the aquatic plants. The fools returned to the farmer and said that his mother was ready to leave the place. The farmer went to see the body. After tying a rope around his waist the framer said to the fools to hold the other end of the rope. He said, "I am going to push the body and making that flow with the current. When I will indicate pull me with this rope." The farmer pushed the body and giving the jerk to the rope indicated the fools to pull him. The fools thought that farmer was asking for that rope. They left that and the farmer was washed away in the water current.

The fools were free now. They returned home and became the owner of the wealth of the farmer. They spent their life without working for any one.

## WAITING FOR THE GOD

In a village there lived a theist. He used to worship the statue of the god daily. One day he went to a temple and sitting near the statue said, "My god, you have given me every thing. I do not want any more wealth. I want to see you. Please appear before me." The god said to him, "Alright today in the evening I will come to your house."

The man ran towards his home. He cleaned and decorated his house with his family members. He told every body that one special guest was coming to his house in the evening but he did not disclose as to who the guest was. He told all not to allow any other visitor to enter his house.

After some time a blind beggar came to his house and said, "Give me some thing to eat. I am hungry for the last three days."

"Kick this beggar out of my home. My guest can come at any time. This is not the right time to entertain this beggar." The man shouted and his servant sent the beggar out.

The man was eagerly waiting for god. One lame man came to him for some economical help. That man refused to help him and said him to leave the place as soon as possible because he was expecting his special guest at any time. It was late evening now and that man was losing his patience. At the same time a crippled man came to him for help. The man got angry and said, "the guest I am waiting for is not coming instead he is sending all kinds of peculiar specimens to me. Throw this man out of my house." The servant got that man out.

In night the tired man slept. In his dream he said to god, "You had told a lie to me. You did not come."

The god replied, "I had come to you thrice in the form of beggar, the lame and the crippled man. You did not recognize me, instead you treated me badly. Still you are telling me a liar."

The man had realized his mistake.

## THE FOX

There was a Miyaji (a Mohammedan). He was the neighbour of an old woman. The Miyaji had a mare and the old woman was the owner of a buffalo. Both the animals were *gabbin* (pregnant).

One day Miyaji said to the old woman, "Let us sell our animals in the city. We will get more money because the buyers give more money for a pregnant animal." The old woman agreed for it and both of them proceeded towards the city. It became dark before they reached the city. They decided to spend night under a tree. The old woman slept soon but Miyaji was not sleeping. At mid night both the animals delivered their babies. Miyaji wanted to do mischief with the old woman. He saw that the old woman was sleeping. He put the buffalo-calf near the mare and the mare-calf near the buffalo. After that he went to sleep.

In the morning both of them woke up. The old woman was surprised to see a mare-calf near her buffalo. She said, "How it is possible that a buffalo delivers a mare-calf?" Miyaji kept mum. When the old lady saw that the mare of Miyaji had delivered a buffalo-calf, she started quarrelling with him.

"It is your trick. You are harassing me. How can your mare deliver a buffalo-calf and my buffalo delivers a mare-calf?" The old lady said to Miyaji.

Miyaji was not ready to accept that he had exchanged the babies of the animals. He just said, "Some times miracle can happen. Any thing is possible in this world. What is wrong in this if your buffalo has delivered a mare-calf?" they decided to go to a third person for justice. An old man was sitting out side his hut. Both of them went to him. When they were telling about their animals to that old man his daughter came and said, "My father is blind and deaf. It would be better if you people go to the fox that lives nearby."

The old woman reached the fox with Miyaji. The fox heard their pleas carefully and said, "I will give my verdict in the evening. Come to me in the evening."

It was evening and both of them once again went to the fox. Seeing them the fox said, "I can not say any thing right now. Come to me tomorrow in the morning. I am tired and do not want to do anything but to sleep."

Miyaji became angry. He asked, "What work have you performed? Pretending to be tired you are harassing us."

The fox said, "I am not harassing any one. What I am telling you is true. Today the forest was blown up into flames. The fire spread up to river. The fire of the forest got extinguished but it took time to extinguish the fire of the river. I am tired." The old woman as well as Miyaji was surprised. They asked the fox, "How can fire take place in the river?"

The fox replied, "If a buffalo can deliver mare-calf and a mare can delver a buffalo-calf, why not fire can engulf a river?"

Miyaji was ashamed. He told the truth to the old woman.

## DEATH OF A DEMON

Many years ago there was a mountain near a village. That mountain was the abode of a cruel demon. It was his daily routine to come down from the mountain, go in the village after crossing a forest and pick up any man, woman, or child from the village for his food. He was a cannibal demon and the villagers were afraid of him. One day that demon caught a young woman. The woman was beautiful and innocent in looks. The demon could not kill her. He said, "I do not want to kill you but I will not let you go to your home. If you will try to escape I will kill all the villagers. Living here you will have to cook for me and boil the persons I will bring."

Since the woman was helpless, she accepted the duty given to her by the demon. She was an intelligent lady. She started planning to kill the demon and to save her co-villagers from the demon. She thought that at first she should take the demon in her confidence and for that she got a trick

One day she said to the demon, "I want to marry you. I take care of your house just like a wife."

"It is not possible. I can not marry you. You are a human and I am a demon. How can a demon marry a human? Above all you are a married woman and are the mother of children," the demon said.

"I do not know who is demon and who is human. You will have to marry me otherwise I will kill myself by eating poison", the woman said.

The demon did not want to lose that woman so he agreed for the marriage. Both of them got married. After a few days the woman asked the demon, "How much do you love me?"

"I love you very much. I would like to die rather than give any trouble to you", the demon replied.

The woman said, "I love you, too. When you go down in the village, I remain scared. What will happen if any one kills you?"

"Do not worry for my death. No one can kill me." The demon said proudly.

"How can you say so confidently that no one can kill you?" The woman asked.

"I have hid my life in a secured place. My life is in a parrot. There is a tree in an island in the sea. A cage is hanging from the tree and the parrot lives there. If any one kills the parrot I will die immediately. However, it is difficult to reach the parrot and no one knows the secret of my life", the demon said.

The woman was happy. Her trick had worked and she knew how to kill the demon. The next day when the demon went to the village the woman came down in the forest. In the forest four wood cutters were cutting woods. She gave some gold to them and said, "Brothers, make one flying cot for me."

"Sister, come here after a week. We will make the flying cot in a week", the wood cutters said.

After a week the woman again went to the wood cutters. Her flying cot was ready. Once again the woman gave them some gold and asked, "Brothers are you ready to help me? I am going to perform a difficult task?"

"You are my sister and we are ready to help you any time. We are ready to go with you", the wood cutters said. Sitting on the flying cot they all went to the island in the sea and killed the parrot. The demon died by the killing of the parrot. The woman was free now. She returned to the cave of the demon, collected all his wealth and returned her home in the village.

The villagers were happy to see her alive. She told every one what she did with the demon. When the villagers came to know that the demon was dead they started dancing in joy. The husband and the children of the woman were happy to find her back home. They were not poor any more because the woman had brought the wealth of the demon. They led luxurious life throughout their life.

## TWO BROTHERS

In a village there lived two brothers. The elder one was rich but the younger brother was poor. Though the brothers lived separately, their houses were near each other. The younger brother never asked for economic help from his elder brother.

One day there was no food in the house of the younger brother. He was sick and had not gone out to work for the last four days. His children were hungry and were crying. Even then he was not ready to go to his elder brother for help. At last when his three year old son fell unconscious he could not control his emotion and went to his brother for help. At that time his elder brother was not at home and his *bhabhi* (brother's wife) was sitting in the courtyard.

"*Bhabhi*, will you please give me some barley? My children are hungry. I was sick and could not go out to work and earn, "the younger brother asked.

"Why should I give barley to you free? First go and plough my field then only I will give barely to you", the woman said to him.

The younger brother ploughed the field till evening but his *bhabhi* did not give barley to him and sent him to search her bulls. The younger brother was searching the bulls near the field of his elder brother. It became dark and he saw one man watering the field of his elder brother.

"Who are you? Why are you watering the field in night?" The younger brother asked that man.

"I am the luck of your elder brother", the man replied.

"Where is my luck?" The younger brother asked that man. That man gave the address of a remote place and said, "Your luck is there. Go there and call him with you."

When the younger brother went to that remote place he saw that his luck was sleeping covering his body with a shawl. The younger brother woke him up and asked him to come with him. His luck who had taken the form of an old man said, "You go home, I will follow you."

When the younger brother was returning home, he met a businessman on the way. The businessman asked the younger brother, "Who are you? Why are you so sad and tired?"

The younger brother told that man about him and said, "My children are hungry? I have nothing to eat." That businessman took the younger brother to his home. He fed him well and gave him good clothes. When the younger brother was ready to leave, the businessman gave him wheat, rice, oil, sugar and spices and called him with his family members to meet him tomorrow.

The younger brother reached home and the entire family ate together. The wife of the elder brother was watching every thing. She told her husband, "Your brother is a thief. He has brought every thing after stealing."

The elder brother scolded his wife and said, "Do not be silly. My brother is poor but he is not a thief."

The next morning the younger brother went to meet that businessman with his family members. The businessman welcomed them all and gave good clothes to them. He sent them off giving a small cart full of grains, a pair of bulls, seeds and some money. He said to the younger brother, "I am giving these things to you because it is giving me pleasure in doing so. You can return to me what I have given to you when your good time comes. Even if you will not return I will not feel sorry for it."

The younger brother returned home with every thing. Once again the wife of the elder brother felt jealous seeing the happiness of the younger brother. She said to her husband, "This time your brother has killed some one. From where does he bring so many things?" Once again the elder brother scolded her and she kept mum.

The younger brother started living comfortably. His children started going to school. He constructed his house and purchased agricultural land. He saw the seeds given to him by the businessman and worked hard in the field with his wife. The businessman had given cotton seeds to him.

After harvesting he loaded all the cotton on a bullock cart and went to the businessman. He said, "I do not know where to sell this cotton and have no idea about the price. You take it all and give me what so ever you think I deserve."

The businessman smiled and gave him rupees three hundred thousand. The younger brother requested him to take back the amount he had spent on him and his family members. The businessman was not ready to take that but he took rupees fifty thousand for the satisfaction of the younger brother. Slowly the younger brother became a rich farmer.

The luck of the younger brother had helped him in the form of a businessman.

## THE VERACIOUS

There was a businessman. His only son Rakesh was a lethargic boy. After the death of his father he did not take proper care of his business and slowly he spent all his money. He became a poor boy. One day he had nothing to eat. He planned to steal goods from someone's house.

When he was going to steal he met a saint. The saint asked him, "Where are you going?"

Rakesh said, "I am going for a theft."

"I am happy to know that you have courage to tell the truth. You are a courageous veracious boy", the saint said smilingly. He further said, "I am going to tell you four points that will always help you."

Rakesh said, "I am listening to you carefully tell me what do you want to say."

The saint said, "Always tell the truth after the theft. Secondly, cover the body of sleeping persons. Thirdly, sit maintaining some distance from the crowd. Fourthly, where people are engaged in preaching always stay there for a while." Rakesh noted the points in his mind and promised the saint he would follow his instruction in future. He went to a businessman and asked for some work. The businessman engaged him as his helper. Though Rakesh was a lethargic being the son of a businessman he had good idea of business. His advice helped his employer a lot. After a month the businessman paid Rakesh handsomely. With money Rakesh purchased gorgeous dress and wearing that started moving in the village.

The villagers asked him who was he and where was he going. Rakesh replied every one that he was a thief and was going for a theft. Villagers thought he was a crazy young man. While he was moving in the village he saw a saint preaching sitting under a tree. Rakesh sat there maintaining some distance from the crowd. That very day a theft had occurred in the palace of the king and the army men were searching for the thief. They came near the tree where the saint was preaching. The army men asked the people sitting there, "Have you seen any thief?" The villagers recalled what Rakesh had told and said pointing towards him, "That man sitting there claims that he is a thief." The army men took Rakesh to the king.

The king asked, "Who are you? Whose dress are you wearing?"

Rakesh replied, "I am a thief. If you think it is your dress and I have stolen it you can take it back." The king laughed at the words of Rakesh and said, "You are not a thief. You are an honest man. I engage you as my personal attendant. I need persons like you."

One day the king was going some where else. He asked Rakesh to take care of the palace and the people in his absence. In the absence of the king the queen was very happy. She had developed illegal relationship with the minister of the king. The absence of the king had given her an opportunity to meet the minister freely.

One day Rakesh saw them sleeping together. He covered their body with his shawl. When they woke up the minister got frightened. He said to the queen, "What will happen now? Rakesh has seen us together. He will disclose our relationship in front of the king."

The queen said, "Do not worry. I will handle every thing well. Rakesh will die before he opens his mouth in front of the king."

When the king returned he found the queen lying on bed and sobbing. The king wanted to know the reason. The queen said, "In your absence, the man engaged recently had come to my room with bad intention. When I screamed he fled away leaving his shawl. Here is his shawl." Saying like this the queen gave the shawl of Rakesh to the king. The king became furious. He wanted to kill Rakesh.

He called his army men and said, "Tomorrow in the morning, hang the person to death that enters in the garden first." In the morning he called Rakesh and said to him to bring flowers from the garden as he was going to temple." Rakesh went to bring flowers. The queen was happy thinking that soon Rakesh would be killed and no one would disclose about her relation with the minister to the king. When he was near the garden he saw a group of people worshiping lord Vishnu under a tree and one man was telling about the god. Remembering the advice of the saint Rakesh sat there maintaining some distance from the crowd.

After sometime the queen called the minister and said, "Go and see in the garden. Our enemy must have been hanged till now." The happy minister went to the garden and the army man hanged him to death. He was the first man that entered the garden. Rakesh was busy hearing the *katha* (story) of lord Vishnu. The queen waited for the minister for some time and went to see what had happened with him. When she saw the dead body of the minister she started crying sitting near that. In that process her nose ring fell down there. After sometime the queen returned to the palace.

When the *katha* (story) was over Rakesh went to the garden and returned to the king with the flowers. The king was surprised to see Rakesh alive. He went to the garden and asked the army men who had entered the garden first. The army men said, "O king first the minister came here and we hanged him to death. After that the queen came here. She cried hugging the dead body of the minister after that she went back. Rakesh was the third person to enter. The king went to see the dead body of the minister and he found the nose ring of the queen there. He understood every thing. He went to the queen and asked her the truth. The queen accepted every thing. The king hanged her at the place where the minister was hanged.

Rakesh became famous as a veracious man.

# Folktales of Munda

## MUNDA: AN INTRODUCTION

Munda tribesmen are found across Jharkhand, Bihar, Orissa, West Bengal, Chhattisgarh, and Assam states of India and into parts of Bangladesh. They speak Mundari, which belongs to Austro-Asiatic language family (Anderson 2001).

Munda tribesmen are generally thought to be indigenous people of the Indian subcontinent. However, biologists (Riccio et. al. 2011) after studying the genetic drift of Munda population, also suggest their possible origin in Southeast Asia.

The term Munda given to this community designates the name of the leader of the tribal community. The Munda call themselves *Hodoko* which means 'Human Beings' (Hoffman 1937).

Historically the Munda tribesmen were hunters but gradually they became agriculturists. They also work as labourer in the field, or in the construction work (Roy 1912).

Though one fourth of the Munda tribesmen follow Christianity, they follow *Sarna* religion. They believe in the supreme power of *Sing-Bonga*, which means Sun-God (Roy 1912, Sahay and Singh 1998). A significant number of Munda tribesmen also worship lord Shiva. *Mage, Phagu, Karam, Sarhul,* and *Sohrai* are the major festivals celebrated among the Munda (Sachhidananda 1979, Srivastava 2007).

*Sarhul,* the festival of flowers is celebrated in the month of March-April which is an important festival for the Munda tribesmen. On the occasion of this festival *sal* (sohrea robusta) flowers are brought to the *Sarna* (religious place) and the *pujari* (sacred specialist) propitiates all the gods of the Munda tribesmen. On full moon day of *Push* (December) month the Mage is celebrated by them. In this festival the spirits of the deceased ancestors are worshipped. They celebrated *Phagu* in *Phagun* (February-March). This festival is characterized by communal hunt, and the worship of village deity. The festival corresponds with the Holi (festival of colours) festival of the Hindus as the Munda tribesmen, too, sprinkle colour on each other. For the prosperity of the village the Karma festival is celebrated in the month of August-September. During this festival, the un-married youths of the village, singing and dancing bring sapling of *Karma* (adina cordifolia) tree from the forest. The saplings are planted in the village. They drink rice beer and dance all night. In October-November, they celebrate *Sohrai*. In the night, earthen lamps are lighted and on the following morning, the cattle shed is washed and sprinkled with rice beer. They decorate their cattle and worship them. Every festival has a story behind its celebration, which show their primitive faith and give solidity to celebration.

The Munda tribesmen consider the famous personality Birsa Munda as their god. He was the man behind the millenarian movement that rose in the tribal belt of modern day Bihar and Jharkhand during the British period in the late 19th century. His activities made him an important figure in the history of the Indian independence movement. His achievements in the freedom struggle became even greater considering he accomplished this before he was 25 years old. When he was only twenty years old, his activities in the tribal areas of Jharkhand state (earlier Bihar) had already begun to worry the British establishment to a considerable extent. He was finally caught by the British on the 3rd of February 1900 when he was only 25 years old. He died soon afterwards in mysterious circumstances on the 9th June 1900 in Ranchi Jail.

## THE CREATION OF LAND

In the beginning the earth was all covered with water and at first god made only such animals, which could live in water. After sometime god wanted to create land and separate that from water. He called the crab and ordered him, "Bring some soil from under the water."

The crab tried several times to bring some soil with his pair of chelae, but as soon as that reached the surface the waves washed off the soil. The crab complained to god, "O my god I tried several times to bring the soil in both chelae, it was all washed away by the waves. What can I do now?"

Now the god asked the turtle to bring some soil. The turtle dived into the water and came back with heaps of soil on its back but just as he was pushing his head out of the water the waves washed out the soil. The turtle also complained, "God, I had brought a back full of soil but when I came out of the water, it was all washed off by the waves."

At this the god turned to the earthworm and said, "We have seen the crab and the turtle failing to bring even a bit of soil. I want you not to fail and fetch some soil."

The earthworm went down and from the bottom picked up some soil and filled his mouth. After that he came out wriggling.

The god asked, "Earthworm, have you brought any soil?"

The earthworm disgorged the soil out of his mouth into the hand of the god and said, "Yes my god, here is the soil."

"Well done earthworm", the god said to the earthworm.

The god spread that soil with a blow and separated the land from the sea. The land grew all kinds of herbs, plants, and trees. After the vegetation the god created the animals and his last creation was man in his own image.

[With a little variation there are several versions of this story prevalent among the different tribes in India. Oraon tribesmen have a counterpart of this story as well].

## SOHRAI FESTIVAL

Once upon a time there lived two kings in two separate villages. Among the kings one was not as rich as the other was. The poor king had seven sons. After the death of the king his eldest son succeeded the throne but he neither improved the condition of his village nor of himself and remained poor. One day one of the other brothers succeeded him but he too failed in his role and no improvement took place. When the younger brother was persuaded to become the king he agreed but put one condition that he would be obeyed implicitly.

One day the younger brother who had become the king ordered his brothers, "Go out, bring any animal dead or alive." The brothers found a dead snake and brought that to the younger brother. The dead snake was put on the roof of the house. By mere coincidence, on that very day the rich king was returning from his hunt and halted near the tank in the village of the poor king. He took bath in the tank and forgot to take his diamond ring which he had put on the bank of the tank. After going back to his house he missed his ring and immediately returned to the tank and asked a lady who was taking bath there if she had noticed any ring there. The lady replied, "An eagle had come and had flown away with something from the bank. However, I am not sure whether that was a ring or something else".

The eagle had flown away with the ring towards the house of the poor king. Seeing the dead snake on the roof he dropped the ring there and flew away with the dead snake. The poor king thus came in possession of the ring. The rich king went to him and said, "Can you help me in finding out the ring please?"

The poor king returned the ring to the rich king but put a condition that no one would light any light on the day of *sohrai* (cattle worship) festival. The rich king agreed and did not let others to light any light during the festival day and to worship their cattle. The cattle felt very sore about it.

They saw lamps lit in the house of the poor king and went there. The *mahua* (bassia latifolia) tree under which the cattle were kept also went with them to the house of the poor king. The goddess of wealth, Lakshmi also accompanied them.

The poor king welcomed them warmly. He drove the cattle in the cowshed and goddess Lakshmi was also called inside the house. But there was a problem to keep the *mahua* tree inside the room. Therefore some branches of the tree were cut and planted in the cowshed. The cattle were given boiled *urad* (horse-bean) to eat. Thus, the wealth and prosperity of the rich king came to the poor king who became wealthy and at the same time the rich king became poor.

[The Sohrai festival is celebrated all over Jharkhand the every next day after the *Deewali* (festival of light) festival. On this occasion the houses are lighted with earthen pots. The cattle are worshipped and given to eat boiled *urad* lentils for about a week before the festival day. Vermilion is applied on their horns and they are decorated with colours. Branches of *mahua* tree are also worshipped and the *Sing-Bonga* (supreme deity) is propitiated]

## THE WILD BUFFALOES

Many years ago there lived a poor boy in a village. He used to graze cattle of the villagers and in turn the villagers used to give him a handful of corns to eat.

One day while grazing the cattle he saw a heron pecking at the eyes of a tiger, while the tiger was taking rest. The heron out of mischief plucked out the eyes and the tiger became blind. Out of pain the tiger roared and the heron flew away. The boy wanted to make sure that whether the tiger was blind or not. He threw some of the wild fruits he was eating, towards the tiger. On being hit the tiger asked, "Who had hit me."

"It is me. I have thrown fruits towards you", the boy gave out his identity.

"Have you seen what the heron has done with me", the tiger asked further.

"Yes I have seen the deed of the heron", the boy replied.

"Do not say any thing about me and the heron to any body otherwise you would suffer", the tiger warned the boy.

The boy agreed that he would not tell about the tiger to any body and took away his cattle from there. At night when the villagers assembled and one after another started repeating some story or riddle, the poor boy said that he too had a story to tell. The villagers laughed and wondered what story he would tell. The boy told them the story of the tiger and the heron and the heron had made the tiger blind. The villagers were amused much and patted the boy. They all retired to sleep.

The tiger was curious to know whether the boy had kept his promise or had repeated his story. He smelt his way to the village and overheard the boy repeating the story. He wanted to take revenge and picking up the boy while he was sleeping, went into the forest. The boy managed to catch hold of a branch of a tree and quickly went up the tree in the forest and escaped from the fury of the tiger.

The herd of wild buffaloes used to come and rest under the tree every evening. In the morning when the buffaloes went away the boy came down and swept the place clean. After eating the forest fruits he again concealed himself high upon the tree. That evening when the buffaloes came back they were surprised to see the place swept and clean. This went on for several days. The buffaloes were curious and one morning one of the buffaloes said, "Today I am going to keep myself concealed at some distance. I will find out who cleans this place daily and will solve out the mystery."

All the buffaloes agreed with that buffalo and leaving her there alone went away. The buffalo hid herself at some distance. When the boy came down the tree as usual, the buffalo too came out of her hiding. The boy was frightened but the buffalo assured him that no harm would come to him. From that day the boy lived happily with the buffaloes and had plenty of milk to drink.

The boy became healthy and strong. One day while he was taking bath in the forest a lock of his beautiful dark hair came out. The boy made a cup of leaf and putting the lock of hair in that cup floated that down the stream. The leaf-cup floated down the *ghat* where the local princess was taking her bath. The princess picked up the leaf-cup and was struck by the beautiful shine of the hair. Her maids told her that the hair was of a healthy youth. The princess was much attracted and wanted to meet the boy.

The princess went back home and began to pine for the youth. The king was told about it and found that his daughter had become thin and morose. The king called his pet crow and said, "Go and find where the boy is? If possible call him to the palace."

The crow went in the forest and found the boy. The crow implored the boy, "Please come to the palace."

When the boy refused to accept his invitation, the crow took his flute which was made up of the horn of buffalo and flew back to palace. After seeing the flute the princess became more anxious to meet the boy.

The boy was very angry because his flute was taken away by the crow. He went to palace and complained to the king about it. The king said, "You will get your flute back if you agree to marry the princess."

The boy agreed to marry the princess and got back his flute. He played the flute and all the buffaloes came to the boy. The boy married the princess and lived happily in the palace. The wild buffaloes also lived with him and became tame.

## THE OLD COUPLE

There was an old couple in a village. They were very poor and used to manage to live by begging. The old man used to go round to beg rice or *jwar* (millet) in the village and the old woman to collect edible leaves, roots and spinach from the forest. They used to cook the grains with the spinach and eat that with relish. In this way they lived quite happily.

The old man had a fun of wit. Sometimes he used to visit the king of the village and amuse him with some story, if he was otherwise unsuccessful in getting his need of the day. In turn the king used to give him some alms. However, he never used to accept any alms from the king if he had already got enough grains for the day. For his ready wit and simple need, the king liked him immensely.

One day the old woman said to her husband, "Today ask for some uncooked rice from somebody. I want to eat *pitha* (a sweetmeat made be rice flour and jaggery) today."

The old man went round and refused to accept any thing as alms other than uncooked rice. He returned to old woman with a handful of rice. The old woman ground flour of that rice, and made three large *pithas*. Now they started quarrelling on the issue as to who should eat the two *pithas* and who will have only one. The old man claimed for the lion's share and the lady refused to hear him telling as the original idea was her. To solve out the problem they decided that both would lie down and whoever rose last should have the two *pithas*. The *pithas* were put by and the couple stretched themselves wrapped up.

Not seeing the old beggar for two mornings the king sent a man to find out what had happened to them. The servant of the king peeped into the room and thought they were dead. He went back to the king and said that the old couple had died. The sad king ordered for their funeral. The king's men prepared for the funeral and carried the old couple to the pyre. When the fire was lit the old man jumped up first and immediately after that the old woman too jumped up shouting, "I have won, I will eat two."

The men present there were stunned and thought they had turned into ghosts. The couple went to the king and told their story. The king had a hearty laugh. He asked the old couple to stay in his out house as his perpetual guests.

## THE STUPID TORTOISE

One day a man was going to perform some work in another village. On the way he found a large tortoise crossing the road. The man got hold of the tortoise without caring for his protest and said, "I am lucky to get a large tortoise. I will have some meat after a long time."

The man came to a river which he had to cross every time to go any where from his village. The river was flooded and no boat could be seen.

The tortoise said to man, "If you agree to spare my life and set me down in the river I can take you across the river."

The man agreed and sat down on the back of the tortoise. The tortoise ferried him cross. The man set free the tortoise in the water. On his return journey the man came again to the river and asked, "Who is in the water to take me across the river."

The tortoise came up to the bank and let the man be seated on his back. In the midstream the tortoise said, "A few hours back you wanted to eat me. I am going to drown you right now."

The man started thinking the way to save his life. He saw a jackal at the other bank and said to the tortoise, "Before you drown me, please ask the jackal if you should."

The tortoise shouted, "Look brother jackal, this man wanted to eat me a few hours back. Should I drown him right now?"

The clever jackal replied, "Look, I am deaf of one ear. Come nearer the bank and tell me."

The tortoise swam nearer the bank and again asked the same question. Again the jackal replied, "A little nearer please. I can not hear you properly."

The tortoise came very near to the bank and repeated the question. The jackal told the man, "What are you gaping at, jump down and run to the bank."

The man did so and escaped. The tortoise told the jackal, "Well brother, you will be taught a lesson."

From that day the tortoise began laying traps to catch the jackal. One evening the jackal came to the river to drink water. The tortoise swam under the water and caught the foot of the jackal. He laughed and said, "Now, I have caught you, run and see."

The quick witted jackal replied, "You have not caught me. It must be a root you have caught."

The tortoise immediately let the foot free and seized a root near by. The jackal escaped laughing at the tortoise. A few days later, the jackal was again at the bank of river to warm him. He wanted to know if the tortoise was nearby. He thought, "Other days it used to cry *okka, okka,* but today it is silent."

Mimicking the tortoise cry the jackal shouted, "*Okka, okka*."

The response came soon, "*Okka, okka*." The jackal laughed and said, "So you are here." He fled from there.

The tortoise could not catch the jackal any way. Since that day there is enmity between the tortoise and the jackal.

[The tribesmen believe that the tortoise and the jackal are born enemies. The enmity between the two persons in Jharkhand is often referred to as the relationship between a tortoise and a jackal.]

## THE PLOUGH

When the god made the image of man and breathed life into that he felt that he must give the man a tool to till the field and raise the crops for his subsistence. He got indulged for a long time in making a plough. After taking a large tree, he carved out of that a plough with its shaft, grip, and handle all in one piece. He was so heavily engaged in his work that he even forgot to come back home and meet his consort. She called a mosquito and ordered him, "Go and see what the god is doing. Call him here."

The mosquito went and started bussing round the ear of the god, but the god did not respond and remained busy in continuing his work. Having failed to disturb the god the mosquito returned to the consort of the god. At this the consort of the god became angry and called a tiger and sent that to perform the job in which the mosquito had failed. The tiger went near the god and started rustling the leaves and making noise. This way he wanted to disturb the god. The god taking a small piece of wood threw that at the tiger and said, "Be gone wild dog." At once the piece of wood became a wild dog and chased the tiger away, and that is why even today tiger is afraid of wild dog.

After a long time the god finished his work and proudly took the plough home to show that to his wife. His wife saw the plough and said laughing, "So this is the plough you have made and taken so much time in making it. It would be useless to our children."

The god asked, "Why you are saying like this? Can you explain the reason?"

She replied, "It would be difficult for any one to spend so much time in making a huge plough like the one you have made."

"I do not agree with you", the god protested.

His wife then said, "You throw the plough on the earth and see how it fares."

The plough was thrown out on the earth and was broken in to pieces. The god was very angry that the plough was broken. She pacified him and said that she would make a better plough which would not need a big tree and would not break even when thrown on the earth. The god agreed and his heavenly consort started making a plough. She made the plough, the shaft, the handle and the grip in separate pieces. Having cut holes in the plough, she joined the pieces together and all this was done in a very short time.

When the plough was ready she made her husband to throw that on the earth. The god threw the plough on the earth and that was not broken. The man on earth took up the plough and immediately started ploughing.

The god said to his wife, "You have beaten me. However from today I pronounce that no woman shall undergo the hardship of making the plough. The man will make it and let woman not even touch it."

Since that day women were forbidden to touch the plough.

[The tribesmen of Jharkhand believe that the god and his wife were *Sing-Bonga* and his consort; they also believe that they were lord Shiva and his wife Gaura.]

## THE WELL WISHER PARROT

Many years ago there was a demon that used to change into human being and as a mendicant used to visit the villages. He had made the king of the village his friend by his clever ways and frequent visit to him. The king used to ask the mendicant for something or other and he was fulfilling his wishes. This way the mendicant made the king to depend more and more on him. Finally the demon made the king agree to give his daughter as well as half of his kingdom to him in marriage.

The princess had a talking-parrot that had a quality to see the past and the present. The parrot told the princess, "Your husband is not a mendicant but a devil that is evil as well."

While the princess was going to her husband's house she insisted that she would take the parrot with her. The bridegroom first opposed her decision but finally agreed with her. For some days the demon lived with the princess as normal human but after that he started his routine of going out. In the day he used to go out and hunt the beasts and eat them up. He never touched the food cooked by the princess.

One day the demon could not get any beast of prey. He returned home very hungry. The princess gave him food she had cooked. The small quantity of rice and curry could not satisfy the hunger of the demon. He pounced on the princess and swallowed her up in one gulp. The parrot saw all this and flew away.

The parrot came to the palace of the king and told the king what had happened with his daughter. The angry king took his army and attacked the house of the demon and killed him. As the demon had swallowed the princess in gulp, his stomach was ripped open and the princess came out alive. The king took back his daughter to his house after demolishing the house of the demon. The parrot also lived happily with the princess at the house of the king.

## THE KING AND HIS FOUR SONS

In a village there was a king. He had four sons. One day the goddess of wealth appeared before him and said, "I am with you till you are alive. One day a snake will bite you and you will die. After your death I will leave your kingdom."

The worried king started thinking not only for the safety of his life but about the welfare of his village and the villagers as well. He wanted to kill the snake first. He called his sons and ordered them to take the charge of giving the protection to him at night. He also instructed them to kill any reptiles coming to him.

First night when the elder son was guarding the king while he was sleeping not a single creature came near the king. Second night the second son took the charge to protect the king in the night and he too did not see any creature coming to the king. The third son also did not see any creature. The fourth night the youngest son was standing near the sleeping king with a sword in his hand. At mid night he saw a snake creeping on the cot of the king. He killed that snake with his sword but a drop of poison fell down on the neck of the queen, who was the step mother of the four brothers. The youngest son thought he had saved his father and he was going to lose his mother. He wiped out the poison with a cloth. The queen woke up and saw the activity of the youngest son. The queen was not good natured and always wanted to get rid of her step children. She got an opportunity to get rid of the youngest prince.

The next morning she complained to the king that the youngest prince was trying to steal his necklace and to strangle her or may be he had some bad intention for her. The king became very angry. He immediately wanted to punish his son but was not sure about the type of punishment that should be given to him. He wanted to ask from his sons and called them one by one.

First, he asked his elder son, "If any body does something forbidden to him, what punishment should be given to him?"

The elder son replied, "If he had committed any thing wrong consciously then after digging a ditch his half body should be buried and half body should be bitten by the dogs. But my father without knowing the fact he should not be punished otherwise you would have to regret for it." In the support of his point the eldest son told a story in front of every body. The story went like this:

A king had a parrot. The parrot brought a divine fruit for his master. While the parrot was bringing the fruit he had to take shelter on the branch of a tree in night and at that very time a snake had made the fruit poisonous. When the parrot gave the fruit to the king, the king gave one piece of the fruit to his dog. After eating the piece of the fruit the dog died. In anger the king killed the parrot. He was not ready to hear a word of his parrot who wanted to say some thing to him. One of the servants of the king buried the fruit in the garden. After a few day a tree grew up there where the fruit had been buried. The king made a boundary wall around the tree in order to prevent any human or animal to eat the fruit of that tree. One day an old couple came to the king and asked for the fruit of the tree. The couple wanted to end their lives. The king gave them the fruits. After eating the fruits the old couple became young. The surprised king called another old man and forced him to eat the fruit. He became young too, after eating the fruit. In great shock and remembering his dear parrot the king died.

"Therefore my father no one should be punished without knowing the reason of his deeds", the eldest son said to the king. After this the king called his second son and asked the same question what he had asked his eldest son and the reply of the second son was also the same as of the eldest son. He told some different story to make his point clear:

Once there lived a goldsmith. His daughter-in-law had the power to know about the past and the future happenings. One day in the night she dreamt that a corpse was floating on the water of the river. That corpse had a diamond ring in his finger and he was calling some one to take the ring. She woke up and proceeded towards the river. She was unaware of the fact that her husband was following her. After going near the corpse she wanted to remove the ring but failed. Then she applied her mouth and took the ring. Her husband who had concealed himself behind a tree watched every thing but misunderstood that his wife was eating the corpse. He returned home and told his father, "You have married me with a devilish. In mid night she was eating a corpse."

The frightened father suggested his son to send his wife to her parents' house. Now the husband after taking some edibles with him proceeded towards his in-laws' house with his wife. On the way the lady told her husband about the corpse and the diamond ring. She gave that ring to her husband. After covering some distance she heard that a cow was telling that there were lots of gold and silver coins buried in the mud and the cow was unable to bear the flame of the wealth. The lady told her husband, "We will get many opportunities to visit my parents' house. At this place lots of wealth are buried. Let us dig out that wealth first."

The husband dug out the wealth and both of them made two bundles of gold and silver coins. Carrying one bundle each they returned home. The lady reached home first. When the goldsmith saw his daughter-in-law he thought she might have killed her husband. In anger he attacked her with an axe and beheaded her. Coming near the dead body the goldsmith found the bundle of gold and silver coins. Meanwhile his son entered the room and saw the dead body of his wife. He said to his father, "Oh father you have killed my wife, who was so good. Where will I find such a noble wife?" He told about the corpse, the diamond ring and the coins to his father. Both father and the son started crying and died in regret.

The third son told another story to make point clear that one should make clear every thing before punishing any one. The story goes like this:

A king had a dog. He sold out his dog to another king for four hundred coins. Soon after buying the dog the king got a profit of four hundred coins in his business. He thought that god had returned the price of the dog and he should now return the dog to his real master. He wrote a letter to the first king and attached that with the neck of the dog. He made the dog free and insisted him to go to his real master. When the first dog owner saw the dog he thought that the dog would have run away. In anger he killed the dog. After that he saw the letter. In regret he started crying and died.

At last the king called his fourth son. The young son told what had happened in the mid night. The king found the dead snake on his cot. He understood that the queen was wrong. He appreciated his sons telling that due to them only he had given the chance to his fourth son to make his stand clear otherwise he would have killed him immediately.

He killed his wife for telling lies and lived happily with his sons.

## THE WISE JACKAL

There was an old tiger that was not able to see clearly. One day while looking for food the tiger fell into a well and in spite of his best efforts could not come out. Sometime after a *bhisti* (water carrier) came there to fill his goat-skin bag with water. The tiger requested the *bhisti* to pull him up. He told the *bhisti*, "Let down your goat-skin bag for me in the water. I will get into it and then you can pull me up." This was done and the tiger was pulled up out of the well.

Instead of being grateful the tiger wanted to kill the *bhisti* and eat him up. The *bhisti* said, "I have saved you from death and you want to eat me up. This is not fair. Let us refer this matter to the mango tree nearby for a decision."

The tiger agreed and both went to the mango tree and put their case. The mango tree said, "Yes tiger, eat him up. I give delicious mangoes to the men as well as shed all through the year. Yet men chop off my branches for fuel."

The tiger then told the *bhisti*, "Well, you have got the decision, now you must be prepared to be eaten up."

Just then a jackal was passing that way and asked them, "What is the matter?"

They put their respective cases and requested the jackal to give his decision. Having heard the cases, the jackal told the tiger, "I am a little surprised that you could get into this goat-skin bag. Will you please demonstrate it to convince me of the truth of your case?"

The tiger replied, "That is simple." As soon as he got into the bag the jackal pulled tight the goat skin-bag and the tiger could not come out. The *bhisti* beat the tiger to death.

[The proverbial cunning of the jackal has won him the epithet of a *pundit* among the tribesmen of Jharkhand].

## THE MILK MAN

In a village a poor man used to graze cattle of a rich man. While grazing cattle in the forest he used to see many birds and animals and wanted to talk with them and learn their languages. One day he came to know that one of the cows used to offer her milk to the statue of lord Shiva which was erected under a tree. The man thought that if his master would come to know about the loss of milk he would beat him severally. He became angry with lord Shiva who was accepting the milk silently. He started beating the statue with a stick. Now it became his daily routine to beat the lord Shiva daily while returning home after grazing the cattle.

One day he forgot to beat the statue. While he was having his dinner he recalled his mistake and immediately went to beat that taking a stick. He was in so hurry that he forgot to wash his hand. When he reached near the statue lord Shiva appeared before him and said, "Whatever boon you want, I will give you but do not beat me."

The man agreed and stopped beating him, and then lord Shiva told him to come tomorrow after taking bath. He went home and told his wife, "O dear! Shiva has called me tomorrow to give a boon."

Early in the morning the man went to take his boon. He said, "Shiva I do not want wealth. Give me the power so that I can understand the languages of animals and birds."

"Go home. Here after you will understand the languages of cattle as well as birds. But do not let anybody know about this boon." Lord Shiva told the man and disappeared from there.

When the man returned home his wife asked about the boon but the man did not want to let her know about the boon. When his wife insisted him to tell about the boon he said, "Horns will grow in the head of queen."

The wife of the man went to the queen and started noticing the horns in her head. When she did not find any horns then went nearer to the queen to inspect closely. The queen asked, "O lady! Why are you looking at me so curiously?"

The innocent lady replied, "Oh queen! My husband has asked the boon to grow horns in your head from the Shiva I am looking for those horns."

The queen became angry and said, "Oh my god! So much insult of me. I had not imagined." She went to the king and narrated every thing to him. The king said his army to arrest the poor man. The army went arrested the poor man from his house and proceeded towards the palace. On the way the man heard a heron was saying, "There are lots of fishes in this tank and each fish has a diamond in her stomach. Is there any man who can take all the diamonds and give me the fishes?"

The man replied, "O heron! Today the king is going to kill me otherwise I would have given you all the fishes."

After covering some distance he heard a cow was saying, "There are lots of gold buried at the place where I am standing. Is there any man who can take all the gold?"

The man replied, "Oh cow! Today the king is going to kill me otherwise I would have taken the gold."

Third time he heard the crowing of a crow, "Underneath the mud there is a pot filled with diamonds and two frogs as well. Is there any man who can take all the diamonds and give me the frogs?"

The man replied, "Oh crow! I would have done so, but today the king is going to kill me."

This time the army men asked the poor man about the talking conversation between him and the crow. The soldiers promised to set him free if he told the truth.

The poor man told about the pot filled with diamonds to the soldiers. After digging the earth the soldiers took out the pot filled with diamonds. They gave the frogs to the crow and set the poor man free. After that they went to the king and giving him all the diamonds said what had happened on the way. The king appreciated the decision taken by the army men to let the poor man free and taking up the diamonds. The queen was not happy. To please his wife the king forced the poor man to work in the palace and take care of the cattle.

One day a heron sitting on the branch of a tree asked the poor man, "I am able to control my twelve wives but you man can not control even a single wife, why?"

The poor man replied, "Time has changed and it is just like so."

The king was also there. He asked the poor man what was going on between him and the heron. The poor man told every thing to him. The king set the poor man free and refused to hear his wife in this regards.

The poor man took all the diamonds from the stomach of the fishes and gold of the cow. He lived happily with his wife and left the job of grazing the cattle.

## THE HUNIPURTI CLAN

In a village a man had sown cotton in his field. When the capsules of the cotton were ripe, the man and his wife came to pick the cotton from the capsules. The wife put her baby on the ground and got indulged in plucking the cotton. A number of field rats came there to eat the cotton seeds. They found the sleeping baby and carried that into their hole. The mother spent a long time without seeing and hearing the cry of her baby. She said to herself, "I should go and nurse my baby."

She went to the place where she had left her baby but her baby was not there. The scared mother ran to the village and started wailing. The villagers gathered her and asked what had happened to her. The lady told them about her missing baby. The villagers set out on a search. They went to cotton field and found that the baby was sleeping on a bed of cotton. The men were highly pleased and said, "The rats are surely our brothers, they have not only brought the baby but let it sleep on the bed of cotton."

[From that day onwards the villagers started considering rats as their brothers and ceased to eat them. Hence they have been called *Huntipurti* clan and the village where all it happened is considered as the ancestral village of this clan. The tribesmen of the Jharkhand claim that the traditional name of this village was *Tuijutu* village.]

## THE SEVENTH QUEEN

A king had seven wives but he had not become a father. He used to live worried thinking about his heir. One day the sad king was roaming in the forest uselessly. He met a saint there. The saint asked the king, "Why are you so much worried and sad?"

The king told him that he wanted to become a father of a son who could take care of his kingdom after his death. He told the saint about his seven wives. The saint said to the king, "Pluck seven fruits from the nearby mango tree by your left hand and give each fruit to your seven wives by your right. Soon you will become a father."

After plucking the fruits the king gave all the fruits to her eldest queen to distribute among themselves. He also told her about the saint. The eldest queen gave the fruits to every queen except the youngest one. When the seventh and the youngest queen came to them to inquire what they were eating they all refused to say. The youngest queen saw the seeds of the mango fruits near the *siloth* (a piece of stone on which condiments are ground with a mullet). She understood what the others queens were eating. She collected all the seeds and after grinding those seeds drank that.

After a few days the seventh queen conceived the child but nothing happened to other queens. When the king got the news of pregnancy of the seventh queen he became very happy. One day the king was going to hunt in the forest. He told all the queens, "Ring the gold-bell if I am blessed with a son and coins-bell if it is a daughter."

The youngest queen gave birth to a healthy son. The other queens after throwing the child in the garden of the palace kept a boom-stick near her. They rang both the bells together. Hearing the sound of the bells the king returned to the palace. When he saw a boom-stick instead of a child near the queen he became angry and ordered his youngest wife to leave the palace.

A gem holder snake started taking care of the child thrown by the six queens. After a few years the new born baby grew up as a naughty child. In night he started playing with the snake in the light of the gem. However, in this process the plants of the garden used to get trampled. The gardener of the palace complained about it to the king. The king told the gardener to guard the garden in night as well.

In the night the gardener saw the child playing with snake in the light of the gem. In the morning he went to the king and informed him about the child. All the queens were also sitting near the king. They immediately understood who the child was. They made a plan to get rid of the child. In the night they all kept hemp plants under their bed sheet and slept. While sleeping they started whimpering.

"What happened to you all? Why you all are whimpering? How you all will get cures?" The king asked the queens.

"We will be cured only after taking bath after putting the head of the gem-holder snake in the water", they all replied.

The king sent his servant to kill the snake of the garden and bring his head. The servant killed the snake and brought the head. The snake was aware of his killing. Before he was killed he had handed over the child and his gem to a cow named Surhi-Kapali. Surhi was one among the cattle of the king and used to live in the cattle shed of the palace. The cow started taking care of the child.

All the six queens pretended to get cured after taking bath. They thought that by getting rid of the snake they would have got rid of the child as well. The cow (Surhi-Kapali) started feeding her milk to the child in the night. Therefore she started giving less milk in the morning. The milk man complained about it to the king.

"What do you think about the cow? All of a sudden, what happened to her?" The king asked.

"O king! I used to take good care of the cow. I do not know what happened to her", the milk man showed his ignorance. The king ordered him to watch the activity of the cow in the night. The milk man planned to spend his night in the cattle shed. In mid night he saw the cow vomiting the child and the gem. After that she fed her milk to the child. Then the child started playing with the gem. When it was dawn the cow swallowed the child and the gem.

In the morning the milk man went running to the king and told every thing he had seen in the night. When the queens came to know about the child and the gem they understood who the child was. Once again they put hemp plant under their bed sheet and started whimpering while sleeping. The king asked the reason of their whimpering. They told they would be cured after seeing the blood of Surhi-Kapali. The king sent his men to kill the cow and to bring her blood. This was done and the queen got cured.

However, the cow, too, was aware of it. She handed over the child to a mare named Hiraman before being killed. Now Hiraman started taking care of the child.

After some time the prince became young man. One day Hiraman asked the prince to bring her bridle from the bed room of his father.

"What would happen if the king got up?" The prince asked.

"It will not happen. The king is fast sleep. He will never know." Hiraman replied. The prince brought the bridle and riding on Hiraman proceeded towards some unknown place. The villagers tried their best to stop Hiraman but their effort went in vain. After covering a large distance, Hiraman stopped under a tree. The prince came down from the back of the mare and started moving in nearby area. He saw a snake and on the instruction of Hiraman killed that snake. There was a nest of a sparrow on the branch of the tree where four sparrow chicks were waiting for their parents. They saw the prince killing the snake. In the past the snake had eaten many sparrow chicks from the nest. When the parents of the chicks returned with the food they refused to eat that and forced their parents to give the food to the prince who had killed their great enemy. The sparrow parents said, "We have very little food. We can not provide sufficient food to the prince but we can allow you to go with the prince and provide shadow to him."

The prince riding on Hiraman proceeded further. The sparrow chicks were flying over his head. The prince saw a female sheep crying in pain. A spine had pierced into her foot. The prince pulled out the spine and she got relief from the pain. The obliged sheep gave her two kids to the prince. The prince continued his journey and found that a lioness was trapped in a net kept in a field. The princess made her free and she gave one of her cubs to the prince.

The prince reached a new village. The sparrow chicks were flying over his head and the cubs as well as the kids of sheep were following him. The king of that village had called all the young men of his village in the courtyard of his palace. He was going to select any one youth among them for his daughter who was of marriageable age. The prince also came to know about this gathering. Covering his attractive and strong body by a dirty lion skin he joined the gathering of youths in the courtyard of the palace. After some time the king came there with a she-elephant. The she-elephant was holding a garland with her trunk. It has been already announced that the princess would marry the man, against whose neck the she-elephant would put the garland.

After taking a round of the courtyard and watching every individual present there, the she-elephant put the garland on the head of the prince who had covered his body with dirty skin of a lion. Every one present there started shouting that the elephant had become mad. Even the king was not happy with the choice of the she-elephant. On the demand of all the candidates the king asked his men to arrange for another elephant and that elephant, too, selected the same prince. At last the king got his daughter married with the prince.

The next morning the king announced that one person from every house of the village would have to go in the forest to hunt the prey. The prince, too, had to go to hunt. The king gave him an old and wicked mare to go in the forest. The king was thinking that being unable to control that wicked mare the prince would fall down and die. Riding on the wicked mare the prince came to his Hiraman. He fastened the wicked mare there and riding on Hiraman went in the forest.

In the forest he killed all the deer and kept the ears and tails of the dead animals with him. There was a tank in the forest. The prince after taking bath in the tank removed his lion skin and wore good clothes given to him by Hiraman. Near the tank he started taking rest, sitting under a tree.

The sons of the king had also come in the forest to hunt. All the men of the village were hunting in a group with the sons of the king. They all came near the tank. They all thought that the prince, who was taking rest under the tree, was the owner of the tank. No one recognized him. The other villagers requested the sons of the king to take permission from the owner so that they all might drink water from the tank. The sons of the king went near the prince.

"Can we drink water of your tank?" The sons of the king asked the prince.

"Yes, you can but before that you all will have to fulfil my wish", the prince replied.

"What do you want from us?" they all spoke together.

"I will put a burn mark on the buttock of all of you", the prince replied.

The sons of the king had no other choice than to accept the condition of the prince. The prince put burn mark on the buttocks of all of them. After quenching their thirst they all returned to their palace. They also carried the deer killed by the prince with them. In front of the king they all started falsely praising themselves that they had killed all the deer. The prince came there very late riding on the old mare provided to him by the king. With the help of the cub and the kids of sheep he had wounded the body of the old mare. Seeing him the king said to himself, "What a lucky chap he is. Nothing happened to him but to his mare only."

The prince did not say any thing to any body and went to his room provided to him by the king. A lady cook used to bring food for the prince. One day, out of curiosity she watched the activity of the prince secretly. When the prince removed his tiger-skin and went for taking bath she noticed he was not a dirty man but healthy and handsome man. She told about it to the princess of the village who had refused to live with the prince after the marriage. The next day the princess concealed herself in the room of the prince and saw him when he went to take bath. She started living with her husband. When the king came to know about the reality of the prince he became very happy and invited the prince to live with them in his palace.

One day the king was praising his sons saying that they were skilled hunters. They had killed all the deer in the forest in a manner that the ears and tails of the deer got lost in the air. The prince told the king that he wanted to test the skill of his brothers-in-law. He tied a goat and asked them to cut his tail and ears. All the sons of the king tried their best but failed. The prince showed them all the tails and ears of the deer and told them what had happened with them in the forest near the tank. Out of shame the sons of the king bowed their heads. The king spent a few days with the prince with happiness and then gave farewell to his daughter and son-in-law.

The prince returned to his village with his wife. Before reaching the village Hiraman told the prince who he was and what had happened with his mother and with him after his birth. The prince conveyed every thing to his father. The king recalled the incidents as to how the six queens had forced him to kill the snake and the cow and believed in the saying of the prince. He announced about his son in the court of his palace. All the six queens started claiming that the price was their son.

"If you are my mother the milk will flow from your breast and will fall in my mouth", the prince said but nothing happened with any of the queens. They all bowed their heads out of shame. The king called his seventh wife who was living in a hut near the forest. The milk started flowing from her breast and falling in the mouth of the prince. The young man prostrated before his mother.

The king asked his men to dig a well. He forced his six queens to wear rags. After pushing all of them into the well the king closed the mouth of the well. There after he lived happily with his seventh wife, son and daughter-in-law.

## THE GREAT DRUMMER

Many years ago there was a young boy, who was a great drummer and a great dancer as well. He used to dance for hours and his drumming was very attractive. He was so keen to dancing that in a single night he used to go and dance in seven villages and return home before dawn.

He used to go to *village-akhra* (meeting point of the village) and beat the tom-tom, "Ding-dong, ding-dong." Hearing the sound of tom-tom the young girls of the village used to rush out saying, "He has come, let us go and dance."

Adorning themselves with flowers the girl used to dance with the drummer boy and be intoxicated with prolonged dancing. While they remained at the height of the dancing the boy used to sneak away to another village. He used to repeat his performance at other village also and like this he used to go round as many as seven villages and return home early morning dead tired. The girls were frenzied over his skill in drumming and dancing.

The seventh village he visited was on the other side of the Koel River. The villagers had put a bridge of creepers over the river. One night when the river was full the drummer boy, while crossing the bridge to reach the seventh village for his last dance of that night, slipped and fell in to the water and was drowned.

The next morning the young boys and the girls of the seventh village started searching for the drummer boy. They kept asking every one, "What has happened to the drummer boy? He had not come to the village last night to dance"?

Searching the boy they all came near the Koel River. They found the boy was lying dead on the other side of the bank at some distance from the bridge. The boys and the girls of the seventh village gathered together and wept bitterly. The sorrowing young damsels who were the admirers of the drummer boy made a funeral pyre out of their combs and burnt him.

[Dancing to the beats of the *dhol* or *mandal* (type of drum) is a part of life of the tribesmen all over India. They are very fond of putting a comb in the hair while dancing.]

## THE OLD COUPLE AND THE JACKAL

Many years ago there lived an old couple in a village. They had a small bit of land and what so ever they were cultivating on their land was sufficient for their livelihood. The old man used to go to his field early in the morning and the woman after taking cooked food used to follow him in the afternoon.

One day the old lady was going with nicely cooked dish to the field. The smell of the dish attracted some jackals. The jackals put their heads together and hit upon a plan to get the food she was carrying. They ran up to the old woman and accosted her, "O grand mother, let us see what you are taking for our grand father." The old woman was taken in and placed the bundle on the ground and opened it. The jackals fell upon the cooked rice and curry and devoured those up.

The old woman went to her husband crying and told him what had happened with her on the way. The old man wanted to take revenge. The next morning he sent the old woman to the field dressed like a man. In the afternoon he put on his wife's cloth and started walking slowly with the cooked rice on his head. He had carefully concealed a big stick under his *sari* (long clothes of woman). On the way the jackals came again saying, "O grandmother what are you carrying today? Let us see. We give you our words that we will not touch the food for our grandfather."

They surrounded the old man. When the old man saw them coming near enough, he quickly brought out the concealed stick and gave them a sound thrashing. Now it was the jackals who wanted to take revenge. While running away they shouted, "All right old man, you have beaten us. But, see what we do with your plough."

The old man came to his field and fixed nails in the plough and left that there. In night the jackals came and fell over the plough with a view to damaging that, but instead of damaging the plough their bodies were scratched all over. They went away crying, "Grandfather you have beaten us but your beans will vanish."

The next day the old man plucked all the beans and in their places hung small knives on the creepers, borrowing a large number of those from the villagers. At night when the jackals came to pluck the beans, they plucked all the knives instead and were hurt. Finding themselves beaten again, they went away saying, "Okay grandfather you have beaten us once again but let us see where your fowls go."

At this threat the old man quickly removed all the fowls from the fowl-house and sat there at night with a sickle. When the jackals came to fowl-house, one was sent to steal the fowls while the rest concealed themselves in the croft. As the chieving jackal sneaked in to and thrust his head forward, the old man pecked at that with the sickle. In pain the jackal quickly drew itself and ran to his comrades.

"Why did you not bring any fowls?" The other jackals asked him.

The jackal replied, "The fowls were big and started pecking me hard. In pain I ran away to save my life", the jackal replied. The other jackal was sent who was treated in the same manner. In this way, one by one all the jackals except the leader went and got hurt. Finding the other jackals useless, the old jackal who was their leader, ventured himself. As he went in to the pen, the old man gave him a sever pecking with the sickle. The leader ran away and told the other jackals that it was the old man who had kept himself concealed with his sickle and had hurt them.

While the jackals were devising some other way to take revenge the old man was even cleverer. The old couple left the village for a few days and stealthily came back in the night. In the morning the jackals found the old woman bitterly weeping and asked her why she was weeping?

The old man replied, "The old man died in the other village where they had gone. I have come here alone and have to make arrangement for the funeral feast."

The jackals wanted to have a good feast and told her that they would hence forth look after her. The old woman invited them all to a great feast in the evening. She made a very nice curry with a savoury smell and when the jackals came they stared howling together, "O grandmother! Give me first a piece of bread and a good amount of curry."

The old woman said, "This way you all will quarrel and fight with each other. Let me first tie each of you separately and then I will divide the bread and a very large quantity of curry."

The jackals agreed and the old woman tied them separately. The leader jackal was tied to the threshing pestle with a thick rope. After the jackals were securely tied, the old woman gave the signal, and the old man came out with a big axe and started belabouring the jackals one after another. All the jackals ran away after getting a sound thrashing but the old jackal who was tied to threshing pestle could not escape. He, the leader was beaten to death.

[With little variations there are several versions of this story and are popular among the tribesmen of Jharkhand.]

## SOMARA AND BUDHNA

Somara and Budhna were two brothers. They were poor and foolish. They had to work hard to earn their livelihood. Somara used to work with an oil man while Budhna served a potter. Somara had to look after the bulls, to give them proper feeds and drive the bulls round and round around the oil-crushing post. In the evening the master used to give him some food and a small wage. Budhna also had to go here and there and get a lot of clay daily for the potter and also help him in moving out the pottery. The potter treated him badly and gave him a very small wage and scanty food.

Somara and Budhna hit upon a plan to escape their bad luck. They thought it would be better to exchange their places. Somara told Budhna, "My master gives excellent food every day. Rice, fish curry, curd, and sweets. He gives me so much to eat that I have to leave a considerable quantity untouched."

Budhna went a step ahead and said, "The potter liked me so well that he gives me a small breakfast besides the midday meal which is plenty in quantity and good in substance. He has another man to bring the earth from out side and I only help him in moving the pottery."

In this way the two foolish brothers tried each to induce the other to exchange places. One day Somara suggested Budhna, "Brother, why not we exchange our places? Probably, both of us will be happier."

They both told their masters that they would like to exchange their places and their masters did not object. The places were exchanged and from the very first day Somara and Budhna working under different masters understood that they had been rather foolish and that neither was better of than before. However, out of embarrassment they did not like to give up the secret out to the other and they continued slogging at their places.

One day Somara found some money under a custard apple tree while digging the earth. He dug up the money in night and going to Budhna told about that. The brothers took the money and left the village. In new village they jointly started trading and were happy. They promised that they would not try to be fooling one another.

## THE ASUR

Once upon a time, while the earth was in its infancy, *Sing-Bonga*, the supreme god, was engaged in a happy conversation with his consort. Suddenly there was an intolerance atmosphere of heat and piteous cries from the beasts and birds that they were being suffocated by hot fumes. The animals and birds sent a complaint to *Sing-Bonga*, "The furnaces of Asur tribesmen are emanating such extreme heat that the steams and other water reservoirs are dried up and all vegetation are being scorched."

The *Sing-Bonga* got perturbed and sent the fearless king-crow as well as watchful shrike as his messengers to the Asur tribesmen with a warning that if they continued working the furnace for iron smelting, they would be annihilated. The king-crow and the shrike flew to the Asur tribesmen and conveyed the message. The arrogant tribesmen replied, "We do not obey any one's order and do not consider any one superior to ourselves." They threw charcoal dust on the king-crow and ore dust to the shrike. The colour of the birds got changed.

The birds went back to Sing-Bonga and complained, "The Asur tribesmen not only have defied your behest but have made us peculiar by changing our colours."

"Go back to your own caste and you will all look alike", Sin-Bonga said to the birds. Since then all the king-crows are black and all the shrikes are grey.

The Sing-Bonga then selected the golden vulture (*Sonadidi*) and silver vulture (*Rupadidi*) for the same errand. The Asur tribesmen struck the birds with hammers and poked them with iron pincers and drove them out. After this the other messenger birds were deputed by the Sing-Bonga but with the same result. Sing-Bonga then decided to go round himself and teach the Asur tribesmen a lesson. He transformed himself in an itch-covered boy and got shelter with a childless Munda couple called Lutkun Haram and Lutkun Buria. He started playing with the children of Asur tribesmen and smashing their iron marbles with the balls made up of cooked rice husk. This created a sensation and the boy was taken as possessed of supernatural power.

Shortly after, the iron ore was exhausted and the Asur tribesmen asked the boy to find out by divination what kind of sacrifice was necessary to obtain the ore again. The boy ordered a white cock to be sacrificed and when this was done the ore was found again. When the ore ran short again, the boy was approached once more and he ordered to sacrifice a white he-goat and on the third occasion a white sheep. However, the ore ran short again and this time the boy ordered for the human sacrifice. As no human being could be got, the boy offered himself to be burnt in one of the furnaces. The clever boy, who was no other than *Sing-Bonga*, prescribed a certain rituals for the sacrifice. He ordered, "For my sacrifice a new furnace should be built, new bellows should be made from the skin of a white he-goat, new bellow-pipes should be used and two maidens should treat the bellows for three days while I am buried in the burning furnace and to extinguish the fire with water to be fetched in new pots."

When all this was done and the furnace was opened, the itch-covered boy came out as a handsome man wrapt with gold and precious stones. The greedy Asur tribesmen asked him, "From where did you get all these things?"

"I have found them in the furnace. You can also get the similar gold and precious stones if you will enter the furnace and remain there as I have done", he replied.

The Asur tribesmen got lured by the assurance of the handsome man and entered into the furnace. The fire was lit and the women worked the bellows hard for three days and all the Asur tribesmen were charred. All the women wailed a lot. The itch-covered boy who had become a handsome man revealed his own self and asked them if they would in future obey him. The Asur women agreed and there upon *Sing-Bonga* announced that henceforth there would be a Munda called *Pahan* and he would make the offerings. The Asur women had to accept their lot and thence after Asur became a declining tribe.

The popular belief is that the Asur tribesmen are a branch of Munda tribe. There is another slightly different version of this story. It is said that Sing-Bonga left alive purposely two Asur, a brother and a sister, who did not enter the furnace. These two were taught to grow various types of corn and were made to continue the tribe.

[The Asur are a fast declining tribe of Jharkhand. The Asur tribesmen are proficient smelters and had known the technique of smelting centuries before and claim to be the earliest iron smelters in India. They are mostly found in Neterhat plateau in Jharkhand].

## THE SOHRAI FESTIVAL TWO

Long ago, before men had tamed cattle, the forests were full of wild cows and other animals. In those days, man used to till the lands by means of spade only. One day a Munda youth went to the forest and saw a few calves gazing there. The calves asked him the reason for his coming in the forest. The youth replied that he had to dig the land for showing the seeds and there was no body to help him. He was tired and frustrated. He had come to forest to forget about his tension for a while. The calves asked the youth to hide him on the tree as it was the time of their parents to return.

When the parents of the calves returned they requested them to help the youth and to live with him. They agreed and to do so, came along with the youth and began to live happily. In return for the grain given to them for food, the animals pulled the plough. After a few years the man began to neglect the cattle and only the straw was given to them to eat. This made the cattle sore, and they returned to their former abode in the forest. On the way, the cattle met the god who advised them to go back and live with the man and help him in his work. He asked the man to give the cattle their proper share of food at the right hour. From that day man began to worship the cattle and give them grain to eat. That is how the worship of the cattle originated.

[The Sohrai festival is celebrated all over Jharkhand by every next day after the Deewali (festival of light) festival. On this occasion the houses are lighted with earthen pots. The cattle are worshipped and given to eat boiled *urad* lentils about a week before the festival day. Vermilion is applied on their horns and they are decorated with colours. Branches of *mahua* tree are also worshipped and the *Sing-Bonga* (supreme deity) is propitiated.]

## THE BOY, THE DRAGON AND THE MONKEY

A man and his wife lived close to a thick forest. They had two children, one boy and a girl. In the forest lived a big demon who one day not finding any thing else to eat came to the house of the man and started devouring both the man and his wife. The scared children ran out of the house crying. As they were running by a stable, the horse asked them, "What are you crying for?"

The children replied that a dragon was devouring their parents and probably he would eat them afterwards. The horse told them, "Untie me and mount on my back. I will take you both to a safer place."

The children did so and the horse galloped away with them. The dragon after finishing the parents started in pursuit of the children. On the way the children and the horse concealed themselves in a thick cluster of bamboo trees. The dragon passed by the bamboo forest and smelt them. He came back and started uprooting the trees. Once again the horse galloped off with the children and came to a large and deep river. The horse swam across the river with the children on his back but the dragon did not know how to swim. He had to pass over a creeper bridge. As he was ascending the bridge, the creeper snapped. The dragon some how managed to save his life, but failed to over take the children.

Having crossed the other side of the river the horse fell down and died. The children ran away in the nearby forest and started living there. They used to collect fruits and leaves and occasionally hunt small animals to eat. They were almost used to the forest life. One day the king of the land came in the forest to hunt. He saw smoke coming out at a distance and went there. He saw the brother and sister were roasting some tuber to eat. He got struck with the beauty of the sister and wanted to take her with him but the boy refused to give her. The king wanted to get rid of the boy. He ordered the boy, "You are living in my kingdom, go and kill a deer and bring that to me. Otherwise prepare yourself for the consequences."

The boy went out for a deer. He spotted a deer and just as he was going to discharge the arrow, a monkey screamed and the deer escaped. The angry boy aimed his arrow at the monkey. The monkey asked him, "Why do you want to strike me? I will be at your service for whatever you want; please do not kill me."

The boy replied, "I have no enmity with you. The king has asked me to kill a deer for him otherwise he would create trouble for me. I was going to kill the deer but you screamed and the deer escaped."

The monkey assured the boy that he would come to his rescue. On the advice of the monkey the boy tied a halter around his neck and took him to the king and complained that he had prevented him from killing the deer. The king pardoned the boy and asked him to go and kill a tiger. The monkey advised him to make a heavy mace so that they could kill a tiger. Using the trunk of *sal* tree (shorea robusta) the boy made a mace. The boy went in the dense forest and met the same dragon who had killed his parents. As soon as the dragon saw the boy, he caught hold of him but the monkey gave a heavy blow to the dragon with the mace. The dragon said, "Please do not kill me. I will obey both of you."

The monkey ordered the dragon to kill a tiger and the dragon did so. When the king saw that the tiger was killed and the boy had made the monkey and the dragon his servant he got impressed with the boy. He said, "I would like to marry your sister and make her a queen."

The boy agreed. The king married the girl and took her to his palace. He gave half of his kingdom to the boy and the boy ruled over half of the kingdom with the help of the monkey and the dragon.

## THE OLD WOMAN

Many years ago a jackal and a kite lived as friends. They used to go out together looking for food. Once they hit upon a plan to make the villagers fool. They sent a word to them that a neighbouring king would soon come and loot the village with his army. The next morning the jackal took an empty pitcher and marched towards the village beating on it with a fright clamour, and the kite flew overhead screaming as loud as it could. The villagers were scared thinking that the army of the king was approaching. They fled in to the forest leaving all their food behind. The jackal and the kite had a merry feast and they laughed as how they had cheated the villagers.

However, an old woman who could not run away, and hid herself inside her house. When she saw that no army came but only a jackal and a kite, she sneaked off to the forest and reported to the villagers. They came back and surrounding the village caught hold of the jackal and gave that a severe beating with sticks. Then they tied some rags to the tails and set fire to it. The jackal fled for his life; with the tail-tip aflame. He jumped in to a tank and had the fire put out. Since then jackals carry in their tails a black tip and in their minds a dislike of men.

## THE MONKEY FRIEND

One day a woman went to collect fire wood in the forest. She collected a large bundle of fire wood. The bundle was too large for her to pick up herself and put on her head. She was wondering what to do then a tiger passing by came to her and asked, "What is your problem? Why you are standing here so worried?"

"Please help me. Put this bundle of fire wood on my head", the woman requested the tiger.

The tiger replied, "I will do so provided you give your first born child, if a daughter to me in marriage; and if a boy to me as chum."

The woman thought it was a joke and agreed. The tiger put the bundle on her head and she returned to her home. After some time the woman had a son. The tiger came and claimed the boy. The terrified woman concealed the boy and said, "The boy is too tiny to go out. Come after two years."

The tiger agreed and came back after two years. Again the tiger was turned away on some pretext. In this way the tiger was sent away disappointed several times. The boy had a monkey-friend who assured him to help in getting out of the clutches of the tiger. One day the boy was ploughing the field and the monkey was with him when the tiger came to him. The monkey quickly concealed the boy in the heap of hay and said to the tiger, "Wait for a while the boy would come soon after having his lunch from his house."

The tiger was tired and thirsty. He asked for water from the monkey. The monkey asked the tiger to first close his eyes and going near him said, "I will pour water into your throat from a pitcher. I am asking you to close your eyes because I am afraid of their dazzle."

The tiger agreed and as soon as he closed his eyes the monkey took up the plough-shaft having first heated the iron end and thrust that into his throat with all his force. The boy also helped the monkey by hammering the head of the tiger with a big mallet. The tiger goaled and died and thus the monkey saved his friend from the tiger.

## THE WICKED SISTERS-IN-LAW

Long ago there were six brothers and one sister. They were very fond of one another. All the six brothers were married and their wives did not like their sister-in-law. They all were jealous of the love and care the brothers used to shower up on their sister.

Once it so happened that the brothers had to go to far away village to trade. Taking advantage of their absence the sisters-in-law started ill treating the girl and forced her to do all types of hard work. The girl happily performed all the works asked her to do by her sisters-in-law without any complain. Then they thought a plan to kill her. They asked her to go to well and fill the earthen pot which they gave her. The earthen pot had a large hole in the bottom so as fast as it was filled the water ran out. The girl took the pot to the well and being unable to fill that began to cry. A large frog jumped out of the well and asked her, "Who are you? Why are you crying?"

The girl replied, "I am the sister of the six brothers. My last hour has come. If I can not fill the pot with water, I will be killed by my sisters-in-law, and it has a hole in the bottom."

The frog said, "Do not worry. I will sit in the hole and cover it with my body and you will be able to fill the pot."

This the frog did and the girl took water back home. The sisters-in-law were angry, but they could not say anything. Then they thought some thing else. They said the girl to go in the forest and bring a large bundle of fuel woods but she was not be given any rope to tie the fuel sticks. The girl collected a large quantity of the fuel sticks and being unable to carry those sticks with out tying them started crying. A large snake came there and asked, "Who are you? Why are you crying?"

The girl replied, "I am the sister of the six brothers. My last hour has come. If I will not take this fuel home, my sisters-in-law will kill me."

The snake said, "I will curl around the fuel as a rope and the problem would be solved."

This the snake did and the girl was able to carry the sticks home over her head. The sisters-in-law were very much upset. The next day they asked the girl to go to a field where *tuar* (lentils) had been sown and bring back all the grains by the evening. The girl went to the field and found the task impossible to be done. As she wept in frustration a flock of pigeons came and asked her, "Who are you? Why are you crying?"

The girl replied, "I am the sister of the six brothers. My last hour has come. If I will not take all the grains by the evening my sisters-in-law will kill me."

The pigeons offered their help to the girl and soon put all the grains in the basket of the girl. In the evening the girl returned home with the basket full. The sisters-in-law were more enraged and thought out a cruel plan. They gave a large pot to the girl and asked her to bring pot full of tigress milk from the forest. The girl went in the forest and sat down. She did not know what to do. A big tigress came to her and asked, "Who are you? Why are you sitting in the forest so sad and alone?"

The girl replied, "I am the sister of the six brothers. My last hour has come. If I will not take this pot full of your milk my sisters-in-law will kill me."

The tigress allowed the girl to milk her and the girl returned home with a pot full of milk. The sisters-in-law took the girl in the forest taking a ladder with them. They selected a high tree with a smooth trunk, and asked the girl to climb on the tree with the help of the ladder and pluck the fruits. The girl after climbing on the tree started plucking the fruits. The wicked sisters-in-law quickly removed the ladder and came away leaving the girl to jump down and be killed.

The girl was terrified and remained perched up the tree. In the night the brothers returned and sat under the tree to rest. The girl was weeping and her hot tears fell on one of the brothers. He looked up, saw the girl and recognized her. They rescued their sister and the sister told them what had happened with her in their absence. They all returned home and in anger the brothers killed their wives. There after they all lived happily with their sister.

## THE FOSTER PARENTS

In a village there lived a poor man whose wife was expecting a baby. As they were very poor they decided that if the child happened to be a son they would abandon that, but if it was a girl they would bring that up. When the child was born that was a boy and according to their decision the man took that child in to the forest and left him there.

A tiger and a tigress that had just lost their cub found the child. They decided to bring up the human child as their own. They accordingly fed the child and looked after him. The child became a handsome young man. The tiger went to a blacksmith and got made a bow and arrow of iron for his son. The youth used to hunt in the forest with that bow and arrows. One day the tiger decided to arrange for the marriage of his foster son. He went in the neighbouring village and when the daughter of the king came out to have her bath the tiger seized her and brought her in the forest. The girl was at first frightened but was soothed when she was told that she had to marry the young and handsome man. They liked each other at the first sight and the marriage took place.

The pair lived happily for a long time in the forest. After some times the tiger and the tigress died, and they decided to go back to the village. The girl went ahead and saw her parents. The parents were overjoyed to see their daughter alive as they had thought that the tiger had eaten her up. They gave a warm welcome to their son-in-law. The young man found out his real parents and gave them lots of wealth for comfortably living. He became king after the death of his father-in-law and lived happily with his wife.

## THE IMPOSTOROUS EXORCIST

Many years ago an old couple lived in a village. They use to take care of the small children of the village when their parents remained busy in the field. In turn the parents used to give a handful of grains to them. They were living hand to mouth.

One day the old man hit upon an idea to earn more and thought to go to another village to make his idea practical. He said to his wife, "Let us go to neighbouring village and earn there."

"We are not able to work, here in this village we have at least something to eat. What will we do in a new village?" The old woman asked.

The old man smiled and replied, "I have an idea to earn without doing much work. Here in this village all recognize us who we are. In new village no one knows about us. I will become an exorcist and will tell the villagers about their lost thing and will take either kinds or money from them."

"How can you tell them about their lost things? You are not an exorcist. It is a dangerous game. I am scared. You should not do like this", the old woman replied in a worried tone.

"Oh, you always underestimate my skill. Let us go to the new village first and see what I can do there", the old man said.

They went to a new village and started living there. One day when it was about to dawn the old man got up silently and entered in a neighbouring house. The family members of that family were sleeping with their only child. The old man took up the sleeping baby and made him sleep in the heap of hay kept in a field. After that, he returned home and slept. In the morning when the parents of the child got up, they started crying for their child. The villagers started searching for the child. No one thought to go in the field to search the child there.

The old man told his neighbour that he was an expert exorcist in finding out the lost things, and could find out the baby through his magical power. Soon the parents of the child came to know about this fact and they came running to the old man. They requested the old man to tell about their child.

"What will you give me when I will tell about your child?" The old man asked.

"We will give you ten kilos of rice and two kilos of *ghee* (clarified butter)", they replied. The old man closed his eyes and after some times said, "Come with me. I will take you to the place where the child is."

The old man proceeded towards the field and the parents of the child as well as a few villagers followed him. The old man took all at the place where he had made the child sleep. The child was still sleeping there. The mother ran towards him and picked up the child. All were very happy. The parents of the child gave rice and *ghee* to the old man. After a long time the couple ate their belly full. The old woman though not happy with all the happenings did not say any thing to the old man.

After a few days a rich man lost his horse. After searching a lot he did not find his horse. The old man was approached to search the horse. He asked, "What will you give me when I will search the horse?" The old man asked.

"I will give you hundred coins and a sac full of rice", the rich man replied.

The old man agreed and called him after an hour. Actually the old man had tied that horse on a hillock. After an hour when the rich man came they all proceeded towards the hillock and the rich man got his horse back. The villagers were very much impressed with the skill of the old man and he was becoming popular among them.

"What you are doing is not good. One day you will get into trouble", the old woman told her husband.

"Do not worry and eat well. Nothing will happen to me", the old man laughed.

One day the queen of the village lost her necklace. A search was made for the search of that but nothing happened. The popularity of the old man had reached the palace as well. The old man was summoned by the king. Now he realized that his wife was right.

"You were right that one day I would fall in difficulty", the old man said to his wife.

"I had warned you but you did not listen. What will happen now? If you will not tell the correct information the king will punish you", the old woman replied.

There was no way to escape and the old man went to the palace to meet the king. Seeing the old man the king asked, "I have come to know that you are an expert in finding the lost thing. Can you find where the necklace is?"

"I will try my best to find out that", the old man replied.

"In the morning you will have to tell me about that necklace, otherwise you would be beheaded. Stay here overnight alone in a room. You have enough time to use your magic", the king said.

The old man was sent to his room. The worried man started thinking the way to escape from there.

Three maids of the queen had stolen the necklace and when they heard that an expert exorcist had been called to search the necklace they got afraid. They thought they would be killed by the king when caught. They inquired about the exorcist and came to know that a room had been allotted to him. They talked with each other, "We will watch the activity of the exorcist very carefully and when will notice that he has found us we will ask for forgiveness from him."

In the room the old man was moving restlessly. He said to himself, "There is no way to find out the necklace. It would be better to run away from here in dark and start living in any remote village far away from this village."

He sat down on the window and started watching the palace carefully so that he could run out easily. While he was peeping out side the window the cock gave his first crow. The old man got afraid thinking that it was going to be dawn soon. A cock crows three times before it is dawn. He thought to run away from the palace after hearing the third crow. He just said, "It is the first".

As soon as he said like this just then the first maid peeped into the room through a window what the old man was doing. She heard that he was telling it was the first. She lost her sense and ran to her friends and said, "It seems he has recognized us. Just when I peeped into his room he said that it is the first."

After some time the second went to see the old man and when she peeped in the room the cock crooked second time and the old man said, "This is the second." The second maid also ran towards her friends. Same thing happened with the third maid as well. They all decided to go to the old man and ask for forgiveness.

The old man opened the door of his room and wanted to escape from there just then the three maids came to him crying and said, "Please forgive us and do not tell any thing to the king about us. We have stolen the necklace and we are returning that to you."

The old man got flabbergasted but understood every thing. He said, "I had understood immediately that you all three had stolen the necklace. I did not say any thing to the king because I wanted to give you all a chance. Return the necklace to me. I will not say anything to anybody."

The maids returned the necklace to him and went back from there. The old man went in the kitchen and put that necklace in a water-pot. He went to his room and slept calmly. In the morning the army men of the king made him wake up.

The court of the king was full with the people. All were waiting for the old man to come. The old man reached the court with a smile on his face.

"Did you search the necklace?" The king asked.

The old man replied, "I am happy to say that I have found the necklace. Come with me, I will show where the necklace is."

The king and the others followed the old man to the kitchen. In the kitchen he poured the water from the water-pot in a bucket and the necklace came out of the pot. The old man put the necklace in the hand of the king and said, "May be when the queen had come here to drink water the necklace would have slipped in the water. I have used my magical power to search the necklace."

The king was very happy and gave him lots of wealth so that he could spend his whole life comfortably. The old man returned to his wife and in the night they returned to their own village and old business.

## THE FROG AND THE FISH

A Munda youth used to cut wood in the forest and sell those in the village. One day he noticed that the edge of his axe had gone blunt. He went to the bank of river and sitting there started rubbing the edge of his axe with a stone. This way he wanted to make that sharp. While he was busy in his work a small fish came and stung on his foot and swam away. In anger the youth uprooted a new sapling of *bel* (hard apple) plant. The mother tree was standing nearby. She shouted, "Why did you uproot my baby? Now I will shade all my fruits."

The tree started shedding its fruits and one of the fruits fell on a cock. In anger he shouted, "Why did you put your fruit on me? Do not you have any other place for putting down your fruits?" In anger the cock dug the anthill which was there under the tree.

"Why did you ruin my hill? Where will we go now?" The ants shouted in anger and bit that snake lying there.

"Oh my god, I was sleeping peacefully. How dare you bite me?" The snake shouted in pain. In pain he bit a boar that was sitting near there. The boar became furious.

"What have you done with me?" The boar shouted and started running in pain and in this process he dashed against a tree and uprooted that. A bat was hanging upside down from the branch of that tree. In fear that bat entered into the ear of an elephant. The restless elephant started uprooting the trees in the forest.

An old woman used to live in the forest in a hut. One tree fell down on her earthen potteries and broke them all. The angry woman caught the elephant and asked, "Why are you uprooting the trees? Who will bring potteries for me from the village? How will I cook? What will I eat?"

"Do not scold me; it all happened because of this bat. If he has not entered into my ear I would have not uprooted the tree", the elephant tried to prove himself innocent.

The old woman moved towards the bat and asked that why he did so? The bat replied, "I was taking rest on the tree hiding myself in between the leaves. The boar uprooted the tree and in search of darkness I entered into the ear of this elephant. I am innocent."

The old woman, the elephant and the bat went to boar and asked the reason for his deed. The boar said, "I am not a stupid to dash against the tree. It all happened because of that snake."

They all went to snake and that blamed ants for his action. The ants blamed the cock and the cock to *bel* tree.

The tree said, "Go and ask that Munda youth why did he uproot my baby. What else could have I done in anger?"

The Munda youth said, "Yes, I had uprooted the new plant in anger but soon realized my mistake and planted that again. It is the small fish that started every thing."

The fish was standing there ashamed with her head down. The old woman and the Munda youth left the fish unpunished and returned to their respective homes. However, all the animals wanted to punish the fish, which had brought bad name for their community by her foolish act. They all said together, "Fish, we want to kill you. Tell me how you would like to die? We want to kill by making you drown in water. Give your preference; would you like to be drowned in hot water or in cold water?"

The fish requested, "Please throw me in cold water. I do not want to give you trouble of heating the water."

All the animals threw that fish into a pond. Water was the home of the fish. She went underneath and sat down there calmly. After sometimes all the animals realized that the fish had made them fool. They all wanted to catch the fish again but were unable to do so. The animal that put his leg in the water was bitten by the fish. At last the elephant said, "I am going to drink all the water of the tank. Then it would become easy to catch the fish."

The elephant did so and when the tank became dry a frog jumped into the water and caught the fish. He put the fish in a pot filled with water and put that pot on fire. He kept peeping in the pot at regular interval to see whether the fish was cooked or not. Every time when he peeped in the pot he said, "There is lot of water in the pot. It will take time to boil so much water. It would be better if I drink some water." After saying like this he used to drink some water from the pot. Actually the frog had made the fish escape from there. Pretending he was drinking water he had kept the fish in his mouth and silently put her out in a safe place, a ditch full of water. He did not agree with the other animals to kill a fish on her small prank.

Half an hour past and all the animals were anxiously waiting to see the fish boiled. When nothing happened to the fish they all looked into the pond and found that the pot was empty. The frog said to them, "May be while drinking water I would have swallowed the fish as well."

All the animals became angry and gave a severe beating to the frog, due to which patches of marks were made on the body of him.

## THE HELPFUL WOLF

A village king had a dog. The king used to take good care of his dog and loved him very much. He used to give good food to him and make him sleep near his bed. The dog used to take care of his poultry well. He never allowed any jackal to enter in his hen-house and to steal any fowl. After sometimes the dog grew old and became weak.

One day a jackal stole a hen from the hen-house and the dog could not do any thing. The king scolded him badly and that day onwards he left taking care of his dog. The dog became very sad. He tried his best to keep his master happy but failed. At last the king drove the dog out of his home. While the hungry and tired dog was moving in the forest he saw a wolf. The scared wolf said to himself, "Today this wolf is going to tear me. It would be good. I do not want to live any more."

The dog remained standing there and did not try to protect himself. The wolf came to him and asked, "Why are you looking so tired and sad? Do not worry; I am not going to do any harm to you."

The dog told his story to the wolf. The wolf wanted to help the dog and after thinking for a while he got an idea. He asked the dog to listen to his words carefully.

The dog replied, "Say what ever you want to say me. I am listening carefully."

The wolf said, "I will help you in regaining your position in that house. Daily in the morning the queen used to work sitting near her kitchen garden. Her baby sleeps nearby in a cradle. Tomorrow when she will make her baby sleep in the cradle and start performing her work, I will take the baby and move towards the forest. At that time you start barking loudly. She will come to see her baby and when she will not find that in the cradle she will look here and there in search of him. At that time you start chasing me, and after jumping on me pierce your teeth in my stomach. I will leave the baby there and will run away in the forest."

The plan was good and the dog agreed for it.

Next day, the wolf silently took the baby from the cradle and the dog started barking loudly.

"Oh, this dog has returned and now barking uselessly he is irritating me", the queen uttered silently. She went near the cradle to see what was the matter? Why the dog was barking like that?

When she did not find the baby in the cradle she became nervous and started looking here and there in search of him. She saw her dog barking and chasing the wolf, which was carrying his baby. She also started chasing the wolf taking a rung in her hand. At the same time she was calling her husband who was ploughing in the field. The dog jumped on the wolf and pierced his teeth in the stomach of the wolf. The wolf put the baby on the ground and ran away in the forest. The queen took up her baby, who was safe. She hugged the dog, which had saved her baby from the wolf. She called him back home. In the evening she told every thing to her husband. Both were very happy. After that they never neglected their dog and took good care of him.

# Folktales of Oraon

## ORAON: AN INTRODUCTION

The Oraon is the second largest tribal group in India. They live in the states of Jharkhand, Bihar, Orissa, West Bengal, Chhattisgarh, Madhya Pradesh and Andaman and Nicobar Island. A sizable population of Oraon tribesmen are found in north-eastern states of the country as well. In Assam and Tripura they are engaged in the occupation of tea cultivation. The language spoken by them is known as *Kurukh,* which belongs to Dravidian family (Edward 1990). However, they also speak the language of the region they reside in such as Hindi, Bengali, and Oriya.

In majority of cases the Oraon tribesmen are *Sarna*. They follow *Sarna-Dharma* ( Sarna religion) in which *Dharmesh* is the supreme almighty. The followers of *Sarna-Dharma* perform religious rituals under the shade of a sacred grove. They worship the Sun as *Biri* and the Moon as *Chando* (Ghosh 2003). They also believe in a host of spirits. A priest is invited to perform their life cycle rituals. An *ojha* (shaman) is specially called to cure diseases by appeasing spirits. They believe in the clan system and marriage takes place out side the clan (Dalton 1872, Hira Lal and Russell 1916, Roy 2010).

The Oraon tribesmen are very fond of music and dance. They have a rich and vast range of folk songs, dances and tales. *Karma*, *Jadur*, *Dassai* and *Kagha Parva* are their most favourite dances. Both men and women participate in the dance freely. Traditional instruments like *nagada*, *kartal*, and *mandar* (types of drum) are still used by these people.

Traditionally the Oraon tribesmen were wood cutter and wood seller, but now they have become settled agriculturists. They also work as wage labourers and industrial workers. Their staple cereal is rice supplemented with maize, wheat, *madua*, and *gondli*. Both male and female consume *handiya* (rice beer).

The tribesmen have their traditional community council at the village level headed by *Sir-Panch*. They have regional council known as *parha* composed of a number of villages (Roy 1999).

A remarkable feature of Oraon tribe is that it is one of the very few in the world that practices human sacrifice (Sachchidananda 1963). Although extremely rare evidence suggests that the phenomenon is prevalent in the villages of Jharkhand.

During the nineteenth century, British Officials had reported a much broader evidence of human sacrifice prevalent in Jharkhand. According to police records, as late as 1980s, there used to occur a couple of sacrifices a year among the tribesmen, and perhaps slightly more if one assumes that not all the cases got police attention (West 2009).

The human sacrifice is illegal in the country and is treated as homicide under section 302 of the Indian Penal code, but detection of culprit in the villages of Oraon tribesman is difficult. Villagers believe that sacrifices are essential for the fertility of their fields, and hence they do not come forward with any information. In general such sacrifices occur in remote area and around the beginning of the sowing season. This sacrifice is related to *Sarhul* festival, a festival related to fertility of the soil.

The reasons police can distinguish these sacrifices from the other forms of murders are several such as the timing to coincide with the sowing ceremony: the victim is often an orphan or homeless person who will not be missed, the victim's throat is cut with a knife, signs of *puja* (worships) are normally found near the corpse, and part of one little finger has been cut off and remains missing. The last item is presumably a part of the human offering that the *otanga* (sacrificer) buries in his field. Sometimes blood of the sacrificed victim is mixed with seeds before it is sown. It is believed that in the beginning the entire body of the victim was used to be cut into pieces and parcelled out to the various fields around the village. The danger of detection now makes this practice too difficult. The sacrifice is normally offered to a vindictive goddess thought to control the fertility of the soil. If a human victim is not caught in time for the sowing ceremony, it is said that a drop of blood after cutting or piercing needle in to the little finger is mixed with hen's blood as a token offering to this goddess (Sachchidananda 1964).

## THE CREATION OF WORLD

The Oraon tribesmen believe that in the beginning there was no human being but only vast forests and water. Lord Shiva felt that there should be another type of life in the regions of forest and water. He told Gaura, his heavenly consort, "I want to create something."

"It is a good idea. Create man after the image of yours and give him life so that he would offer you food during worship", Gaura advised her husband.

"I will do that but I think it would be better if I create some animal first and then create human being", lord Shiva replied.

Lord Shiva first made the horse and gave life to it. It took eighteen months in making the dummy of the horse and putting life into that. That is why a mare delivers her pony after eighteen months.

After creating the horse, lord Shiva made an image of man. Before he could put life in that image the horse trampled upon that several times, kicked that and destroyed the image.

"Why did you do so?" Lord Shiva asked in an annoyed tone.

"If you will create man he would ride on my back", the angry horse replied.

Lord Shiva created a dog to guard the image of man which he thought to create again. He took two months in creating a dog and that is why a bitch takes two and half months to reproduce its puppy. Finally lord Shiva created another image of man and breathed life into that. That is why a human child is born after nine months. He created a woman also.

The man and woman began giving birth to children and slowly the world was populated. Slowly the people became selfish and greedy. They started quarrelling with each others. Several complaints reached lord Shiva that his children were misbehaving with one another. Lord Shiva became very angry. He rained fire on the earth. As a result of the fire all creations were destroyed and the hills emerged.

After the destruction lord Shiva and Gaura came down to earth to find out whether there was any human being alive. At one place they found a brother and a sister hiding behind a bush. They pulled out them, blessed them and made them forget their relationship. The pair became the progenitor of the human race.

## THE SHINING DARK HAIR

Once upon a time there lived two brothers. The brothers were very poor. They used to live on working as labourers in the field of others or on begging. One day at harvest time they had gone to harvest the field and on their way back home they reached near a stream with muddy bank. They found that a cow had got stuck in the mud and was unable to come out. The brothers pulled the cow out. The grateful cow followed them home and shortly afterwards had a calf.

In a few years the cow had several calves and the calves had claves. The two brothers had a good income by selling their milk. The elder brother got married and started living in a separate home. The younger brother lived in the forest grazing the cattle. The son of the elder brother used to bring food for his uncle every day. Though, it was not necessary to bring food for him. The cow used to bring all sorts of delicacies for him.

One day the nephew of the younger brother went to his mother and said, "Today uncle had given delicious sweet to me. He has many sweets and good things to eat."

The wife of elder brother got suspicious and out of jealousy she beheaded the younger brother while he was sleeping. The grateful cow saw what had happened. After the woman left the place, the cow pushed the head with her horns untill that joined the body and she sprinkled her milk over the body. The younger brother was revived and got up well. He did not complaint to his elder brother what his wife had done with him. However, he took away all his cattle to another part of the forest and began to live there.

The younger brother used to get far more milk then he could sell. He used to pour the surplus milk into an ant-hill that was there under a banyan tree. In fact what the younger brother took for an ant-hill was in fact the abode of snake king. The king of the snake was very pleased with the younger brother. One day the snake king appeared before the younger brother and granted him a boon, "You will have shinning hair and attractive appearance always."

The younger brother used to take bath in a river, and each day after taking bath he threw one of his hairs into the water. Lower down the river a princess of neighbouring village used to take bath. One day she saw the hair floating on the water and picked that up. Seeing the lustre of the hair she vowed that she would marry no one but the owner of the hair. She left taking food and told about her vow to her father, the king of the village.

The worried king called his priest and said, "Go and find out the person who is the owner of shining hair. If you find him, propose to him to marry the princess."

The priest went in the forest in search of the person and soon discovered that the owner of the shining hair was the younger brother. The priest conveyed the marriage proposal to the younger brother. The man became very happy and said, "I am ready for the marriage. I will come with my friends to marry the princess."

He sent the priest back with lots of gold and silver, that the snake king had given to him. On the selected day and at the auspicious hour the younger brother started riding on a cow for the palace of the king. When he was near o the palace the snake king through his magic gave him a long retinue of followers with music horse and elephants. The younger brother married the princess and after the death of his father-in-law, he became the king.

He was very a charitable king and used to donate food, money and clothes to the poor, once in a week. Meanwhile, the elder brother and his wife became very poor. One day they came to the palace of the younger brother to receive charity. They were very much upset and ashamed when they saw who the king was.

However, the younger brother forgave his *bhabhi* (elder brother's wife) and gave them lots of wealth. The elder brother and his wife returned to their own village. Thus younger brother doing much welfare works for his villagers lived happily.

[Shinning dark hair is the mark of beauty and the tribesmen of Jharkhand who keep it shinning with *karanj* oil. They love to comb their hair and usually both the man and the woman like to stick a wooden comb in their hair. It is peculiar that the tribesmen of Jharkhand seldom have grey hair even after growing very old.]

## THE FOOLISH MAN

In a village there was a foolish man. One day he went to bullock market and bought a pair of bulls for his field. On his way home night fell and it became pitch dark. He was far away from his village. Above all he had to cross a dense forest full of wild animals to reach his village. He decided to spend night in the village he was passing through. Seeing an oil-mill by the road, he tied his bulls there and spent his night there.

The next morning while he was untying his bulls, the owner of the oil-mill came and asked him, "Who are you? What are you doing here? Why are you taking away my bulls?"

The foolish man replied, "The bulls are mine. I have bought them at the market. It was getting dark I stayed here for the night."

"No, the bulls are mine. The oil mills have calved to them during night. Do you not see that they are tethered to it?" The oil man insisted.

The foolish man was so dumbstruck that he had no reply to give. He left the bulls and went away crying. When he had gone a little way, he met a monkey who was very wise.

"Who are you? What is wrong with you? Why you are crying like this?" The monkey asked.

The foolish man told the monkey what had happened with him and requested him to help. He told him, "I am ready to arbitrate. Go back to the village where you have left your bulls. Call a few villagers near the oil mill and wait for me. I will come there in the afternoon."

The foolish man went back and collected a few co-villagers of the oil mill man and waited. The monkey had said that he would reach the village at noon. The villagers waited there till evening. In the evening the monkey came with a great air of importance.

The foolish man asked, "Why you were late making us wait for you for a long time?"

The monkey replied, "I was coming when I saw a pond on fire and the fish getting roasted. I waited till the fire went out and had a good feast along with others on the roasted fish. They were such large and tasty fishes."

All the villagers including the oil mill man laughed and said, "What a story. Do you think we are fool? Can a pond catch fire?"

The monkey replied, "It is as good as the story that an oil mill has calved two bulls."

There all were silenced. The monkey ordered the foolish man to take away the pair of bulls. He did so and there was no opposition now.

[With minor variations there are several versions of this story and are popular among the people of other tribes as well. The Santhal tribesmen have a counterpart of this story.]

## TWO FRIENDS

The sons of a king and of a barber were great friends. The step mother of the prince did not like him and she instigated the king to order his son to leave the kingdom. The prince went away to a distant land and his barber friend accompanied him. The barber earned his living by his profession, while the prince started working with a moneylender. The prince had to join the service on a very hard term. His wages were one leaf-plate of rice a day with a stipulation that if he gave up the job he had to lose a span long piece of his skin.

After sometime the prince who had been brought up in luxury found his work very arduous and the food insufficient. Therefore, he decided to leave the moneylender. However, before he could do so he had to allow the moneylender to cut off a span long piece of his skin. According to the terms of agreement the prince submitted himself to the moneylender and the piece of skin was cut off from his body. The dignity of the prince was wounded. He went to the barber and said, "I had to leave the job as well as lose a span of my skin."

The barber vowed that he would be avenged. The barber went and offered himself as a servant to the moneylender. His offer was accepted and it was agreed that which ever party first proposed to terminate the contract should lose a piece of one span long skin. The clever barber worked so badly and ate so much that one day the moneylender in a fit of anger asked him to leave the job and so forfeited a piece of skin. Thus the humiliation of the prince was avenged.

The prince and the barber left that place and went to the land of jackals. They found the king of jackals sleeping in front of his cave. While he was sleeping the barber shaved all the hair of his tail. Then the two friends hid in the cave, drawing a cart in front of the entrance. When the jackal woke up and found that he had been shaved, he thought that *bongas* (spirits) were around and were angry with him. He ran away in terror.

After going for some distance the jackal king met a bear who asked him, "Why you are going in such hurry?"

"Some *bongas* (spirits) have taken possession of my cave and they have shaved off my hair", the jackal king replied in worried tone.

"Is it so? I must find out first before I accept if it is", the bear said. The bear agreed to go back with the jackal and see if he could exorcise the spirits.

On reaching the cave the bear climbed on the cart to offer a sacrifice. As he sat there the barber caught hold his tail and held on it while the prince began stabbing the bear with a knife. The wounded bear started howling and groaning but could not get away.

The king of jackal who was looking on was very happy thinking that the *bongas* had got hold of the bear. At last the bear broke free and ran away, the jackal running after him. Then the jackal met a tiger. The jackal king told his story to the tiger and persuaded him to try his hand for exorcising the *bongas*. The tiger was treated exactly in the same manner as the bear had been. The tiger, too, ran away in agony.

The king of the jackals then resolved to try himself and mounted the cart. The barber stabbed him through with the bamboos and killed him. Then the prince succeeded on the kingdom of the jackals, and also replaced the piece of skin which he had forfeited to the moneylender with a piece of the skin of the dead jackal.

[The *bongas* (spirits) are dreaded and are propitiated by the tribesmen. The jackal as well as the barber have the reputation of being very shrewd by the Oraon tribesmen].

## THE OGRE

Many years ago there lived a rich farmer who was a great drunkard. As he remained always drunk, he never took care of his field as well as his family members. His wife with the help of her son and the helpers used to take care of every thing. One day his wife played a prank with her husband. She made a few villagers and the son sit in one row and asked her husband, "Point out who is you son?"

The man failed to do so. All started laughing at him and the man felt very much ashamed. The wife then pointed out the son and told her husband, "Our son has grown up. You should give up your liquor at least for some time and find out a bride for your son." The man agreed with his wife and promised to her that he would search a suitable bride for his son soon.

The man left the place in search of a bride for his son. He took with him a large sum of money which he concealed in his clothes. He went to a distant village and sitting down near a well he started watching all the young girls who fetched water. He saw a girl among them, who he found suitable for his son. He followed that girl and sat down near her house. When the parents of the girl saw him they thought he was a beggar hence did not pay much attention to him. After sometime the man spoke to the parents of the girl, "I have come here to seek the hand of your daughter for my son."

"Are you able to pay the bride price? You look very poor." The parents of the girl asked. The man asked for a bamboo basket and when the basket came, he filled that up with coins he had concealed in his clothes.

The parents of the girl understood that the man who was seeking the hand of their daughter for his son was a rich man. They gave him water to wash his feet, invited him to a meal and agreed for the marriage proposal. Unfortunately, the man on his way back died suddenly. After waiting for some time the parents of the girl found out that the man was dead. They sent word to the son that the bride-price had already been paid for his marriage. The boy there upon came to the village and married the girl.

However, the son of the rich farmer was an ogre and his parents were not aware of the fact. He used to take the form of the ogre in night and go out. While roving in night, he used to eat up the animals and even man. The wife soon found out that her husband used to slip out every night after she was noticed to be asleep. One day in the night she was lying quietly on the bed and watched her husband with eyes seemingly shut. Thinking that his wife was sleeping, he got up and brought out a small stick from the basket. He touched himself with one end of the stick. At once he became an ogre and left the room. The wife watched him and found that in the early morning he came back and touched himself with the other end of the rod and took the human form and quickly slipped into the bed. The next morning the wife quietly broke the stick and burnt that to ashes.

On the next night when the boy got up and looked for the stick in the basket, he did not find that. His wife said in a very understanding tone, "You should not continue as an ogre. I have burnt the stick to ashes." Thereafter the man lived in a normal manner and both of them were very happy.

[It is a common belief among the tribesmen that during the sleep the soul often leaves the body, takes another form and afterwards comes back to the normal body].

## THE BROTHER IN A MANDOLIN

Many years ago, a brother and a sister lived a wretched life in the outskirt of the village. Every day the brother and the sister used to collect some paddy from the field. The sister after scrapping the paddy and making rice out of that used to boil that. They two used to eat boiled rice with some *jungli sag* (wild spinach).

One day they went to forest and found a date tree laden with ripe dates. The brother after climbing on the tree started eating and throwing the dates down after plucking them. The sister who was under the tree was also eating them. A group of entellus of the forest had their eyes on the dates from before. They came running fast and attacked the boy. The girl ran away for her life. The entellus tore the brother to pieces and he died.

While the girl was running a prince who had come to the forest to hunt saw her. The girl, although very poor, was very lovely to look at. The prince stopped her and asked, "Who are you? Why you are running so?"

The girl narrated details about her and told that her brother had been killed by the entellus. The prince said, "I am ready to take you with me to my palace."

"I can go with you provided I am given vermilion to be your wife", the girl replied.

The prince agreed and got a new dress for her. The girl wore that dress and the prince put vermilion on her forehead and took her to his palace. The girl although was living in comfort had not forgotten her previous life. She used to shed tears for her brother, but she knew that her brother was killed and would not return.

After a few days a saint was passing by the date tree. He saw the skin of the dead boy under the tree. He was in need of a covering for his mandolin, so he picked up the skin and made a covering for the mandolin. The soul of the brother entered into the mandolin.

One day the sister saw the saint from the room of her palace. The saint was playing the mandolin and she was able to hear the word coming out of that:

*"Tu to dare bhag geli re bahin,*
*Saadi karke rahi geli re bahin.*
*Bandra badka, chhotka re bahin,*
*Phad delau hamra re bahin."*

(You went out of fright, sister and married a prince. Entellus tore me to pieces).

The girl recognizing the voice of her brother rushed out to the saint and caught hold of the mandolin. In her hurry the mandolin fell down and broke. The brother came out from the broken mandolin alive. The saint was happy seeing that the brother and the sister were once again united. The prince gave a portion of his kingdom and one house to the brother. Both the brother and the sister lived happily since then.

[With some variations, there are many versions of this story and all are popular among the tribesmen of Jharkhand.]

## THE DANCING MOUSE (ORAON)

A mouse had planted a clump of jute plants by the side of the road, leading to the forest. The jute plants had abundant flowers. The village girls while returning from the forest by that road used to pluck the flowers. The mouse used to chide them and shout, "Do not pluck my flowers otherwise I will put vermilion on you." the girls used to laugh at the impertinence of the mouse and pay no heed to him.

Daily the girls used to pluck flowers and the mouse used to shout at them. One day the mouse managed to get some vermilion. The next time when he saw the girls plucking the flowers, he quickly climbed up and applied vermilion on one of the girl's head. Putting on vermilion on the head of any girl means to solemnise marriage with that girl. The girl began crying but she had no option but to remain as a wife. The mouse was very happy at the trickling tears of girl. He started dancing and asked her to accompany him into his hole or give back his flowers and go to her parents. The girl could not return the flowers that had been plucked days before. She had no option but to follow the mouse.

The girl came up to the hole of the mouse, but she could not enter into that because the hole was very small for her. The mouse again started dancing and said, "Enter, enter into my house, O girl, or else give back my flowers and go back to your parents."

The girl sat out and the mouse ordered her to cook food. The girl brought water and started boiling rice which was stored by the mouse. When the rice was boiled and cooked, the mouse felt hungry. He started dancing and wanted the girl to pour out the rice gruel. The girl poured out the gruel and began to cook the curry. The gruel was kept in an earthen pot separately. The mouse was overjoyed that he had won over the girl and in his crazy dance fell into the gruel and was drowned. The girl did not take him out but took the rice and the curry and went home to her parents.

[This story underlines the custom that applying vermilion on the forehead of the girl means she is married to the boy who does so. Mouse is one of the totems honoured by the Oraon tribesmen. Those who honour this totem have the surname of Tirki, an Oraon word meaning a small mouse.]

## THE ANIMAL FRIENDS

Once upon a time there lived a boy name Lallua. He was a kind hearted boy and every one in the village loved him very much. One day he decided to earn and stand on his own feet. The desire of economic independence was so intense that he immediately went to his father and said, "Please give me some money so that I can start my own business."

The father of lallua gave him 20 rupees. Now he had some money in his pocket, but had no idea as to what he should do. He went out and while passing by a village he found a cat being hotly chased by a number of villagers. On being asked the villagers said that the cat had stolen milk from the house of the king.

Lallua felt pity for the cat and he purchased the cat for 5 rupees. The cat was very grateful and advised him to buy an otter, a rat and a snake as well. With those Lalulla came home. He had spent all his money. His father watched every thing but he did not say any thing to his son as he was playing the game of wait and watch.

One day the snake said to Lallua, "The ring your father is wearing has some magical power. When placed in some milk the ring will produce anything you desire."

Lallua asked for the ring of his father and he got that. He became quite prosperous with the help of that ring and on the advice of the cat, the otter, the snake and the rat got married to the girl name Lalita.

Lalita was not a good woman. She did not like Lallua because she was in love with the *kotwal* (chief police officer) of the King. She was not ready to marry Lallua but her father had forced her do so. The fathers of both the bride and the bridegroom were childhood friends.

One day the *kotwal* said to Lalita, "Find out the secret of the prosperity of your husband. How he is making money without doing any work". The wife found out the secret from her husband. At night when Lallua was sleeping she managed to draw the ring from his finger and eloped with the *kotwal*. Before eloping she sprinkled the blood of a dead animal, given to her by the *kotwal*, on the floor.

The following morning Lalita was found missing and Lallua was suspected to have murdered his wife. He was taken into custody. The animal friends of Lallua followed him in prison. Lallua asked them to search and find out the missing ring. The animals searched and found out where Lalita was living with the *kotwal*. The rat managed to bore a hole in the wall. Crawling on the body of Lalita, while she was sleeping, the rat tickled her nose with the tip of his tail and made her sneeze. The ring came out, which she had hidden in her mouth. The rat ran off with that ring.

However, when the rat was crossing the river he was pounced upon by a kite. The rat dropped the ring into the water. The otter went down in the water and caught hold of the fish which had swallowed the ring and brought that up. The kite pounced on the fish leaving the rat free and took that off. The kite after eating the fish dropped the ring along with the bones under a tree. The snake brought the ring to Lallua. The cat, the otter and the rat followed the snake. Lallua put that ring in some milk and ordered that the bed on which the guilty pair was sleeping should be transported to the king. This was done and the king was convinced that Lallua was innocent. The king made him free from the prison and the guilty pair was appropriately punished.

Lallua got married once again with a nice girl and lived happily with his animal friends.

## BHOLA ORAON

One day Bhola Oraon was going to another village in search of some job. On the way while he was crossing a forest, he felt thirsty and halted near a water-stream to quench his thirst. He saw an old man sitting under a tree. That man was very hungry. Due to hunger only he was feeling giddiness and was unable to move. Bhola gave him food to eat that he had taken from his home to eat on the way. That old man gave many thanks to Bhola and said, "I was on my way home. I fell ill and had to spend two days here. In two days I ate all that I was having for the journey. I am a poor man and can not give any thing to you but I can give you some good advises."

Bhola replied, "I am happy I helped you. I am hearing your words carefully. Tell me what you want to say to me."

The old man said, "If you travel, travel in company; if you sit down, look where you are going to sit; if you visit strangers, be your own guard."

Bhola gave thanks to him and promised he would never forget his sayings and would do exactly so as told by him. The old man left for his home and Bhola went to drink water. He found a crab in the water and recalled the sayings that, "If you travel, travel in company." In order to have a companion on his travel he picked up the crab and thrust that into his turban.

After he had covered some more distance, he lied down under a tree but forgot to check where he was going to lie down. Soon he went in to deep sleep. Under the tree there was a hole of a big snake. The snake came out the hole and advanced with the jaw open to swallow Bhola up. The crab in the turban noticed the snake. Just when the snake was about to strike, the crab pounced on the hood of that and stung there. The snake withered in agony but could not get at the crab. The crab went on pinching the snake until withering in pain he died.

When Bhola woke up, he saw the dead snake and the crab on the hood of the snake. He understood every thing. He gave thanks to that old man and repeated, "If you travel, travel in company." He also realized that he was foolish as he did not check the place where he had rested.

He resumed his journey and came to a place where a number of cheats were sitting in a circle. These cheats had made a clever device. They had spread a mat on the top of a wall which had no curb and had covered that mat with grass. They were sitting on a circle round the well and on the edge of the mat. Their idea was to make a new comer sit in the centre so that he would fall down in the well and the cheats could take away all his belongings.

"Brother, do you not think it would be better to sit with us and talk? We are taking some rest here and sharing our experiences with one another", the cheats invited Bhola in a very sweet tone and asked him to sit down in the centre. Remembering the saying, "If you sit down, look where you sit" Bhola gave a pull at the mat and the cheats who were sitting on the edge of the mat all fell down into the well. Bhola realized how very true the saying was. Once again he gave thanks to that Brahmin.

Bhola continued his journey further and came to a village when it was evening. He stopped at the first house and found every one was weeping. Bhola was curious and asked them, "Why you all are weeping when there is no death in the house?"

They said, "The king has a daughter and it is found that who ever is married to the princess falls dead on the very night of wedding. It is the order of the king that one by one all the young men must be married to her. Today is the turn of our son and so we are crying thinking that our son is going to die."

Bhola said, "I have no objection to substitute for your son and will marry the princess. I am a bachelor and no one need be sorry if I die." This was god send and Bhola was given good food, drink and fine clothes.

The marriage took place that very night and the princess and Bhola retired to their room. The Bhola kept himself wide awake so as to observe every thing. At midnight he noticed a snake came out of the mouth of the princess. He quickly cut the head of the snake and the snake writhed in pain and fell down dead. The princess got up and greeted Bhola as her husband. Early in the morning a number of people assembled, as they used to do always, to take out the corpse. They were well amazed to see the couple came out, together. He fully realised the wisdom of the saying, "If you visit stranger, be on your guard". Bhola lived in the palace with the princess and after the death of the king became the king of the village.

[There is a proverb popular among the Oraon tribesmen: If you travel, travel in company; if you sit down, look where you are going to sit; if you visit strangers, be your guard].

## THE GULLIBLE MAN

There was a gullible man who was very irritated because his wife had not returned from her father's house since long. At last he made up his mind and without giving any prior notice went to his in-laws' house in the evening at about dinner time. Due to his arrival a great commotion prevailed in his in-laws' house and her mother-in-law quickly made tasty fish curry for her son-in-law. Pretending angry the man said that he had his dinner on the way and would not like to eat any more. After a little coaxing the family sat down to their dinner and every one praised the delicious fish curry within the hearing of the son-in-law who tried to satisfy his hunger with a glass of water only.

When every one had retired but the women were still having a conversation the man felt very hungry, the more so as the fish curry had smelt so appetising. He stealthily got up and found his way to the kitchen and started fumbling for the left over of the fish curry and rice which he had heard his mother-in-law had kept for the morning. At last he found the cooking pot and started making a good meal of the fish curry and rice.

However the bad luck of the gullible man did not forgive him, a cat came and wanted to share the fish curry. Quite forgetful of his circumstances the man threw a brass pot, which was near to him, at the cat. The cat mewed and ran away but the sound of the pot falling and the mew of the cat attracted women who made their way to kitchen. The man tried to hide behind the door and on seeing him the women shouted, "Thief, thief." A lamp was brought in and the man was discovered with his hands and mouth smeared with fish curry and rice. They all laughed to their hearts' content and the man had to put up at the jeers of the sisters-in-law. Above all he had a sever rebuke from his wife in the night.

Out of sheer embarrassment the man wanted to run away in the early morning when it was still dark. Once again he stealthily got up and left the home but while going out the household dog took him to be a thief. The dog started barking loudly. There was again a shout, "Thief, thief', and the members of the household came out and found that the dog had caught hold of the dhoti (waist cloth) of the man and had bitten him. Fooled again the gullible man had to come back to his room.

Next morning he left the village with his wife for his own home. He became a wise man in the company of his wise wife.

## THE GREEDY TIGRESS

A cow and a tigress were great friends. The thought of eating up the cow had never occurred to the tigress.

The tigress had given birth to two human children. The boys grew up as sturdy lads. They were also attached to the cow, the friend of their mother very much. One afternoon the cow and the tigress went to a stream to drink water. That day the cow drank water up stream and the tigress down stream. Usually the tigress used to drink water up stream but that day they had changed their positions. The tigress found the taste of the water sweet and thought if the cow could make the water taste sweet by merely drinking it, how delicious the flesh of the cow must be. On the way back from the stream the tigress suddenly pounced on the cow and after killing that ate her up, leaving nothing but bones. At home, in the evening the sons asked her, "Where is the cow? Why did you return alone?"

The tigress replied, "I do not know where the cow is? When we were drinking water in the afternoon she left the place saying she was going home because she was not well."

The next day the boys found the bones of the cow and guessed easily what would have happened. The elder brother said, "If our mother can kill her dear friend the cow, she can kill and eat us the next time."

"Yes, you are right. What should we do now?" The younger brother asked in fearful tone.

"We should forestall her before she could do any harm to us", the elder brother said. When the tigress was in her deep sleep, both the brothers killed her with an axe. After killing the tigress they ran away from there. After passing through the forest and hills they came to another village where they found the people were in great distress. A tiger was devastating the kingdom and killing all the inhabitants and no one had courage to kill the tiger. The king of the village had announced that any one who could kill the tiger would be given half of his kingdom as well as his daughter in marriage. Being the sons of the tigress the two boys had knowledge of tiger ways to fight. Thus they killed the tiger easily. The king gave them half of his kingdom and the elder brother married the daughter of the king.

[Animal giving birth to human children is very common in tribal stories. They strongly believe in the relation of animal, forest and human beings].

## THE BOY NAMED SON-IN-LAW

In a village a blind woman used to live with her grandson. One day two cheats were passing through the village. They came to know about the blind woman and her grandson. They learnt that the boy had silver bangles on his hand, necklace around the neck and rings in the ear-lobe. They went to the house and greeted the old woman as distant relatives of her dead husband. The old woman unable to see their face believed them. The cheats stayed a day with them and while leaving wanted the grandson to accompany them to visit one of their close relatives. The old woman and her grandson did not see through their ruse and the boy got ready to accompany them.

As soon as they had gone some distance from the village the two men started ill treating the boy and loaded him with their bamboo boxes and other luggage. They boy had to carry those luggage on his head. In the noon when it became hot they stopped near a pond. The men went into the village for some work.

"Do not open the bamboo box in our absence. There is a poisonous snake in that." The men warned the boy. They boy was very hungry and thought that he had smelt parched rice and treacle in the bamboo box. Without any fear he opened the box and found that it was full of parched rice, treacle and other sweets. He made a full meal of them. When the two men returned, the boy said that the snake had come out of the box and entered into a hole. The two cheats understood that the boy was very clever but they had to remain silent.

They continued their journey and reached another village. The men sat under a tree for rest and gave the boy two bangles and ordered him to sell those bangles in the village. The boy went in the village and found an oil man extracting oil with the help of a bullock. The boy said to him, "I can offer a pair of men if a good price is paid to me."

The oil man was very happy and settled the deal. The boy shouted to the two men, "Please answer, do you want me to conclude the deal? Shall I sell the both?"

"Yes, sell away both", the men shouted back. The boy asked for the money and got that. He called the two men and when they came near the oil man seized them. The boy escaped from there while the two cheats remained in captivity.

On the way back to his village the boy came to a river which was in high retch. He found that an old woman and her granddaughter were standing by the bank. They were unable to cross the river. The boy asked old woman, "Mother, may I take your granddaughter across first, and take you afterwards?"

The old woman was very pleased and asked for his name. The clever boy replied smilingly, "My name is 'son-in-law'.

The old woman then said, "All right, son-in-law, do so."

The boy swam with the girl and on reaching the other bank walked away taking the girl with him. Seeing the boy going with her granddaughter the old woman started shouting, "Look, look, son-in-law is going away with my granddaughter." A few persons who happened to be there rebuked her, "Why are you shouting if your son-in-law is taking away his wife? You need not bother."

In this way the boy went back home to his grandmother and gave her all the money and presented the girl. He and the girl were married and lived happily. The grandmother of the girl was called back and was given rice and clothes. She had a hearty laugh when she found her granddaughter safe and happily married.

## KARMA RAJA

It is believed that in the beginning dancing was a celestial prerogative and was confined to the palace of the king Indra in heaven. The nymphs were the dancers of the court of Indra. Those days there was no dance culture on the earth. A hornet and his wife used to live in the palace of Indra.

One day the hornet had a flight to the world below. On the earth that hornet came across a beautiful flower. He presented that flower to his wife and forbade her from showing that flower to the nymphs. The hornet's wife was charmed with the sweet smell and the colour of the flower and wanted one such daily. The plant of that flower was in the garden of the king Aja on the earth. Having extracted the secret of its location on earth from her husband, the hornet's wife used to visit the garden daily to take away one flower. One day she could not suppress her exultant feeling and showed the flower to the nymphs. The nymphs were very keen to have such flower and they refused to dance.

King Indra wanted to know the reason why the nymphs would not dance. The nymphs told him, "We also want to have the flower that the hornet's wife gets."

The king Indra called the hornet to know whereabout of the flower and the hornet had to disclose where the flower came from. All of them, including the nymphs, proceeded to the garden of the king Aja seated in the chariot of king Indra. After that it became a daily routine and the nymphs used to visit the garden and pilfer the flowers. Soon the gardener of the garden noticed that flowers were missing and he informed the king Aja that some one was stealing the flowers. The king asked the gardener to spray a special kind of magical ash on the flowers. The next morning the chariot of Indra came with all the nymphs and as soon as they touched the flowers, they all became immobilised along with the chariot. The thieves were caught red handed. The chariot was impounded.

When Indra heard about it, he rushed to the court of the king Aja and disclosed his identity and the identity of the thieves. The king Aja wanted to know why the king Indra was so much ager to appease the nymphs. He asked Indra, "Why do you take so much care of the nymphs? Why are you ready to do every thing only to please them?"

King Indra replied, "The *Karma* dance which the nymphs perform is the source of all my wealth and prosperity. I advise you too, to perform *Karma puja* (worship Karma)."

The king Indra requested the king Aja to release his chariot and the nymphs so that they could be back to heaven. King Aja told King Indra, "The effect of the magical ash would disappear only if a young unmarried girl who is on fast today touches the chariot and the nymphs."

A search was accordingly made for such a girl in the village. Luckily it was discovered that a widow and her unmarried daughter had quarrelled in the morning and they had not taken their meals. The girl was called in and made to touch the nymphs as well as the chariot. The chariot moved as soon as she touched that and king Indra returned with the nymphs to the heaven. From that day the king Aja started the performance of *Karma* dance and became wealthier. Thus began the dancing culture on the earth.

The king Aja had two sons, Anayahiri and Danyashiri, who were the father of Karma and Dharma respectively. There was scarcity of salt in the kingdom of the king Aja and the villagers were facing great trouble due to this scarcity. On the advice of the king Indra, the king Aja sent Karma to Katak (may be Cuttack in Orissa, which is a place of trade and commerce. The pilgrimage road from Jharkhand to Jagannathpuri passes through Cuttack), a big town for bringing salt from there. Karma managed to get large stock of salt from Katak which he loaded on a number of bullock carts and started homeward journey. When he approached his village with his carts full of salt, he sent a message to his brother Dharma about the success of his mission thinking that Dharma would come out immediately to receive him with all due gaiety. But, at that time Dharma was engaged in worshipping *Karma Raja* and asked the messenger to wait. At this Karma in mightily enrage went to the palace of his brother and cut down all the branches of *Karam* and destroyed the articles of the worship. Dharma was very upset at the insolence of his brother. He got himself separated from him the same night because of want of respect for the *Karma Raja*.

Karma went back to bring salt and found that all the bullock carts were empty. He went to his house and found that his building was in ruin and his wife and children were in rags and hungry. Karma and his wife were reduced to great poverty and had to take to the job of field labourer to make the two ends meet. He than realized that all his trouble were due to his bad *Karma* (luck) and that he must worship *Karma Raja* to revive his fortune. Karma then set out to find *Karma Raja* and to worship him.

On the way he met tortoise hanging from a branch of tree. The tortoise was in great pain. When he came to know about the mission of Karma he requested him to pray before the *Karma Raja* for his salvation. He proceeded further and met a woman with a *borsi* (a small earthen pot used as hearth to keep warm in cold weather) fixed on her head. She also requested Karma to propitiate *Karma Raja* and pray for her welfare. Karma then came to a tank which he found full of insects. A crocodile was in the tank with a fully grown palm-tree on his back. The crocodile was in agony and requested Karma to pray for him to *Karma Raja*.

Karma went on and came to a river where he found *Karma Raja* floating on the river. He jumped into the river to touch the feet of *Karma Raja*. As he was sinful he could not reach up to him to touch his feet. He tried for hours but did not succeed. At last feeling tired and dejected he wanted to be drowned. At that point *Karma Raja* took pity on him and saved him. He prayed fervently to him and all his troubles were over. He also prayed for the tortoise, the old woman and the crocodile and they all were relieved of their troubles. Karma recovered all his lost wealth and prosperity. He went back home and found his house as it was before and his wife and children were happy and rich.

Since that day the people of the world began to have great faith in the *Karma* festival and started performing it with great zeal and enthusiasm.

The Karma festival is celebrated both in Jharkhand as well as Bihar. In Jharkhand it is celebrated by the tribesmen and in Bihar by the non-tribal population. In Bihar the story behind the festival starts from the King Indra and the king Aja while in Jharkhand it starts from the two brothers Dharma and Karma. The Bhil as well as the Barela tribesmen in Madhya Pradesh, too, celebrate this festival with enthusiasm.

[This festival is observed throughout Jharkhand on the eleventh day of *Bhado* (August-September). It is observed to bring wealth, prosperity and pleasure in life. This is a community festival, although a few particular households specially observe the festival when they foresee some signs of bad omen. Young girls bring a few baskets (seven, nine or eleven) of mud from the field and two branches of the tree karma (adina cordifolia). The branches are planted parallel to each other in the mud kept in the baskets. It is symbolic of the *Karma Raja* having been installed. The fasting and singing is followed by a lavish *handiya* (rice beer) drinking. Dancing goes on for the whole night moving around the branches. The next morning the dancing is done from door to door and the dancer gets a cup of *handiya* at every place. The festival is over by the evening with songs to propitiate the *Karma Raja*. At the end the branches are immersed in a pond or a river].

## THE REVENGE OF A JACKAL

One day a jackal killed a kid in a village. He was happy and wanted to make a good meal of that kid. When he was going to eat that the crows gathered on a tree over his head and started crowing. The villagers came to see what the reason of restlessness of the crows was. They gave severe beating to the jackal and also took away the body of the dead kid. The jackal was very angry with the crows and wanted to take revenge.

Shortly afterwards came a great cyclonic storm followed by heavy rains. All the birds and animals were in danger of being drowned. The jackal pretended to be sorry for the crows and invited them all to come and take shelter in his den. When they had got in, the jackal killed and ate them all except one which he decided to keep for his breakfast for the next morning. He kept the bird tied to his tail. The bird was clever and kept pecking at the jackal's tail until it broke loose. The tail of the jackal got badly wounded and was swollen. As the jackal went along with his swollen tail he met a potter who was going to market to sell his earthen pots. The jackal told the potter, "I am the messenger of the king, and one of the pots must be given to me. It is the order of the king." The potter gave him one pot. On the way back the jackal met a boy who was grazing goats. The jackal bluffed the boy saying that his father had agreed to give him a goat in lieu of a pot of ghee. The boy gave one goat to the jackal and took the pot which the jackal had filled with sand. The boy soon found that he had been cheated but by that time the jackal had gone far away from his reach.

The other jackals living near the den of the jackal were very jealous when they saw a healthy goat with him. When the jackal was away, they all killed the goat. The jackal found out what his friends had done. He wanted to be avenged. He took the skin of the goat to a cobbler who made a good drum of it. After this the jackal went to the bank of a river and began to play the drum. All the other jackals gathered round him and admired the sound of the drum. They wanted to know as to where from such a fine drum could be got.

The jackal said, "There are many such drums at the bottom of the river and if you tie stones round your necks and jump into the river you would find those drums." The other jackals were duped and they all jumped into the river and thus were drowned. The clever jackal had taken his revenge from all of his enemies.

## FOUR FRIENDS

Four young men were fast friends from boyhood. They used to dance together on the same dance floor and had sworn mutual friendship. When growing up they took to different professions. One of them hawked vermilion, another became a weaver, the third took to wood carving and the fourth became a goldsmith. One day they decided to go and see new places to earn their livelihood. They took their tools and started their journey for the new place.

They visited many places. One day they had to spend a night under a mango tree. After having their meal they decided that as it was an unknown place they would better by turn keep a watch overnight. The wood-carver was the first to keep the vigil while the other three slept. After some time the wood-carver got tired of sitting idle and, taking up a piece of dry wood, he chiseled it into a female figure. He put the woman thus shaped on her feet and woke up the goldsmith to take his turn.

The goldsmith got up and after a while spotted the wooden figure. He thought, "She is a lovely girl but she needs ornaments." So he made a gold chain and put it around her neck. He also made a pair of earrings and bangles and put them on her. He then woke up the weaver and went to sleep. During his vigil the weaver saw the wooden woman, admired her figure and ornaments and started thinking, "Something is missing. Ah, she should have a sari." That very minute he counted up the threads for a sari and wove a garment. Very fondly he wrapped her in it. He then woke up the vermilion-hawker and saying, "Your turn has come, brother, please be on the watch", he retired. The hawker, while on the watch, saw the wooden woman and anointed her forehead with vermilion just at daybreak. The wooden woman came alive and stood there.

The four friends started brawling among themselves as to who should marry the girl. The wood carver said that if he had not given her a shape she would have remained a log. The goldsmith claimed her for the ornaments he had given her. The weaver said, 'I gave her clothes so she is mine». The hawker insisted that he had the best claim.

While the four friends were brawling they saw a holy man coming. They made him their arbiter. The holy man heard the claims of the four friends and said, "He that made her is her father; he that clothed her is her elder brother; he that gave ornaments is her uncle; but he that brought her to life and put vermilion on her forehead is her husband."

The four friends bowed to the decision and the woman became the wife of the hawker.

[The story refers to the custom prevalent among the tribes of Jharkhand that *Sindur-daan* or applying vermilion on the forehead of a girl means that she is married to the boy who does so. The story tries to preserve tradition. Even today marriages are forced this way in tribal society. This custom is also cleverly exploited by couples who have fallen in love. At the weekly fair a boy suddenly appears before a girl and applies vermilion on her forehead. The girl's parents are then forced to recognise the marriage. This story also reveals that fighting for a girl has always been a common practice in Indian society. At the same time the story supports the proverb that one who possesses skills cannot sit idle. The four friends were all endowed with skill, and rather than sitting idle they preferred to work, even at night, and could also enjoy the fruits of their labour].

## THE RUNNING DOG

A jackal and a dog were great friends. One day the dog invited the jackal for dinner. The dog had got hold some fowls and had cooked them. Both had good meal. The jackal then invited the dog but made two conditions. The first was that the dog must come to his den moving and not running and the second was he must reach the jackal's den at sun set. Without thinking much, the dog accepted the conditions.

On the evening of the dinner, the dog started for his friend jackal's den. After a while the dog found that he was not moving but running. He came back to his house and started again, but again he found that he was not moving but running. In this manner he had to come back home several times. By the time he reached the den of the jackal the sun had already set. The jackal had already eaten up his share. He gave bones to the dog to crunch. The dog had no other alternative but to crunch the bones.

From that day onwards the dogs love to crunch the bones, even if there is no meat attached to that, with cracking sound.

## THE SNAKE AND THE GIRL

Many years ago a woman was on a visit to a distant village. On her way home she had to cross a river, When she reached the river she found that in high spate, the water was too deep and the current too strong. She saw no boat or any other mode of crossing the river. She was very worried as night was approaching.

While she was standing in fear and hesitation a big snake came out of the river and asked her, "Lady, what will you give me if I ferry you across the river? I will not take you across the river unless you at least promise to give something to me."

Not knowing what else to do, the woman who was pregnant at that time, promised that if her child would be a daughter she would marry her to the snake and if it was a son, the boy when grew up should become the friend of the snake. The snake accepted the offer and taking her on his back swam her across the flooded river. The woman safely reached her home.

After some time a daughter was born to her. Years passed by and the woman forgot all about the snake and her pledge. One day she went to the river to fetch water. The snake came out of the water and said, "Lady, where is the bride you promised for?"

The woman then remembered her promise and going back to her house she returned to the river with her daughter. When the girl came to the bank of the river the snake seized her and took her under the water. The girl lived with the snake at the bottom of the river and bore him four snake sons.

A few years later the girl felt a yearning for her home, and to visit her mother. Her brothers were surprised to see her, for they had thought she had drowned. The girl assured them, "No, I was not drowned. I am married and have children."

The brothers did not like the idea of having a snake as brother-in-law and expressed a desire to meet him. The sister said, "Go to the bank of the river and shout for the snake."

The brothers went to the river and shouted for the snake. The snake came out of the river and went to their house with them. The brothers gave the snake large quantities of *handiya* (rice beer) to drink. After drinking the *handiya* the snake became sleepy and coiling himself went to sleep. The brothers killed the snake with their axe while he slept. There after the girl lived happily with her brothers in their house.

## BUDHNA ORAON

Budhna Oraon was a potter. Though his wife was very beautiful, she was not a faithful woman. She had developed relationship with the king of the village. The king wanted to house the wife of Budhna to his palace but before he could do so it was necessary to get rid of the husband. Therefore, he planned to kill Budhna by setting him to impossible task to perform.

One day the king called Budhna and ordered him, "Bring the heads of twenty four jackals, otherwise I will hang you to death."

Though annoyed by the order of the king, Budhna went to forest and started digging a large pit in the side of a hill. A jackal came near him and asked, "Why you are digging the pit?"

Budhna replied, "It is soon going to rain fire from the heaven. Those who have no such shelter would be burnt to ashes." At this the jackal became very frightened. Budhna however, assured him that he would allow the jackal and his friends not extending twenty four in numbers, to share the shelter which he was digging. The jackal gratefully ran away and returned along with his twenty three friends. They all went into the pit and Budhna closed the entrance. After some time he looked out and said that the rains of the fire was over. He then came out first and took his stand at the opening of the pit. As the jackals came out one by one, he went on cutting off their heads with a sickle. In this way he beheaded twenty three jackals. The last jackal, however, saw what was happening with his friends. He dogged the sickle and escaped.

Budhna took twenty three heads to the king. The king pretended to be angry and said, "If you do not at once produce the twenty fourth head, you would be beheaded to compensate for the missing number."

Budhna asked for a little time, and cursing the king silently proceeded towards the water pool which was in the direction where the last jackal had left. He had also taken a pot of honey with himself. He smeared his body with honey and lied down by the water pretending to be dead. After a while the jackal that had escaped passed that way with a friend. Thinking it was a dead body the second jackal proposed that they should eat that. The first jackal warned his friend that it might be a plot and narrated how twenty three of his friends had lost their lives at the hand of that very man. The second jackal was, however, too greedy to listen to the advice and went up to the supposed corpse of Budhna and having smelt that started licking that. Finding the taste of honey very pleasant the jackal started licking the body all over beginning from the feet. As soon as that came up to the waist and within the reach of Budhna, he got up and stabbed the jackal with the knife he had concealed and took the head to the king.

The king then hit upon another plan. He ordered Budhna to bring a pot of tigress's milk. Once again cursing the king from his heart and taking some bread, Budhna went into a forest and soon found in a cave a pair of tigress cubs. The tigress was away hunting. Budhna told the cubs that he was their *mama* (maternal uncle) and gave them bread to eat. The cubs liked the taste of the bread and ate that to their fill. Budhna hid on a tree near the cave. When the tigress returned the cubs did not suck her milk as usual and the tigress asked, "Why you both are not sucking milk? What is wrong with you? Are you all right?"

"We are fine. Our *mama* had come and fed us something very tasty. We are not hungry", the cubs replied. The cubs showed her Budhna on the tree. The tigress wanted to know what he had given her cubs to eat. When he told her that it was the bread the tigress wanted to taste that.

"Give me some bread to eat. I would like to taste that", the tigress requested Budhna.

"I can give you the bread, too, but there is one condition", Budhna said. "What is that condition?" The tigress asked.

"You will have to give some of your milk to me", Budhna said.

The tigress agreed for it. Having milked the tigress, Budhna gave her a loaf of bread and ran from there as fast as he could. Finding Budhna too clever for him the king persuaded his characterless wife to put her husband dead. The wife of Budhna installed an idol in her house and prayed daily in front of that to make her husband blind and die. One day Budhna heard his wife's prayer. The next morning he hid behind the idol and when his wife came to pray, he answered from behind, "Your request is granted. In two days your husband would become blind." The faithless wife was happy and sent word to the king. Two days later Budhna started pretending to have become blind. The wife sent word to the King that Budhna was blind hence he must visit her any time. The king came accordingly and when they two were together Budhna killed them both with an axe.

He buried the body of his wife, and put the body of the king in a field belonging to a neighbour. Early morning the owner of the field came and he saw some one in the field. He thought that a thief had come to steal the crops and hit the supposed thief on the head with a stick. He was shocked to find that he had apparently killed the king. In great anxiety and worry he consulted his friend, Budhna.

"What should I do now? The king is killed by me?" He asked Budhna.

"Do not worry. Put the body among the buffaloes belonging to a herdsman", Budhna advised his neighbour.

In the evening the milkman came to look at his buffaloes. Seeing the body of the king he thought it was a thief stealing the milk of the buffalo. He inflicted a severe blow with a stick on the thief and the body fell down. When he found that the body was that of the king and he had apparently killed the king, he became nervous. In great fear he went to his friend Budhna for help. It was finally decided to dispose of body by putting that into a well.

The next day there was a hue and cry and a search was made for the missing king. The body was found in the well by an old Brahmin who had gone there to take bath. Arrangements were made for the cremation of the body and a funeral pyre was erected. Budhna took it as an opportunity. He dug a pit in the ground under the pyre and hid himself in that. When the body had been cremated and the mourners were still present near the pyre, Budhna began to speak from the pit in a loud voice. The mourner thought that they were hearing the voice of the king from the heaven declaring that Budhna had always been a true friend of the king. It was king's desire that Budhna should be given half of the kingdom and the hand of his daughter in marriage. The people felt that this must be done. The supposed wishes of the king were carried out and Budhna lived in luxury for the rest of his life.

## CATTLE WORSHIP

A villager had seven sons. They all got married one after the other in view of their age. The wife of the youngest son, although very young in age was very wise. Seeing that the wants of the family were growing, she told her husband, brothers-in-law and to her father-in-law, "We have failed to make a good living in this village; let us go away elsewhere so that we may live in happiness."

The family accepted her advice and collecting their meagre household goods left for a distant village. The village where they arrived was in an uproar, for the queen had just lost her necklace. She had gone for her bath and removing the necklace, she had kept that near the well. A kite had come down with a sweep and had carried the necklace. The maids and the queen had raised a hue and cry to make the bird drop the necklace but without success.

The kite went away with the necklace and strangely dropped that at the place where the family of the seven brothers and their father were taking rest. The wife of the youngest son saw the necklace first and kept that with her. The queen was very much upset at the loss. The king announced by the beats of drum that whosoever found the necklace and brought it back would get five villages. The wife of the youngest son heard the announcement and told her neighbours that she could find out the necklace. The villagers were amazed and soon took her to the queen.

The king asked her, "My dear girl, have you got the necklace? If so, give it back and you will get five villages."

The girl replied, "O king, I do not want the five villages, but I want only your favour."

"Your desire would be fulfilled if possible", the king said to her.

The girl said, "The favour I ask is that on the night of cattle festival no one should be allowed to light the lamp. On that day we alone will light one lamp."

The king said, "This is a very simple request and I grant it." The girl gave the necklace to the queen and returned home. Her husband and brothers-in-law all thought that she was extremely foolish in not asking for the villages. The girl, however, assured them that all would be well and asked them to wait till the festival of the cattle worship which was coming only after two days.

On the festival day no lamps were lit in the village except the house of the seven brothers. The bullocks, the cows, the calves, he and she buffaloes, goats and sheep lost their way in darkness. Perceiving one steady light, all the cattle of the villages entered in to the house of the girl. According to the customary tradition all those cattle who passed her threshold of by their own accord became hers. The family became very rich and spent their days in happiness. The girl explained to the family that not knowing the intricacies of running the villages, they would have been in great trouble if they had taken the five villages. They knew how to manage the cattle and make money out of them; it was better to take the cattle. They all agreed that the young girl was extremely wise. There was no end to their happiness hereafter.

The cattle worship festival is known as Sohrai festival by the tribesmen of Jharkhand. Both the people of tribal and no-tribal origin celebrate this festival a day after the festival of Deewali (festival of light). On this day the cattle are given a bath, often anointed with oil and colour and are given special feed and they are worshipped as well. Cattle are considered as wealth in India and are worshipped all over India to propitiate the goddesses of wealth.

## A NEW PAIR OF SHOES

Once upon a time there lived two cheats in a village. They were friends. One day one cheat said to the other, "We have cheated the villagers around to such an extent and for long; no one in this village is ready to believe us."

The second cheat said, "You are absolutely right. Let us go to another village and find new victims to cheat at."

They went long way and reached the kingdom of another village. They came to know that the king of that village had died on the previous night. Both of them got an opportunity to cheat the sons of the king. They waited for king to be buried. After the burial was over, they dug a pit near the grave in which one of them concealed himself. The other cheat went to the sons of the king and after making a show of grief told them, "The king had borrowed fifty coins from me when he had come to my village. I have come here to take back my coins."

The sons of the king replied, "We know nothing about the loan. How can we believe your story? What is the proof that you are telling truth? We will not give any coin to you."

The cheat protested that his words were true and he said, "The spirit of the king will confirm the truth about the loan if they will only go to the grave and invoke the spirit."

The sons of the king agreed and all of them went to the grave. The cheat number one shouted, "O king, please tell your sons if you had borrowed fifty coins from me."

The reply came from the pit, "Yes, I had taken the coins and my sons should repay the loan."

The sons of the king were duly impressed and when they went back to palace, they paid money to the cheat. The cheat who got the money wanted to cheat his friend as well. He left the village silently without pulling his friend out of the pit. After waiting for a considerable time the other cheat managed to lift himself from the pit and came to the palace of the king. He asked about his friend from the sons of the king. They showed him the way the first cheat had gone.

The second cheat brought a new pair of shoes and taking a short cut went ahead of his friend. On the way he left behind one of the pair and concealed himself. When the first cheat came to the place, he saw the shoe, but as there was only one of the pair he did not pick it up, and went ahead. By that time his friend had gone further ahead and placed the other one on the way and as before concealed himself. On seeing this one, the first cheat thought that he must also collect the first one so that he might have a new pair of shoes. He concealed his bundle in the bushes and went back. While he was away his friend took the bundle and ran away with that.

## THE CUNNING JACKAL

A camel and a jackal were friends. They used to live in a forest. The camel was wise whereas the jackal was very cunning. He used to take maximum advantages from the camel and used to roam from one place to another sitting on the back of the camel. The camel was good in nature and used to put a lot with the jackal.

One day the jackal told the camel, "There is a sugarcane field on the other side of the river. Let us cross the river and eat sugarcane." The camel agreed and crossed the river with the jackal on his back. They entered the field and started eating sugarcanes. The jackal had a small stomach so he got satisfied soon. The camel was still hungry. The jackal wanted to play some mischief and started howling. The camel requested the jackal to stop howling till he had eaten to his belly full of the sugarcanes. The jackal did not listen to the camel and said, "It is my habit to howl after eating. I can not help you."

Hearing the howling of the jackal the owner of the field came to the field with a big stick. The jackal hid himself some where. The camel was too large to hide, and was severely beaten and driven away. When the farmer went away the jackal came out and went to the camel. The wise camel did not say anything to the jackal. On the contrary he welcomed the jackal as usual.

On their return journey the jackal again sat on the back of the camel to cross the river. When the camel reached in the middle of the river he stopped. He told the jackal that he felt like rolling in water. The jackal requested him not to do so, but the camel began rolling saying that he had the habit of rolling and could not help it. The jackal was drowned in the river and died. The cleverness of the jackal with wicked intention cost his life.

## THE BROTHER BORN AGAIN

In a village there lived two brothers named Haru and Gopa. They had lost their parents when they were kids. An old woman relative had taken care of the brothers and she, too, had expired.

One day they decided that one of them should marry, because they needed a girl to take care of the house especially in their absence. The younger brother Gopa said to his elder brother Haru, "Brother! If you will marry first, there will be no problem, but if I will marry first then it may create problem."

"What the rubbish you are talking? There would be no problem if you marry first. Go and find a suitable girl for yourself", Haru said to Gopa.

Both the brothers kept persuading each other to marry first but failed to decide as to who would marry first. At last the younger brother said, "We will go to search the girl. You are elder than me, so first you will go to search a girl and second day I will go. This way we will go day after day till we find a suitable girl. The person who will get the girl first will marry first."

The elder brother agreed with the plan and next day went out in search of a suitable partner for him but did not find any. The girls he met were either handless or lame or crippled. He returned home in the evening and said to his younger brother, "I have failed in finding any bride for me. Tomorrow it is your turn to go out."

The next morning when the younger brother went out he met a very beautiful and good natured girl. He married that girl and returned home in the evening. The girl started taking care of home. The brothers used to spend the day in hunting and collecting fruits, tubers and fuel from the forest. The younger brother was very happy with his wife. The happiness of the younger brother made the elder brother jealous. After a few days an ill thought came to the mind of the elder brother. After killing his brother he wanted to marry his wife.

One day the elder brother told his younger brother, "O brother, let us go to some other forest for hunting today."

The younger brother agreed and went with his elder brother to another forest which was far away from their hut. They reached a hilly forest and the elder brother as he had planned earlier played a trick with his younger brother. He sent his younger brother towards the foothill and he went to the top. He was in look out for a tactical opportunity to strike his brother. As soon as he got a chance he shot dead his brother with his gun. Poor younger brother died on the spot.

However, the younger brother had guessed the ill thought of his brother. He had given one *dona* (leaf made cup) milk and one *dona* water to his wife. He had told her, "At the moment the milk turns into blood and the water into milk then understand that I am not alive."

The wife of the younger brother, too, was suspecting about some ill happening. In the absence of her husband she used to watch both the *donas* very carefully. As soon as the elder brother killed the younger brother the milk kept in the *dona* turned into blood and the water into milk. The lady understood what would have happened with her husband. She locked herself in a room and started crying bitterly.

The elder brother returned home in happy mood, thinking that now the wife of his younger brother was his. After coming home he ordered the wife of his younger brother to open the door. The wife asked about her husband. At first the elder brother did not tell the truth but at last he told the truth. The wife of the younger brother got an idea to get rid of her brother-in-law. She said, "Now I will not marry any one other than you. However, before the marriage, we should perform the last rites of the dead body you have left in the forest. Let us go to the forest and search the body first."

The elder brother was not willing to perform the last rites of his brother but he did not say no to the lady. He thought of making her fool by not going to the right place where he had killed his brother and return home after spending an hour in the forest. Both of them proceeded for the forest. The lady was in a palanquin and the elder brother was on a horse. Very soon the lady discovered that the elder brother was not going in the right direction and was making her fool. She started wailing:

*"Jaha gidhva mandraye hey Ram, ho Ram*
*wohi ghodwa ke bhej, hey Ram, ho Ram."*

(Where ever vultures are hovering, there only you send the horse, hey Ram)

After hearing the song the elder brother started riding the horse in the right direction. When they covered some distance they found the leg of the younger brother. The elder brother had cut the body of his younger brother into pieces and had thrown the pieces at different places. Seeing the leg the lady started wailing again:

*"Godwa jaha jutba sobhta tha hey Ram, ho Ram,*
*Jutba jo much, much karta tha hey Ram, ho Ram,*
*Uhi godwa chal gayal hey Ram, ho Ram."*

(The leg where there used to remain shoe giving the sound of much, much, that has gone hey Ram).

They proceeded further and got the waist of the younger brother and once again his wife started wailing:

*"Wo kamarwa jaha dhoti sobhta that hey Ram, ho Ram,*
*Wo kamarwa chala gaya hey Ram, ho Ram."*

(The waist where there was a beautiful waist cloth, has gone hey Ram).

When they moved further they got the head of the younger brother and his wife wailed:

*"Ek sir jaha lal pagdi tha hey Ram, ho Ram,*
*Wo sir chala gaya hey Ram, ho Ram".*

(The head where there was a red turban, has gone hey Ram).

Like this the lady collected all the body parts of her late husband and said to her brother-in-law, "You go and bring some fire and I will collect woods for the pyre."

The elder brother went to bring fire. Meanwhile the lady collected the woods, made a funeral pyre and sitting on that with the body parts of her husband requested to god, "O god if our love for each other was true, then please put fire on the pyre."

The pyre got fired and the lady burnt herself with the body parts of her husband. When the elder brother returned he got only ashes. He realized his mistake. He had lost his brother as well as his sister-in-law. He started crying bitterly but no one was there to hear his cry. After sometime he got up and taking some ash put a mark on his forehead. He did not return his home and spent night in the forest. He began wandering from village to village begging and singing:

*"Haru and Gopa do bhai the hey Ram, ho Ram,*
*Ek aurat ko pane ke liye hey Ram, ho Ram,*
*Haru ne Gopa ko maar dala hey Ram, ho Ram".*

(There were two brothers named Haru and Gopa. For a woman Haru killed Gopa hey Ram).

The dead couple, Gopa and his wife were born again in the same village and became husband and wife in their new birth as well. Living in a big house they were leading good life.

One day while begging the elder brother came to the house of his younger brother singing his favourite song, "There were two brothers..."

Hearing this song Gopa recognized his elder brother of previous birth. He came out from his house and told his brother, "You had killed me in my last birth and my wife had burnt herself with my body. In this birth I am happy with my wife."

The elder brother also recognized his younger brother. They started crying and the elder brother who was an old man now asked for forgiveness. He promised that he would not do any thing wrong with them and he had suffered a lot for his deed. The younger brother forgave his elder brother. He called a barber who saved the hair, beard and moustache of Haru. The younger brother asked his brother to take bath in hot water and gave him good clothes to wear and food to eat. Thereafter Gopa lived happily with his wife and brother Haru, who was now a fatherly figure to the young couple.

## THE LION AND THE JACKAL

A lion and a jackal were good friends. One day the jackal told lion, "You know men are very clever."

The lion who was proud of his strength replied that he would like to snatch the cleverness from the man and asked about the whereabout of man from the jackal.

The jackal said, "Friend! If you want to snatch cleverness from the man then come with me. I will show who the man is".

Both the friends started searching for a man. They saw a child. The lion asked, "Is this a man?"

The jackal replied, "No friend! He will become a man after a few years."

Then they saw an old man. Again the lion asked, "Is this a man?"

Once again the jackal replied, "No friend! He was a man, now he is old."

At last they saw a man who was armed with a gun and a sword. The jackal told the lion about the man they were searching. After seeing the man the lion swoop on him to overpower him. When the lion made the swoop the hunter shot at him with his air gun and then pierced his sword into his stomach. The lion ran away to save his life. Seeing this, the jackal passed the sarcastic remark, "Tell me friend! How do you find a man?"

The lion replied, "You told truth my friend. Man is clever. First he shot me with a black stick (gun). I felt burning sensation but I did not want to let him go free. Then he pierced his stick (sword) in my stomach. After this I ran away, otherwise he would have killed me."

## TO GUARD A CORPSE

In a village there was a king. He was a king for name sake. He had lost his wealth and except four horses he had nothing to show that once he was a king. The king had four sons. After becoming young the four brothers decided to earn and give rest to their parents.

All the brothers riding on their own horses proceeded towards another destination. In the village they reached, a rich man had died and his son had announced to pay four thousand coins to any fellow who would guard the corpse in the cremation ground whole night. When the four brothers came to know about this announcement they decided to take up the task. They went to the son of the rich man and showed their willingness to guard the corpse. After signing the agreement the brothers proceeded towards the cremation ground taking four *masal* (torch).

The elder brother told, "O brothers! There are four *pahar* (duration of three hours time) in a night. If we guard each *pahar* one by one it would be dawn."

First the elder brother started guarding the corpse. After some time the corpse told, "O son of the king! I want to fight with you."

The elder brother replied, "You do not have any reason to fight with me. Why do you want to fight with me? Keep quiet and sleep otherwise I will cut you into pieces."

While they were talking the torch which was kept near the leg of the cot of the corpse got extinguished. In the darkness the elder thought that the corpse would have run away. He started groping for the corpse and at last found that. He wanted to light the torch but there was no fire. The elder brother tied the corpse with his horse and proceeded towards the village in search of fire. On the way he saw a *diya* (oil lamp). Near that lamp some witches were trying to make a dead child alive. The elder brother forced his horse to jump in between the witches. Out of fear the witches ran away and the elder brother returned to cremation ground with the dead child and the oil-lamp. It was the end of first *pahar* of the night. He made his second brother get up and went to sleep.

Now the second brother started guarding the corpse. After sometime the corpse repeated the desire to fight with him and he too replied the same as his elder brother had told to the corpse. Again the torch got extinguished. The second brother tied the corpse with his horse and proceeded towards village in search of fire. On the way he saw the flickering of the oil lamp. He went near the oil lamp and found that a devil was sitting there. When she saw the second brother she started crying. The second brother asked for the reason of her crying. She replied, "In the morning the king is going to hang my son to death. It is the rule of the king to hang any person if he does any thing wrong. I have come here to offer water to my son."

The second brother asked the devil on his shoulder. He was ready to reach her near her son. However, the devil was playing game with the second brother. He started eating the arm of the second brother and in this process blood started flowing from his arm. When he felt pain he asked the devil as what she was doing. She replied that it was water flowing from her pot, but in the light of the lamp the second brother saw the blood and understood every thing. Taking his dagger in his left hand he tried to kill her. The thigh of the devil got mutilated. She had concealed a diamond in her thigh. The second brother took the diamond and returned to cremation ground with the oil lamp and the diamond. The devil had managed to escape. Now it was the turn of the third brother to guard the corpse. The second brother made the third brother get up and he went to sleep.

When the third brother was guarding the corpse same thing happened with him as well. The corpse wanted to fight with him and he refused. The torch got extinguished and he went in search of fire. He saw an oil-lamp in the palace of the king and when he went near it he saw that the king and the queen were sleeping and a poisonous snake was moving to bite them. He killed the snake and covered that with a *borsi* (an earthen fire pot used to keep the room warm). He returned to cremation ground with the oil lamp.

The younger brother became ready to fight with the corpse. The corpse guffaw and said, "I will fight with you near the cave where the souls of dead men live. My soul is also there."

Both of them came near the cave of the soul. There were many souls in the form of corpses and they all started fighting with the younger brother. While fighting it became dawn and all the souls returned to their respective cave. Before going back to their cave they all praised the bravery of the youngest brother and gave him eight pots of gold coins. The younger brother was unable to carry those pots alone. The corpse that had gone with him said, "Put the pots in the tank and take them home later on when no one watches you."

The younger brother dipped the pots full with gold coins in a nearby tank and returned to the cremation ground with the corpse. In the early morning the sons of the rich man came to the cremation ground to perform the last rites of their father. The four brothers refused to give the corpse to the sons and asked for four thousand coins. The sons of the rich man refused to pay the money to the brothers and said in grouch tone, "What is the proof that you had guarded the corpse in the night?"

The sons of the rich man and their family members snatched the corpse from the four brothers and cremated that. All the four brothers went to the king for the justice. The king asked them to prove their claim. The brothers narrated what had happened with them in night and in proof the elder brother gave the dead child to the king and the second brother gave him the thigh of the devil. The third brother told about the snake and the king's men brought the dead snake from the bed room of the king. The younger brother said that when he went to guard the corpse it was already dawn. The king convinced with the four brothers ordered the sons of the rich man to pay the money to the brothers.

The four brothers returned home and started taking rest. The younger brother told them what had happened with him in the night. The brothers were happy and when it became dark they all went near the tank and brought the eight pots filled with gold coins from the tank. They family had become rich once again. There after the four brothers lived in luxury with their parents.

# 7 Folktales of Santal

## SANTAL: AN INTRODUCTION

The Santals are the largest tribal group in India. They live mainly in the states of Jharkhand, West Bengal, Bihar, Orissa, and Assam. They are also in significant number in the neighbouring countries of Bangladesh and in Nepal (Troisi, 1976). The language spoken by them is called Santali, which is a part of the Austro-Asiatic family. This tribe also has its own script called Olchiki (Chakrabarti 1994). Apart from Santali they also speak Bengali, Oriya, and Hindi.

The Santal tribesmen of India have a typical life style. Their basic needs are fulfilled by forest trees and plants. The tribesmen are also engaged in fishing and cultivation. These tribesmen possess a magnificent skill of making musical equipments, mats, and baskets out of the plant.

The Santhal tribesmen believe in supernatural beings and ancestral spirits. Their rituals consist mainly of sacrificial offerings and invocations to the *bongas* (spirits). They believe that there is a close bondage between the forest, the forest animals and the human beings. This belief is depicted in many of their folk tales. The story of the Santal ancestors Pilchu Haram and Pilchu Budhi is also popular among them.

The Santal tribesmen like music and dance as well. Santal music differs from Hindustani Classic Music in significant ways (Prasad, 1980).

Before the advent of the British rule in India the Santal tribesmen used to reside peacefully in the hills of Jharkhand, Bengal Orissa, and Assam. Their life was based on cleaning the forest, and in hunting for subsistence. The agents of the new colonial rule along with the local and greedy moneylenders claimed their rights on the land they resided. They cheated them by luring them into debt by goods lent to them on loans. However, they tried to repay these loans, but they never ended. Through the corrupt measures of the moneylenders, the debts multiplied to an amount for which a generation of Santal family had to work as slave. This loss of the freedom that they enjoyed once turned them into rebel (Orans 1965).

On June 30, 1855 two great Santal leader Sidhu Murmu and Kanhu Murmu, moralised several thousand Santhal tribesmen and declared a rebellion against the British Colonists. Although, the revolution was brutally suppressed, it marked a great change in the Colonial rule and policy. The day is still celebrated not only among the Santal but by the others as well, with great respect and spirit for the thousands of the Santal martyrs who sacrificed their lives along with their two celebrated leaders to win freedom from the rule of corrupt moneylenders and the British operatives. In order to commemorate the sacrifice made by the two great Santal leaders Sidhu and Kanhu, a university has been named after their names in Jharkhand, India.

## THE TIGER AND THE KING

Many years ago there was a Santal king. He had one son and seven daughters. One day the king went into a forest to cut grass. He spent several hours in cutting grass and as a result he collected a huge quantity of grass. After finishing his job he tied up a big bundle of the grass that he could possibly carry on his head, and still there remained a large quantity of surplus grass.

"What should I do now? I have spent several hours in cutting grass. I do not want to waste my labour. I can not leave the remaining grass here", the king was thinking like this. As he was wondering what to do, a tiger came up by that way and asked the king, "What I can do to help you?"

The king explained his difficulties to the tiger. The tiger said, "I can carry the grass on my back, if I am rewarded."

"What would you want in reward?" The king asked.

"I would like one of your daughters in marriage", the tiger replied.

The king thought that he had seven daughters and he could give one of his daughters without any problem. He agreed to this deal. The tiger carried the load of surplus grass on his back to the palace of the king. After reaching the palace the king felt ashamed to give away his daughter openly to the tiger. He asked the tiger, "Go and wait near the *jharna* (water spring) in the forest. I will send my daughter to the *jharna*. You can take her away from there."

The tiger agreed to that and went away from there. He patiently waited near the *jharna*. The king called her youngest daughter and said, "Go to the *jharna* in the forest and bring some water from there."

The innocent girl went there and the tiger carried her away. After sometimes the son of the king missed his sister and came to know that his sister had not returned with the water from the *jharna*. He went in search of her and ultimately came to cave in the forest and found the tiger finishing the remains of the girl whom he had killed. The son of the king ran back to the king and said, "My sister has been killed by the tiger."

The king was embarrassed. He said, "I will punish the tiger."

The next day the tiger boldly came to the palace of the king and wanted to see the king. The king's men took him to the king. The tiger said to the king, "The wife given to me has died; hence I want to have another wife."

The king understood that the tiger was very cunning and if he would fulfil his demand he would lose all of his daughters. He thought out of a plan and told the tiger to stop at his palace for the night. The tiger was glad at this proposal and after the dinner he went to sleep on a cosy bed. The king asked his son to boil a few large vessels of water. His son did so. The king and the son poured the scalding water over the sleeping tiger and thus killed him.

[Like any other tribesmen the Santal tribesmen, too, feel nothing odd in their king's going to the forest to cut grass or to collect fuel. The tribesmen believe that there is a close bondage between the forest animals and the human beings. The Santal tribesmen also believe that many of the *bongas* (spirits) can take the form of animals and call on mankind for good or evil purpose].

## THE CLEVER CHICKS

In olden days a jackal and a hen lived like brother and sister. Actually the jackal was very cunning. He was playing a trick for an opportunity to kill and eat the hen. One day both of them prepared liquor and the jackal made the hen overdrunk. Under the spell of intoxication the hen started shaking her head and her chicks started crying. Finally the hen fell down on the earth and slept. The jackal got the chance for which he was waiting so long. He grabbed the hen and ran into the forest. In the forest the jackal ate the flesh of the hen and drank liquor. The chicks of the hen became orphan but they became cautious of the jackal.

Two days after the death of the hen the jackal, with an intention to eat the chicks of the hen, went to them and said, "My nephews, why you all are so sad?"

"Uncle, my mother died two days back", they replied.

The jackal pretending to be sad said to them, "Oh, it is very sad but do not worry. I am always with you."

Before leaving the place the jackal asked the chicks, "By the way where you all are going to sleep tonight?"

"Uncle, tonight we are going to sleep in the hole of the wall", the chicks replied.

"Okay sleep well and take care", the jackal said and went back.

The chicks understood the intention of the jackal. They put knives, spines and sickle in the hole of the wall and slept some where else. In the night the greedy and cunning jackal pounced in the hole of the wall and got his claws injured. In pain he ran away from there. His claws were bleeding profusely.

Next morning the jackal again went to the chicks to know their welfare as well as the place where they were going to sleep that night.

"Uncle it is very cold. To night we will sleep in the ash of the hearth", the chicks said to the jackal.

The chicks put burning coals underneath the ash of the hearth and slept else where. The foolish jackal, searching chicks in the ash of the hearth burnt his claws and stomach badly. In anger and pain he started jumping out. The chicks who were sleeping in the cage were watching every thing. They started laughing at the foolishness of the jackal. In anger the jackal closed the door of the cage and carrying the cage he ran in to the forest.

"Today I am going to eat all of you. You all have harassed me very much. Due to you only I got my claws hurt. I had bled a lot. Now you all have burnt me almost half", the jackal said.

The chicks made a plan jointly and said, "Uncle you can eat us but fulfil our last wish. Do not eat us one by one. It will give much pain to us seeing our brothers dying in front of us. We want to die together. So eat all of us together. Put the cage with a jerk on a stone and kill all of us together."

"Alright, I will fulfil your last wish", the jackal said and dashed the cage on a rock. The jerk made the cage open and all the chicks, except a weakest one, flew away.

"I will eat you", the jackal said after grabbing the weak chick.

"Yes you can but see my wings. They are dirty. First, make me clean after giving me a bath and then eat me", the chick replied. He gave bath to the chick and the chick started shivering in cold. The jackal wanted to make the chick dry. He started blowing the chick with his mouth. The chick's wing dried up and he was able to fly. After a while the chick flew away putting his dung in to the mouth of the jackal.

The cunning and greedy jackal was left regretting.

## A DAY DREAMER

Many years ago a Santal boy was engaged by an oilman to carry oil pots in a basket over his head for fifty paisa as wages. The Santhal boy was carrying the oil pots to the market and the oilman was following him. On the way the Santhal boy began day dreaming. He mused, "For one half of my wages, I will get some chickens. I would rear the chickens and sell both the eggs and chickens at a good profit. With the money thus earned I would buy some goats and go on breeding goats for a year. A large number of goats and kids thus raised will be sold out at a very good profit and then I would go in for some cows. In a year or so I would make again a good business from the cows and sell the whole lot there after buying buffaloes. Having thus amassed plenty of money, I would marry and have children."

And so he went on musing that his wife would come and say, "Darling, come on dinner is ready." He would shake his head, "No, no, not now", and while musing like this he vigorously shook his head and the basket fell on the ground. All the oil was spilled on the ground. The oil man rushed to him and gave him substantial beating, besides wailing his loss.

The Santal boy said in a sad tone, "You have lost only some oil. However, I have lost my chickens, goats, cows, buffaloes, wife and children."

"What do you mean? How did you lose all of them?" The oil man asked in a surprised tone.

The Santal boy described his day dream to the oil man. The oil man had a hearty laugh and he did not have any more complaint against the Santal boy.

## RAMU AND SHAMU

Ramu and Shamu were two brothers. They were very poor and had nothing to eat. One day Ramu said to Shamu, "Let us go to village chief to ask for some grains and some money as loan. We will start our own business and will repay the loan soon."

Shamu agreed to this and both of them went to the village chief. The village chief gave one sac of grains and ten coins to each of them. The brothers were happy. Planning for their future, they were returning home carrying their bag on their back. On the way they came near a river. Ramu said to Shamu, "Wait here for a while, I am coming soon."

In the absence of Ramu, Shamu took some grains from Ramu's sac and put that in his own. Ramu returned soon and both of them started their return journey. When Ramu lifted his sack he found that a bit light in weight. He guessed what would have happened in his absence. He asked Shamu about it and Shamu denied taking out the grains. They started fighting with each other and ultimately Ramu killed Shamu.

Ramu came home and with the money he had received from the village chief, purchased some chickens. After a few months he sold those chickens and eggs and brought goats. He did well in business and after a few years purchased land, cows and bull and became a well to do farmer. Shamu took birth as a he-calf from one of the cows of Ramu. When he grew up as a bull Ramu wanted to plough his field with Shamu the bull. The bull refused to plough the field and Ramu gave beating to that. Shamu the bull said, "In my previous birth I was your brother Shamu. I had stolen grains from your sac and I have taken birth as a bull in your very home."

In anger Ramu killed the bull and buried his head in the field with his horns out of the mud. The horns used to warn people against stealing the crops from the field.

[Thence the Santal tribesmen burry the horn of their dead animal in their respective fields so as to protect their crops from the evil eyes as well as from thieves.]

## SABAI GRASS

Once upon a time there were six brothers who lived with their only sister in a village. The brothers used to spend their days in the forest hunting while the sister managed the domestic chores.

One day while the brothers had gone for hunting the sister went to collect some spinach to cook for the dinner. While she was busy in her work she cut her finger and a few drops of blood fell on the spinach. She cooked the spinach and served to her brothers in the night. The brothers found the dinner very tasty particularly that night. The sister said that a few drops of her blood had fallen on the spinach.

In the night when the sister slept, the brothers talked with one another, "If the blood of our sister can make the spinach so tasty, she herself must be very much tasty so let us kill and eat her."

The brothers conspired to kill their sister the next morning. The youngest brother, Lita, was not willing to do so, but he dared not to oppose them. The next day the brothers told their sister, "Today come with us in the forest. You can pluck beautiful flowers in the forest."

The girl without suspecting any thing foul went with her brothers in the forest. In the forest the brothers made her climb on a tree and then shot her dead with an arrow. They cut the dead body of their sister into pieces and sent Lita, to fetch water from a river. Lita went to the river and by sitting on a branch of a fallen tree started wailing. As he was wailing a large frog came out of the water and said, "Why are you weeping? What is wrong with you?"

"My sister has been killed by my elder brothers and now they are going to cook her", Lita replied.

"Do not worry. Every thing will go Okay", the frog said and gave a big fish to Lita. Lita returned to his brothers with the fish. When his brother told him to cook, he hid the pieces of his sister and cooked the fish. The brothers ate that thinking it was their sister's flesh. When they finished eating they went in the forest for hunting. After covering some distance, Lita said that he had forgotten to bring his arrow and must go back to take that. He went back to the place where he had hidden the pieces of the body of his sister. He joined up the pieces and wept loudly. The forest goddess felt pity on that boy. She gave life to the dead pieces and his sister stood up alive. Lita went to another forest with his sister and both of them lived there.

One day a king hunting in the forest passed by that way and saw the girl. He took her away from the forest and married her. He took Lita with him as well. He married his sister with Lita and gave him half of his kingdom.

The king decided to dig an enormous tank and people came from far and near to work at it. The five elder brothers of the girl, who had become poor, also came there along with others. When their sister saw them she forgave them. Not only this she gave them gold, silver and clothes. However, the brothers were so ashamed and repentant that they could only kneel on the ground and beat the earth with their hands. As they continued to do so the earth opened and swallowed them up. Their hair got stuck out of the ground and became the *Saba*i (ischaemum angustifolium) grass which exists even today.

[*Sabai* grass is an indigenous product of the hill of Santal Pargana. This grass is used for making papers.]

## THE TRICK OF A FATHER

There was an old farmer. He had four sons but all were lazy, dullard and worthless fellows. The farmer couple always remained worried thinking about the future of their sons. One day the famer fell ill and he understood that his end had come. In his last days he called his sons and said, "My dear son I have buried gold in the field. After I am dead dig out the gold and live happily."

The sons were happy thinking their future was secured. They had nothing to do but to lead an easy life with the help of gold. They prayed to god to kill his father so that they can take the gold and enjoy the life. After a few days the farmer died. The sons, though very happy, pretended to be sad. The death rituals of the farmer were performed and his sons were eager to dig out the field.

One morning they all went to the field and dug out the field but found nothing. They dug one by one all the fields but did not find any gold.

"That old man was a liar. He made us fool", they all talked with one another.

"My sons since you have dug the field sow grains there. I have some seeds. Do not let your hard works go in vain", their mother said to them. They all agreed with their mother and did sow the seeds in the field.

After a month they yielded good crops and filled their godown with grains. They stored the grains for their use and sold the surplus. In this way also they earned good money. Now the four young men understood the meaning of their father's saying.

Here after they worked hard, took good care of their mother and lived happily.

## THE ORIGIN OF THE WORLD

In the beginning there was only water. Thakur Jiu (the supreme god) created a few aquatic animals such as crab, crocodile and tortoise and put them into the water. Then he created two dummy human beings, one man and one woman. As he was going to put life into the dummies a horse came from the sun and destroyed the dummies. After this Thakur Jiu, taking his own flesh from near his chest made two birds and put life into them and the birds flew away. However, the birds returned after some time and complained to Thakur Jiu, "We kept moving every where but did not find food and place to take rest."

Thakur Jiu ordered the crocodile, the crab, and the whale to bring up the earth from underneath the water and create a surface. They all failed. At last Thakur Jiu assigned this task to an earthworm.

"I can do it with the help of tortoise", the earthworm said. With the help of tortoise the earthworm brought out the earth. The tortoise stood on the water with his leg chained. The earthworm came down and reached the subsoil with his tail on the back of the tortoise. The earthworm started eating the soil with his mouth and pushed that out from his hind portion. The soil got stuck on the back of the tortoise and in this way the earth was made. Thakur Jiu gave different form to the surface of the earth. There were hills, valleys and the fields on which various trees like the *sal* (shorea robusta), *karam* (adina cordifolia) and *mahua* (bassia latifolia) grew up.

Thakur Jiu separated the earth from the water and asked the birds to build their nest and lay eggs. The birds did so. When the bird hatched her eggs two human beings, one man and another woman, came out. The birds got frightened and went to Thakur Jiu for instruction.

"My god, what should we do know? How can we take care of human children?" The birds asked Thakur Jiu.

Thakur Jiu giving some cotton to the birds said, "Squeeze the juice what you eat and feed the babies with the help of the cotton."

After sometime the children grew up and the birds complained to Thakur Jiu that they could not live on the tree.

"Go and search suitable place for the children and put them there", Thakur Jiu said to the birds. The birds took a round of the earth and found a place called Hihiri Pipiri for the children. Thakur Jiu also found that place suitable for the children. The birds carried their children on their back to Hihiri Pipiri and left them there. They then flew away to unknown place.

Now these two persons were called Pilcu Haram and Pilcu Budhi. They lived in complete peace but without any clothing. Naran Buru, another manifestation wanted to do some mischief with Haram and Budhi. He took the form of an old man, Lita by name. He went to Haram and Budhi and introduced himself to them as their grand father. He prepared a spirituous drink and asked them to drink it. They drank that drink and became drunk. That night they behaved like husband and wife.

The next morning Lita visited them again. Before the arrival of Lita, Haram and Budhi had got up and realized for the first time that they were nude and were ashamed. When Lita asked them to come they replied they could not do so because they were naked. Lita asked them to use the leaves of fig (ficus indica) and clothes themselves. They two did what they were asked to do and Lita disappeared. They two lived as husband and wife and had a number of children. Through them the original seven clans of the Santhal tribe were brought into existence. The place Hihiri Pipiri was too small to accommodate all of them. They started migrating. Similarly at another place a new race of man and women sprang up. They also had to migrate from place to place to find suitable accommodation. This way the world began with man and woman.

## THE DISHONEST OILMAN

There was an oilman in a village. He had fixed up his oil crusher in one of the rooms of his house. One day a man, riding on a mare, was passing the through village of the oilman. The man wanted to take some rest and thus with the permission of the oilman tied his mare in the room where the oilman had fixed his oil crusher.

In the night, the mare gave birth to a baby mare. The oilman came and started dancing and shouting, "My oil crusher has given birth to a baby mare."

The rider was speechless. The behaviour of the oilman had made him nervous. The oilman was not ready to give the baby mare to the rider.

A jackal was passing through the village. When the rider saw the jackal he called him and said, "Brother, help me. Do justice. The oilman is not ready to give baby mare to me."

"No, I do not want to stay here. If I stay here for long, the dogs of village will tear me", the jackal replied in a hurry.

"Oh, do not worry for the dogs. I will take care of them but solve my problem", the rider replied.

The jackal agreed to help him. At first, he heard the saying of each party and then started shouting, "The fishes in the sea are burning. Run fast, the fishes in the sea are burning."

The oil man gave a hearty laugh and said, "You, the king of fools, what are you saying? How can you solve our problem possessing such a foolish mind? How can fishes burn in the sea?"

"If a crusher can give birth to a baby mare, why not a fish can burn in the sea water?" The jackal asked.

The oilman had no answer to this argument. He handed over the baby mare to the rider. The rider gave thanks to the jackal and left the village immediately.

[This story shows the relation between the wild animals and the human beings. Santal tribesmen think jackal is an intelligent animal that can solve any problem. Human being talking with animals and birds attracts the tribesmen very much]

## THE DREAM OF A POTTER

In a village there lived a potter who was a very hard working man, though he was very lean and thin. He used to make earthen pots in one day and go to sell them in the market next day, carrying those pots in his *behangi* (a bamboo-and-string-basket for carrying things on the shoulder). Since he was a weak person, he did not carry more pots at a time.

One day he put more pots in his *behangi*. It was a market day and some festival was in the offing as well. In the process of putting more pots in the *behangi* he got delayed so he was going fast to the market.

On the way he started musing, "Today I have put more pots in my behangi therefore I will earn good money. I will buy salt, spices, and oil for two rupees. For one rupee I will eat *mudhi* (puffed rice) and *jalebi* (Indian sweet meat) and will take for my children and wife as well." His *behangi* was giving the sound of "*Achchha*", "*Achchha*" (good, good) and he was thinking his *behangi* was supporting him.

He continued musing that his children will start fighting with each other to eat more *jalebi* than the other and he would slap one and kick the other. Thinking like this he waved his hand and leg in the air. He removed his hand from his *behangi* and while acting like kicking the child kicked a stone. He fell down and before that his *behangi* slipped down from his shoulder. All his earthen pots were broken and he remained standing regretting at his dream.

[Giving the example of this story, Santal tribesmen never put more loads on any thing. They do not think too much about future.]

## THE GIRL INSIDE A DRUM

Many years ago a village came under a stroke of drought. The villagers were craving for food and water. They moved to another place in search of food. In a family there were six members besides two sisters.

One day the two sisters went towards a forest in search of fruits. The forest was far away from their house but they did not care as they were hungry. In the forest they ate some wild fruits. Since it was night they slept in a cave and next morning they ate the fruits again. They were thirsty and to quench their thirst they made frantic search for the water but did not find any drop of water. The tired sisters sat under the shadow of a tree. The sister saw a heron. The elder sister said to her younger sister, "Wait for me sitting here. I will follow this heron and will find out water. After quenching my thirst I will bring water for you."

The elder sister following the heron went far away and reached near a water stream. She drank water and wanted to take that for her sister. However, it was night and she decided to stay there. Next morning she, taking the water in a leaf made cup, returned to the place where she had left her younger sister.

Her younger sister waited for her elder sister long and when it became night she returned to the same cave where she had spent the last night with her sister. The owner of the cave was a big and old monkey. Previous night that monkey was not in his cave and the sisters were safe but now he had returned. He killed the younger sister and ate her up.

When the elder sister returned to the tree where she had left her younger sister, she found no one there. She thought her sister might have returned home. She also returned home. However, at home she found that her sister had not returned.

Her family members as well as other villagers understood that she was killed by some wild animal. They wanted to take revenge from the animals. The next morning they all went in the forest and killed many animals. That old monkey, who had killed the younger sister, was also killed by an old drummer. The drummer covered his drum with the skin of that old monkey. As soon as he played his drum the younger sister started singing from the drum:

*"Dhin, dhinadhi Didi re,*
*Pani labat, labat kidhar gele re.*
*Ek to budo bandra,*
*Mujhe maari delo re".*

(My elder sister, you had gone to bring water but where did you go. One old monkey killed me).

The drummer became very happy. He thought he would roam around the whole village playing the drum. The girl would sing and he would earn good money.

The next morning he was playing the drum and earning money. When he reached near the house of the girl her family members recognized the voice of the girl.

The elder sister of the girl, her two brothers and parents came out and requested the drummer to play the drum again. The drummer played the drum. The family members of the girl got surprised and understood that there was some mystery with the drum. They requested the drummer to spend the night at their house. The drummer agreed to their request. He was tired so he hanged his drum from a peg and after the dinner, he went to sleep early.

While the drummer was sleeping the elder sister of the girl put some sticky and soggy jaggery on the bed of the drummer. When the drummer turned his sleeping side the jaggery got stuck in the waist cloth of the drummer. Early morning when he woke up and saw his waist cloth, he thought he had passed motion on the bed. Out of shame he left the place without telling any thing to any body. Even he left his drum there and never returned to ask for that. The family members kept the drum in a safe place.

The village had come out from the spell of drought and all were busy in their respective work. All the family members of the girl used to go out for their work in the morning. After their departure the younger sister used to come out of the drum and after performing the house hold chores and taking bath used to go inside the drum. In the evening when the family members returned they used to find their home clean with all the work done. They all were ager to know who was doing it all.

One day one of the brothers of the girl hid himself in the house when others went to work. He got surprised seeing his sister coming out of the drum and doing all the work. In the evening he told every one what he had seen. The next morning, both the brothers hid themselves in the house while others went to work. As usual the younger sister came out of the drum. As soon as she came out, one of the brothers ran towards her and caught her tight on the other hand the second brother threw the drum on the earth and broke that. The younger sister could not enter into the drum and they all lived together happily there after.

[The happy end of the story makes it popular. Santal tribesmen admit that any thing can happen in a story. However, they also claim that if god wants he can make the dead alive. The separation of any one gives much pain to them and if a dead person comes alive they will not ask for anything then.]

## THE GIFT

One day a farmer went to his field with his plough and the bull. Before coming out of his house he tucked the share of his plough in his waist cloth. In the field he started searching for that and got tired.

"Is any one there who had seen the share of my plough?" He shouted.

He received no reply from any one. After some time he shouted again, "I will give my daughter to the person who will tell me where the share of my plough is."

A tiger emerged out o the bush and said, "Dear farmer you have tucked the share of your plough in your waist cloth."

The farmer was happy to have found that. Now the tiger asked for his daughter. Though the farmer was not willing to do so, he had to fulfil his promise. In the worried tone he said to the tiger, "Go and wait near the water stream in the forest. In the evening I will send my daughter to the stream and you can take her away." The tiger agreed to this and went away from there.

In the evening he said to his youngest daughter, "My daughter, your mother is busy doing another work. Take the pot and bring water from the water-stream by going into the forest."

His daughter taking the pot proceeded towards the water-stream to fetch water. His younger brother was playing with bow and arrow out side the home. When he saw his sister going to fetch water he said, "I will also come with you."

Both of them went to the forest. The brother was going ahead of his sister with his bow and arrow in his hand. Near the water stream the tiger was hidden behind the heap of dry leaves. When the brother and the sister reached near the stream a heron came and sat on the heap of dry leaves to catch a frog. The brother said, "Sister, stop for a while. At first, I will kill this heron with my arrow. Then only you can fetch water."

The bother shot at the heron but that flew away and the arrow of the brother pierced the eye of the tiger that was hidden behind the leaves. The tiger jumped out and died.

The sister hugged her brother and said, "Brother, you have saved my life today. What would have happened if you were not with me? At the time of my marriage I will tell my husband to give a healthy bull to you." After fetching water they returned home safe.

Next year the farmer settled the marriage of her daughter. She had not forgotten her promise made to her brother. She sent her message to her in-law's house to give a healthy bull to her brother otherwise she was not going to marry the boy. They happily presented a healthy bull to the brother of the bride and the marriage took place without any interruption. All were happy.

[Even today the Santal tribesmen follow this tradition and present a bull to the brother of the bride given by the family members of the groom. It is considered a good omen for a happy marriage.]

## THE YOUNGER BROTHER

There were seven brothers in a family. The elder six brothers were very cunning. They used to make fun of their younger brother because he was a lame. The elder six brothers divided their parental property among themselves and except a goat they did not give any thing to their younger brother. They argued that their younger brother was a lame and was not able to defend his property against going to wrong hand. They gave the goat to him because that was very dear to him.

The younger brother used to spend his day in working in the field of his elder brothers and evening in playing with his goat. He always remained happy, though he had nothing. His elder brothers were jealous of him. They planned and killed his only friend his goat and gave the skin of the dead goat to him when he returned home in the evening. The sad younger brother went into the forest and climbing on a tree wept loudly. He was not willing to return home and remained on the tree itself thinking about his goat.

In the mid night a group of thieves came there and sitting under the tree started distributing their booty among themselves. The younger brother was in his half sleep. The skin of the goat slipped from his hand and fell on the thieves. Out of fear the thieves ran away leaving their money there. In the morning the younger brother came down and taking all the money, returned home.

His elder brothers saw him with money. They came to him and asked, "Brother, who had given money to you? Where from you got so much of wealth?"

The younger brother replied, "I have sold out the skin of the goat in the city and got money."

The elder brothers again felt jealous of him. This time they burnt his hut and put the ashes in the sac. In the evening when he returned home they gave that sac to him. When the younger brother saw his burnt house he understood every thing. He did not say anything to his brothers and went into the forest. Climbing on a tree he wept bitterly. He had no home to return so he decided to spend his night there. In the middle of that night a group of thieves came there and sitting under the tree started dividing their booty among themselves. The younger brother put down the sac full of ash on the thieves. They ran away from there shouting, "Ghost", "Ghost". In hurry they left their money there.

In the morning the younger brother returned home taking all the money. His elder brothers enquired about the money from him. He said smilingly, "I have sold the ash of my burnt hut in the city and have earned good money."

The elder brothers burnt their huts as well and putting the ashes in the sac went to city to sell that. In the market no one purchased their ashes instead the buyers gave substantial beating to them. They returned to their village. The villagers laughed at them. They handed over every thing to their younger brother and left the village forever.

The younger brother got married with a good girl and lived happily with his wife and children.

## THE CROCODILE AND THE JACKAL

There was a jackal. Daily he used to go to a river to drink water. One day a crocodile caught his leg. The crocodile was not able to open his mouth that's why he started shouting "Hun", "Hun", in pleasure.

The jackal playing a trick said to him, "Why are you telling "Hun", "Hun? Say "Yes" and "Yes". Then only you can eat me."

The crocodile got caught in the game of the jackal and as soon as he opened his mouth to say "Yes" the jackal freed his leg and ran away from there smilingly. In anger the crocodile said to him, "Next time I will teach you a lesson."

"Tomorrow I will graze in the field. Come there. We will meet again", the jackal said to him.

The next day when the jackal was in the field the crocodile reached there. It was cold and the crocodile was shivering.

"How do you remain warm in the cold? How do you protect yourself?" The crocodile asked the jackal.

"I used to sit in the heap of hey", the jackal replied. Both of them sat in the two separate heap of hey. The clever jackal came out secretly and put fire around the heap of hey in which the crocodile was sitting. The crocodile was not able to run fast. He got burnt and died.

The jackal ran away from there.

## THE GIRL REFUSED TO MARRY

Many years ago there lived a boy, who was the patient of elephantiasis. One day the parents of the boy called a middle man who was an expert in searching groom/bride for any one.

"See brother, no one is ready to give his/her daughter in marriage to my son. Please do some thing I will give you enough money if you arrange for the marriage of my son", the parents of the boy said to the middle man.

"Okay, I will do that but you will have to follow my instructions carefully" the middle man said and the family members of the boy agreed for that.

The middle man said to the boy, "Look young man, start making rope of hey when the family members of the girl come to see you. At that time you can easily hide your leg under the heap of hey."

On the selected day the family members of the girl came to see the boy and according to the earlier plan the boy started making rope, hiding his leg in the heap of the hey. In order to free himself from any blame the middle man said to the father of the girl, "See the groom, see the rope and see the leg behind hey."

The girl's father thought that the middle man was saying that the groom was a hard working man and he had immersed himself in work. He could not understand the meaning of the words of the middle man and fixed the marriage.

On the marriage day, the marriage procession came to the bride's house with the groom. The friends of the girl described about the elephantiasis of the groom to the girl. She went to her father and said, "I am not going to marry this boy. Even I do not want to see his face."

The father of the girl said, "It is not right time to refuse the marriage. You will not have to see the face of the groom when he will put vermilion on your head. I will arrange for that. After the marriage you can refuse to live with him."

The girl agreed for it. During marriage, when the time of putting vermilion mark on the head of the girl came, her father put a curtain in between the bridegroom and the bride. Thus, the girl did not see the face of the groom. After the marriage was over the girl refused to go with the boy.

[Among the Santal tribesmen there is a custom to put a curtain in between the bride and the groom at the time when the groom puts vermilion mark on the head of the bride. Due to this custom the tribesmen consider this story as real happening.]

## THE NEW EXORCIST

In a village there lived an old man with his wife. One day the old man was making *pua* (sweet flour cake). The old man was sitting out side the hut with some pebbles. When the old woman put the batter of the flour in the hot oil it used to make the sound of "*chhan*". The old man hearing the sound used to put one pebble separately. After sometime the old woman came out with the cakes and divided those between the two in equal number. When the old man compared the number of the pebbles with the cakes he found the pebbles were more in number. The old woman had preserved some cakes for the next day.

The next morning the old man asked the old woman, "Where have you kept the remaining flour-cakes?"

The old woman got surprised. The old man was not in the kitchen when she was preparing the cakes. "How did the old man come to know that I have kept some cakes for today? May be he is an *ojha* (exorcist)", the old woman thought. Both of them ate the remaining cakes and the old man left for his work. The old woman spread all over the village that her old man was an exorcist.

The next year the village faced a severe famine. The king of the village ordered his minister to call every available *ojha* (exorcist) of the village to his palace. Among the other exorcists the old man, too, was taken to the king by the army men. The king gave warm welcome to all of them and said, "Now you all can take rest. Tomorrow in the morning you will have to tell when it is going to rain here."

All of them went to sleep. The old man thought it would be better to escape from there rather than to lose face in front of every one in the morning. He jumped out of his window and ran towards his hut. It was pitch dark and the old man was not able to see any thing. He fell down into the well of the garden of the palace. In the well two frogs were talking that it was going to rain in the third half of the next day. The old man was happy because now he was able to answer the king correctly.

"Help me, somebody please help me", the old man shouted from the well. The army men heard his alarm for help and pulled him out. He told them a lie that he was walking after the dinner and fell down into the well.

The next morning all the exorcists were called in the court of the king. While all of them were unable to tell when it was going to rain in their village, the old man said, "My king, do not worry for the rain at all. It would rain today in the third half of the day."

It was bright morning and there was no sign of rain. All present there started laughing on the verdict of the old man. The king said, "I will hang you to death, if it will not rain today."

In the afternoon black clouds covered the sky and it rained heavily in the evening. All the ponds, wells and lakes of the village were filled with water. The king, the villagers all were very happy. The king gave lots of money and gifts to the old man and he became a famous exorcist. He lived happily with his wife.

## THE JUDGEMENT

A boy was in love with a girl. The girl loved him too. Many times the girl had said to the boy that they should marry because her father wanted her to marry soon. Though the boy loved the girl, he was not ready for the marriage.

"No, I will not marry you though I love you", the boy said to the girl. The girl was annoyed with the behaviour of the boy. She told about her love to her father because he was searching a groom for her. The parents of the girl went to meet the parents of the boy. The father of the boy gave warm welcome to them. He called his son and asked, "Are you ready to marry the daughter of the man who has come to our house?"

"Father, I love the girl but I will not marry", the boy replied.

"What is this nonsense? You are saying that you love the girl but will not marry her, why?" The father asked him in anger.

"No I will not marry", the boy replied simply.

The family members of the parties decided to have a fight between a cock and a buffalo. They said to the boy, "If the buffalo kills the cock you will have to marry the girl."

The fight took place between the two and the cock striking in the eye of the buffalo killed that. The marriage between the two did not take place. The boy belonged to Tudu clan and the girl to Besara clan.

[Even today the marriage alliance between the two clans of the Santal tribesmen is not permissible at all.]

## THE DECEITFUL RABBIT

Once a man was going to his in-laws' house through a forest. A rabbit was following him. After sometime the rabbit asked the man, "Where are you going?"

"I am going to my in-laws' house", the man replied.

"Where are you going?" The man asked the rabbit.

"I am following you", the rabbit replied.

"Why?" The man asked again.

Pointing towards the image of the man the rabbit said, "Your hands are going to fall. I will take those hands and will eat."

The man laughed and said, "You fool, it will not happen. You can not separate an image from a man and above all you can not eat an image."

The rabbit was much ashamed of his foolishness. After sometime he said again, "Let us play a game. If you will lose I will eat you and if you win you can eat me."

The man agreed.

"Let us climb on a tree. The person who will fall first will be considered defeated", the rabbit said. The man agreed to it and climbed on a strong but dried tree. The rabbit climbed on a green tree. Soon the rabbit got tired. He wanted to play a dishonest game and said that he had told earlier that the person would be considered defeated whose tree would fall first.

The man said, "Rabbit, you are not only fool but dishonest as well. Today I will eat you completely."

That man killed the rabbit and ate that after roasting in fire. He did not bother even to remove the intestine of the rabbit from its body.

[The Santal tribesmen eat the rabbit with its intestine. They even burn the hair of the rabbit and mix that with their food. They believe that if they will throw the hair the rabbit will run fast and they can not hunt that easily.]

## SAUBHAGYA

Saubhagya was the only sister of her four brothers. She was the youngest among them. All the elder brothers of Saubhagya loved her very much. With times all the brothers got married one by one and the family members increased from five to nine. When the sisters-in-law of Saubhagya noticed that their husbands loved their sister more than them they felt jealous. They wanted to take revenge from the girl and teach her a lesson.

One day the four brothers said to their wives, "We are going to another village to earn money. In our absence take good care of Saubhagya."

The sisters-in-law of Saubhagya were happy. They had got an opportunity to teach her a lesson. One day in the morning they gave a pot to Saubhagya which had a hole in the bottom and asked her to fetch water from the near by water stream. Saubhagya went to the stream and cried loudly. A frog came out from the water and asked, "Why are you crying like this?"

"How can I fetch water in a pot which has a hole in the bottom? In the absence of my brothers, my sisters-in-law will beat me", Saubhagya replied.

"Do not cry, I will help you", the frog saying like this jumped into the pot and sat on the hole. Saubhagya fetched water home and poured water in another pot. The frog went back.

Next day the sisters-in-law of Saubhagya ordered her to bring fuel wood from the forest. They did not give her any rope to tie the bundle of the woods. Saubhagya collected the woods and started crying. A snake came to her and asked, "Why are you crying like this?"

"My sisters-in law without giving me rope ordered me to bring the woods? How can I take a bundle to these woods home on my head?" Saubhagya replied.

"Do not cry I will help you", the snake said and coiled around the bundle of wood sticks. Saubhagya carried that bundle home and the snake went back. The sisters-in-law of Saubhagya were getting impatient because she was not giving any chance to them to punish her. All of them then conspired to kill Saubhagya.

One day they all went to the forest with Saubhagya. They made Saubhagya climb on a tree. After putting poisonous and spiny bushes around the tree they all returned home laughing and joking. Saubhagya was unable to come down. She remained on the tree hungry and thirsty. Fourth day her brothers were returning home. While crossing the forest they reached near the tree on which Saubhagya was living. They noticed some thing on the tree. After removing the bushes one of the brothers climbed on the tree. He found his sister on the tree and brought her down. All the brothers gave her water to drink and food to eat.

After sometime Saubhagya narrated to their brothers what had happened with her. The brothers were angry and were in a mood to punish their wives. While they were planning how to punish their wives a prince of neighbouring village came near them chasing a rabbit. When he saw the girl he immediately fell in love with her and wanted to marry her. The elder brothers of the Saubhagya agreed for this marriage. They all returned home. The prince was with them. On reaching home, leaving Saubhagya and the prince out side the home, they all went inside and asked their wives, "Where is our sister?"

Their wives kept mum. They never thought their husbands would return so early. In anger the brothers wanted to cut the heads of their wives with sickle. Saubhagya and the prince stopped them from doing so. Saubhagya requested her brothers to forgive their wives. The sisters-in-law of Saubhagya asked for forgiveness from Saubhagya.

After a month the marriage of Saubhagya was solemnized with the prince and after a week he returned his home with his wife. They all lived happily here after.

## THE DARLING SISTER

Kalbatiya was the darling sister of her six elder brothers. Her brothers used to take good care of their sister. The brothers were hunters and they used to spend their day in the forest. In the evening while taking dinner they used to talk about the forest such as presence of beautiful flowers, water-stream and sweet berries. The talk of the brothers had made Kalbatiya desirous of seeing the beauty of the forest. She also wanted to go to the forest with her brothers but due to fear of wild animals the brothers were not ready to take her with them.

One day Kalbatiya adopted an inflexible attitude to go to forest with her brothers. The brothers had no other choice but to take her with them. They all tied a thread around waist of their sister and the other end the other end of the thread around their own waist. They did so to remain in touch with their sister always. Breaking of the thread meant their sister was in danger.

In the forest Kalbatiya climbed on a tree and started plucking flowers while her brothers got engaged in hunting. The tree on which Kalbatiya had climbed was the abode of a big python. The python swallowed her slowly and the thread broke down. Her brothers understood that Kalbatiya was in danger. They rushed towards her. Near the tree they saw a big python. One of the brothers in anger trampled the head of the snake with a stone and killed that.

"Brothers, I am in the middle of the stomach of the python", Kalbatiya said. The brothers cut open the stomach of the snake with their knives and Kalbatiya came out. She climbing on the tree started singing song:

*"Chhah bhaiyao ki piyari bahena,*
*Uske maje ka keya hai kahena.*
*Ped par baithi hai who rani,*
*Suno suno sab uski kahani".*

(There is no end to the joy of the sister of six brothers. She is sitting on a tree and singing song. Listen every one her story.)

After sometime Kalbatiya said, "Brothers I am thirsty." Her brothers ran here and there in search of water. One of them brought water in a leaf made cup from a water-stream and Kalbatiya quenched her thirst. She again climbed on the tree and started singing song:

*"Chhah bhaiyao ki piyari bahena,*
*Uske maje ka keya hai kahena.*
*Ped par baithi hai who rani,*
*Suno suno sab uski kahani".*

(There is no end to the joy of the sister of six brothers. She is sitting on a tree and singing song. Listen every one her story.)

At some distance from there some wood cutters were cutting wood. They heard the song of Kalbatiya. They came to see who was singing the song. They saw Kalbatiya and were charmed by her beauty. They wanted to take her with them. A good fight took place between the brothers of Kalbatiya and the wood cutters. The wood-cutters were more in number. They killed all the brothers of Kalbatiya and captured her. When they were taking her from there forcefully she requested them, "Do not leave the dead bodies of my brothers lying like this. Please perform their last rituals."

The wood-cutters after collecting wood made six funeral pyres and burnt the dead bodies of the brothers of Kalbatiya. While the pyre was burning Kalbatiya said to wood-cutters, "Look above. Today you will see some more shinning stars in the sky."

When the wood-cutters looked above, Kalbatiya threw sands in the eyes of them and jumping in one of the pyres immolated her. The souls of her brothers were waiting for her. They all were united once again and left for heavenly abode.

## THE CLEVER BOY AND THE BEAR

One day a bear was playing hide and seek game with a chameleon. All of a sudden the bear said to the chameleon, "If you will not arrange for my lunch, I will kill you."

"How can I arrange your lunch at such a short notice? You are my friend and you should not talk like this with me", the chameleon replied.

"I do not know any thing. I will kill you if you do not arrange my lunch", the bear said.

Gnashing in anger the chameleon bit the thigh of the bear and got stuck there. The bear started moaning in pain. A Santal boy was passing from there. The bear called him and said, "Brother, help me. Save me from this chameleon."

"Why should I help you? You will eat me and my goats as well", the boy asked.

"No, I swear, I will not do any harm to you", the bear replied. The boy with a stick, removed the chameleon and the bear after giving thanks to the boy, went away.

In the evening after returning home the boy locked the goats in a room and lying on a cot in the courtyard started eating parched grains. He was tired and so he slept with his parched grains on his bed. In the mid night the bear came to him and started pulling the bed with the boy on that. The boy got up and understood every thing. He started eating the remaining parched grains while making noise "kit", "kit", "kit".

"This sound is coming from where?" The bear asked.

"Do you remember the chameleon? He is with me with his relatives and friends", the boy replied.

The bear had not forgotten the pain due to the biting by the chameleon. He ran away in another forest leaving the boy there. The boy slept again peacefully.

## THE COTTON TREE

There were seven brothers and one sister in a family. The sister was the youngest one. The brothers loved their sister very much. They had fixed her marriage in a well to do family. The in-laws of the girl were kind hearted and the groom was not only kind hearted but was meritorious also.

Before the marriage of the girl took place, the brothers of the girl decided to dig a pond. They dug a deep and broad pond but for want of water. There was very little water at the bottom of the pond and the brothers wanted to see their pond full of water. They all went to an *ojha* (exorcist) and told their problem to him. The *ojha* closed his eyes for a while and said, "If you all sacrifice your sister in the pond that will be filled up with water."

The brothers, thus decided among themselves, "Although our sister is so dear to us, we can not let our labour that we have put in digging the pond, go waste, hence let us kill her." Although the younger brother was hesitating in giving support to his brothers, he could not oppose them. The brothers conspired to kill their sister by befooling her and sending her to the pond.

The next morning the brothers said to their sister, "Sister, we have dug the pond but water is not emerging up sufficiently from the earth. Let us do some thing to please the *bongas* (spirits)."

"Yes brothers, you are right. Let us go and make some sacrifice to please the *bongas* (spirits)", the sister replied. They all went near the pond.

"Sister, you descend inside the pond and bring the available water, whatsoever, up to the brink of the pond. By then we make our cart ready", the brothers assured their sister. As soon as the sister went down to the half of the dried pond, her brothers shot her dead with their arrows. The pond was filled with water and the dead body of the sister went underneath the water. The brothers returned home; but for the younger brother all were happy. They did not tell any thing to the villagers about the absence of their sister. The marriage of the girl was scheduled to be solemnized after a week only.

After a week, on the selected day, the marriage procession came to the house of the brothers. They told them, "Our sister has gone into the forest to bring fuel." The groom and his party waited for the girl for long. In the evening, the brothers said to the groom, "It seems our sister has been killed by some wild animals. You better please return home."

The groom and his party started their return journey with heavy heart. On their way home they reached near the same pond which was dug by the brothers of the girl. They saw a beautiful lotus flower in the pond. They all wanted to pluck that but failed. At last when the groom went to pluck that, the flower automatically came into his hand. The groom kept that flower in the empty palanquin which was meant for his bride. When the bearer lifted the palanquin, they found that heavier. They then peeped into the palanquin to find that the bride was sitting there in. They all became happy and returned home singing and dancing. The brothers of the girl did not know that their sister was alive.

After a year the brothers of the girl faced many adversities and became poor. They had to take to begging. While begging, they reached the same village where their sister was living and thus they reached her home. The girl recognized them and started crying. Her in-laws wanted to know the reason for her crying. She said, "The seven men standing begging outside the home are not the beggars but are my brothers themselves."

Her in-laws called them inside. They gave them oil, warm water and new clothes to take bath. After that they were given food to eat. When they finished eating their sister appeared before them. Seeing their sister, they all bowed their head out of shame. They started crying and beating the earth with their hands. As they continued to do so the earth opened and swallowed them up. The sister tried to save them and in this process the soft and silky hair of the younger brother got stuck on the earth and in course of time, they grew up as cotton trees.

## KARMA AND BALMA

Karma and Balma were two brothers. One day they had gone into the forest to collect some edibles. They spent whole day in collecting sweet tubers, and it was night when they started their return journey. In dark cold night they lost their way in that dense forest. When they were wondering what to do, Karma saw a bonfire.

"Let us go there and warm up our body in the bonfire", Karma said to Balma. Balma agreed to it and they went near the bonfire. There they found that the bonfire was burnt by a tiger who was warming his body sitting there. Although scared they went near the tiger and asked, "*Mama* (maternal uncle), can we sit here?"

"What will you give for sitting near my bonfire?" The tiger asked.

"We will give you roasted birds", they replied. In fact they had told a lie to the tiger as they had no birds but only sweet tubers. The tiger allowed them to sit there. While the brothers started eating sweet tubers they gave burnt coal of bonfire to the tiger to eat. The mouth of the tiger got burnt but he thought that when the human could eat such birds why not he.

After the dinner they all wanted to sleep. The tiger slept in his den while Karma and Balma slept at the opening of the den because it was warm there due to the bonfire. The tiger had planned to kill the two brothers in their sleep and enjoy their flesh. In order to know whether the brothers were there or had left the place the tiger played a trick. He kept his tail rolling over the bodies of the brothers from time to time. Karma and Balma knew of it and so they, pulling the tail with a jerk, uprooted that. In pain the tiger ran away from there. The brothers roasted the tail and ate that as well.

"Brother, I am going to kill the tiger. I have found his tail very tasty and I want to enjoy the whole tiger", Karma said to Balma. In the morning they followed the drops of the blood of the tiger and found that the tiger was hiding behind a bush. They overpowered the tiger and returned home pulling the tiger on the ground. When they came out of the forest Balma said to Karma, "Brother, the tiger is still alive. The children of the village will get scared. Let us kill it by hammering its head with stone."

"Yes, you are right. We should kill it first", Karma said. Both of them went to bring stone and the tiger got an opportunity to run away from there. When Karma and Balma returned they did not find the tiger there. Once again they went into the forest in search out the tiger.

In the forest the frightened tiger told every animal, "Two hunters have arrived in the forest. They are very brave and intelligent as well. Look at me. What they have done to me." All the animals wanted to see Karma and Balma. They also wanted to teach them a lesson.

In the forest Karma and Balma were roaming in search of the wounded tiger. Karma said to Balma, "Brother let us climb on the tree and see where the tiger has gone." The brothers climbed on a tree. Meanwhile, all the animals also came near the tree searching Karma and Balma. The tiger saw the images of Karma and Balma falling on the water of the pond. He said to other animals, "Look every one. Here are the two brothers."

They all jumped into the water but found nothing. In anger and anguish the tiger started growling keeping his head up. He saw the two brothers sitting on the tree and informed all the animals about it. The animals wanted to reach near Karma and Balma. They climbed one above the other; the tiger was on the top. When the tiger wanted to grab the two brothers Karma cut open the stomach of the tiger with his knife. The tiger was tied and all the animals ran away from there. Karma and Balma came down and cut the tiger into pieces. After roasting the pieces of the tiger they enjoyed eating that. It was night. They decided to spend night in the forest and climbed on the tree. Karma took the intestine of the tiger with him whereas Balma took the remaining pieces of the tiger duly wrapped in a big leaf and tied that with grass made rope.

In the night the prince of the neighbouring village came near the tree with his four friends. They were going to attend the marriage of one of the relatives of the prince. The price and his friends wanted to spend night there and slept under the tree. When it was about to be dawn, Karma put down the intestine of the tiger on the prince.

"The stomach of the prince ruptured and he died", the friends of the prince started shouting and ran away from there.

"No, I am okay and alive", the prince shouted and followed his friends. They all left their belongings under the tree. Karma and Balma collected all the coins, clothes, ornaments and sweets. They made a bundle of all the things and carrying that bundle on their back moved towards home. Karma also took a drum which was open from one side. On the way Karma saw a beehive. He put all the bees in the drum and Balma took the honey. The brothers were happy. They had lots of edibles, besides clothes, coins and ornaments with them. They came near a well and wanted to take some rest there. While they were taking rest a girl came there to fetch water. Seeing the brothers she said, "Do not waste your time in taking rest and run away from here as soon as possible. Soon a demon will come here and he will make both of you his slaves. I am a princess but he has made me his slave and does not allow me to go home. He follows me every where. My family members think that I am dead."

The girl was right. The demon came there soon. Karma threw bees towards the demon and the bees started biting him. Meanwhile, the princess burnt a wood and pierced that into the eyes of the demon. Balma cut the nose and ears of the demon. This way they all joined to kill the demon. Karma and Balma took the princess her home. Her family members were very happy to see her alive. The princess narrated about Karma and Balma to her parents as to how the two brothers had saved her from the demon. They were impressed with the bravery of the brothers. They gave their daughter to the brothers in marriage. Karma and Balma returned home with the princess. They all lived happily hereafter.

[In this story two brothers married a girl and this indicates the validity of the polyandrous system among them. However, these days the system of polyandry is not prevalent among the Santal tribesmen.]

## THE SPEAKING BED

Kunja was a lazy and malingerer boy. He was just like a cat that loved fish but feared to wet her paws. He used to spend his day in flying kites and playing with the children of the village. His elder brother had tried to make him understand his responsibility many a time. He had told him to earn because he was not a kid but a grown up boy Kunja had not taken the advice of his elder brother seriously.

One day the elder brother of Kunja said to his wife, "Today do not give food to Kunja. When he will ask for food, send him to earn first."

In the evening when Kunja returned home and asked for food from his *Bhabhi* (elder brother's wife), she refused to give him food. Kunja started shouting at her. At last she gave him food. By that time the elder brother of Kunja returned home and did not let Kunja finish his dinner and scolded him badly. Sad Kunja left home and went to another village. A farmer gave shelter to Kunja there hence he started living there. The farmer had one daughter. No one was ready to marry the daughter of the farmer due to the reason not known. Kunja agreed to marry her and the farmer solemnized their marriage. After getting married Kunja thought it was his right to stay in the farmer's house. He became lazier and spent his day in eating and sleeping.

The farmer wanted to teach him a lesson. He gave him an axe and said, "*Beta* (son), go some where else and earn for yourself and your wife."

Kunja and his wife went to a forest, made a hut and started living there. One day the wife of Kunja said, "Cut some wood. We will make furniture and will sell that furniture in the village."

The couple started making furniture and selling those in the village. Soon Kunja became expert in his work. One day when he was cutting wood in the forest he found two trees talking with each other. He, by way of cutting wood from the talking trees made a beautiful sleeping cot and presented that to the king of the village. The king paid him handsomely for that.

In the night when the king was sleeping on the bed the two legs of the bed started talking. The king got alert and started listening to their talk carefully. The first leg said, "Today I had gone to the department of the queen. I found every one enjoying, singing and dancing there."

"I had also gone to queen's apartment today but what I saw there is more serious", the second leg said.

"What had you seen there?" The first leg asked.

"The queen is in love with the minister of the king. I found both talking and the minster conspiring to kill the king. He was asking the queen to help him and when the queen refused he slapped on her cheek. The fingers' print of the minister is still there on the cheek of the queen", the second leg said.

The king heard every thing and went to queen's room to find out the truth. The queen was sleeping. Her cheek was red and the fingers' print was present on her cheek. The king understood that the words of the second leg were true. He ordered his men to kill the queen as well as the minister.

The next morning he called Kunja and gave him half of his kingdom besides his only daughter in marriage. Thus Kunja became the ruler of the half of the village. He called his first wife from the forest and lived happily with both the wives ruling over the whole village after the death of the king.

[This story indicates towards the system of polygamy which is not very common among the Santhal tribesmen.]

## THE SAL TREE

A Santal youth used to graze cattle of a rich man. One day in the evening when he was returning home he noticed that one of the calves was missing. Afraid of being scolded by his master he went into the forest in search of that calf. When he failed in finding out the calf he decided to spend the night in the forest and climbed on a tree. He was having his bow and arrows with him. He was not aware that the tree on which he had climbed was the abode of spirits.

In mid night many women from the nearby villages came and assembled near the tree. They were not simple women but were the witches. Chanting some spells they called the spirits, one tiger and one tigress. They all started dancing and after some time the women called some more spirits to appear before them. The witches and the spirits were dancing while the tiger and the tigress were the observers. The Santal youth was very much scared of the scene. Since the tiger and the tigress were sitting idle the man thought to kill them and shot his arrows on them. The tiger died after some roaring, but the tigress attacked the women witches thinking that it was because of the jealousy of these women and through their conspiracy that her mate had been killed. The tigress took revenge by killing all of them and died after a short while. Her roaring was so terrible that cows and calves rushed to the village for safety and the villagers, too, could not sleep. The boy came down from the tree in the morning and went back to village.

After coming home he saw the missing calf present in the cattle shed. He took a breath of relief. When his master saw him he shouted in anger, "Where were you in the night?"

The youth replied that he spent the night in the forest. Although the master was angry, he too was worried. His wife was missing after dinner last night and the baby of the master was crying for his mother. The youth understood the situation. The one of the women killed last night as a witch was the wife of his master. He felt pity for his master. He went close to his master and said, "I can tell about your wife, who was not a simple woman but a witch. But before I do that, you should promise me that henceforth you will not scold me on flimsy ground for minor faults."

The master became angry and started shouting, "How dare you call my wife a witch?" He wanted to hit the youth who in a loud voice of protest said, "I pity you, I pity on you. Your wife was a witch. She is dead and her dead body is lying in the forest."

Meanwhile the other people also gathered there and the youth told the whole story in front of them. Then it was revealed that a few other women of the same village as well as of other villages were also missing since last night. The boy took them all with him to the forest where the women as well as the tiger and the tigress were lying dead. The villagers were convinced that the women were witches. The bodies were burnt to ashes. After that the villagers planted a *sal* (shorea robusta) tree on the ashes. Within a year the tree became grown up and it was full of flowers.

[The *sal* tree with flowers represents the victory over the devil. The Santal tribesmen like to tuck the flowers in the locks of their hair.]

## THE BANANA TREE

Once upon a time there lived a king in a village. The king was a very unfortunate man. He had no child and his wife was in love with a black cobra before she got married to the king. Even after the marriage she used to visit that black cobra.

One day the king came to know about the black cobra. Pretending to be going to the forest to hunt, the king went near the black cobra and concealed himself behind the bush. After some time the queen came there and started talking with the black cobra. The king shot an arrow at the black cobra and killed that on the spot. The queen's heart was overwhelmed with sorrow. Immediately there after a supreme command was given to the queen, "Bury my head in front of the entrance of your palace."

The queen brought the head of the black cobra and buried that in front of the entrance of the palace. After a few days a tree sprouted on that spot. The queen was the only person who could recognise what the plant was of.

After the death of the black cobra there was always a dispute and conflict between the king and the queen. The queen always tried to defeat the king in arguments by asking him questions. One day the queen asked the king to tell the name of the plant present at the entrance of the palace. The king tried much, but could not give the answer. The question was asked with a condition that any boy who failed to answer the same would be killed with an arrow. The king had failed to answer to the queen and that arrangement was made for piercing arrows into his body by the people of the village. The king called all his relatives for the last meeting before he was dead.

The house of the younger sister of the king was quite far away and on the other side of a dense forest. For coming to meet the king she would have to cross the forest. In the forest she was taking rest with her children under a tree. She heard a female vulture on the tree speaking to her children. The vulture was saying, "My babies, tomorrow you all will have to fly away from your nest in search of food."

"Why tomorrow?" The children asked their mother.

The mother answered, "Tomorrow when the king would be killed, I would get some human flesh. We have a tradition that after giving human flesh to babies of the vulture, they have to move away from their nest, in search of their own food."

The baby vultures asked their mother, "Why is the king to be killed?"

The mother said, "There is a tree in front the entrance of the palace of the king. The queen had asked the name of the plant to the king the king could not answer. For this reason the king is going to be killed."

The baby vultures asked again, "What is the name of the plant?"

"The plant is a black cobra that was killed by the king", the mother vulture replied.

After hearing these conversations between the mother vulture and her babies, the younger sister of the king ran towards the palace. At the palace of the king not only the Santhal tribesmen but Munda and Ho were also ready to pierce the body of the king with their arrows. The sister of the king after reaching there secretly told the name of the plant to her brother. As a result finally the king succeeded in answering the queen. Now it was the turn of the queen to be killed with the bow and arrows.

Every one was waiting anxiously. The queen was made to stand at an open space near the palace. As the time came to releasing the arrows the body of the queen suddenly disappeared and the plant existing at the entrance of the palace appeared there. The arrows got stuck on the plant.

[The plant was known by every body and it was called as *kaira*. In the language of Santal the fruit banana is called *kaira*. The tree present at the entrance of the palace of the king was a tree of banana. It is believed that this incident had happened on the next day of *Makar Sankranti* (a festival celebrated by Indian community in January). The Santhal tribesmen practise the piercing of banana tree on the next day of *Makar Sankranti* with great enthusiasm.]

## THE CUNNING JACKAL

In a forest there lived a jackal. He was very clever and cunning as well. Giving trouble to another animal and then to laugh at him was his habit. All the animals of the forest were looking for a proper opportunity to teach him a lesson but he was so clever that he did not give them any chance to do so.

One day while roaming near the bank of the river he saw a boat of the local king on the river. He wanted to do some boating in the river but thought that he would enjoy the boating if he had some company. He saw a crane in the water that was looking for the fish. The jackal threw a piece of wood towards him and shouted loudly, "Fish."

The crane immediately caught that piece. The jackal started laughing at him and said, "I was joking with you but now I am serious. I know about a place in this river where you can find lots of fish. If you are ready to come with me I can take you there."

The crane was well aware of the mischievous behaviour of the jackal. He said, "No! I will not go with you. May be it is your trick. You will put me in trouble and will laugh afterwards."

The jackal replied, "I am serious. There is a boat in the river. Do not waste time. Come with me. I will take you there."

The crane agreed and went with the jackal. After some time of boating the jackal slept and the crane kept asking the place he had promised to take him for the fish. The jackal was enjoying the restlessness of the crane and smiling. The crane understood that the crane had made him fool. With his strong beak he made a hole in the boat and flew away to the bank of the river. Water started filling the boat and now it was the time for the jackal to get nervous. He cried and asked for help but no one was there to help him. The jackal jumped into the water and started trying to return to the bank.

A crocodile was passing through there. When he saw the jackal he said, "I am hungry. I will eat you first."

The jackal was clever. He said, "I am thin. You can not enjoy eating me. However, I have killed an elephant a few hours before. If you will take me to the bank of the river by making me sit on your back, I will take you near the elephant."

The crocodile agreed and the jackal sitting on his back safely reached the bank. He said to Crocodile, "You stay her. I am going to bring water. Then we both will go to elephant and eat him."

The jackal had not killed any elephant. He had made the crocodile fool, only to reach safely on the bank. He did not go to bring water but hiding himself behind a tree started watching the activity of the crocodile. When he noticed that the crocodile was sleeping he brought a creeper and tied him with a tree. The crocodile asked, "What are you doing? Why you are tying me?"

The jackal laughed and said, "You were a fool who trusted me and helped me. Now I am going to kill you."

The crocodile requested him not to do so but the jackal kept beating him till he was dead. He thought, "I can not eat all the flesh at a time. I have arranged for my one week's meal. It would be better to hide the dead crocodile at a safe place."

When he was trying to hide the crocodile, one tiger jumped at him and said, "Today I am going to eat you."

The clever jackal quickly thought out the idea to make him free from the clutches of the tiger. He said, "I am thin. You can not fill your stomach by eating me. However, if you eat this crocodile it would be sufficient for you. If you will bring some water I will boil the flesh of this crocodile and then it would be easy for you to eat it."

The tiger agreed and said, "If you make me fool, the consequence would be very bad. I am going to bring water, till then arrange for boiling the crocodile."

When the tiger went to bring water the jackal hid the crocodile in a ditch and covered that with dry leaves. After that he climbed on a tree. When the tiger returned he searched for the jackal.

The jackal started laughing loudly and said, "You foolish old tiger, why should I give my prey to you? Do you think I am stupid? You are a fool who trusted me and left me free."

The crane was also sitting on the tree. Seeing him the jackal said, "How did you like the fish my dear friend? You all are idiots. You can not do anything to me."

The angry crane attacked on the tree and caught him in his claws. The tiger started shaking the tree. The jackal was not ready for this attack. He fell down on the ground and the crane did not let him run from there.

The jackal began to cry and beg for forgiveness but the crane did not leave him. The tiger slapped him so badly that one of his eyes and all the teeth came out.

The tiger said, "I am not going to kill you, but here after you will not try to make any one fool."

The jackal left the place and after that no one ever saw him again in the forest.

# 8 Nature and Forms of the Folktales

The folktales may vary from tribe to tribe, the condition and purpose of telling tales may change from land to land, yet everywhere it ministers to the same basic need that is entertainment. Tribal people with very limited resources of other forms of entertainment in their area such as television, computer, movie-theatre and so on find telling stories as one of the most satisfying pastimes. Like in any other non-tribal society, in tribal society too, children, men and women gather around the person who tells stories. They satisfy their eagerness and needs for information or amusement, for incitement to heroic deeds, for religious edification or for release from the overpowering monotony of their lives through hearing various types of stories.

The folktales collected from all the tribes have been grouped into three categories and are presented in Table 8.1. This categorization has been done on the basis of their structure which helps us in understanding the popular trend of tales in tribal societies.

**Table 8.1**

**Structural Classification of the Folktales (in number)**

| No. | Structure | Bhil | Barela | Korku | Munda | Oraon | Santal | Total |
|---|---|---|---|---|---|---|---|---|
| 1. | Myth/Legend/Origin | 14 | 2 | - | 6 | 2 | 9 | 33 |
| 2. | Ordinary/Joke/Formula | 14 | 18 | 17 | 16 | 17 | 14 | 96 |
| 3. | Animal Tales | – | 3 | 1 | 3 | 5 | 3 | 15 |
| 4. | Total | 28 | 23 | 18 | 25 | 24 | 26 | 144 |

The ordinary formula and humorous tales are very popular among the tribal people. It makes them laugh and forget about the miseries of their life for a moment. Curiosity to know about the past brings eager listeners to the tales which deals with the history of their folk hero. Legends grow with the telling, and often a great heroic past evolves to gratify vanity and tribal pride. The elder people feel elevated by telling stories of their ancestors to their younger generation. Religion also plays a mighty role in the society of every tribe in the encouragement of the narrative art.

Tribal people live very close to forest and the wild animals. Animals play a large role in many of their folktales. In their stories animals think and act like humans. Such tales are usually designed to show the cleverness of one animal and the stupidity of another. Animal tales full of humour are liked by tribal people especially by their children very much hence are popular in their community. When animal tale is told with an acknowledged moral, it becomes a fable. Senior story teller tells animal story with a moral to their children not only to entertain them but to educate them with certain values as well. Children like the stories of talking animals and birds especially when they solve problems of human beings or become friends of any boy or girl.

Anthropologists (Kluckhohn 1965) suggest that five themes occur in the folktales of all the societies: catastrophe, generally through flood; the slaying of monsters; incest; sibling rivalry, generally between brothers; and castration, some times actual but more common symbolic. In tribal society also, we find the story of catastrophe through flood, the slaying of monsters, and the sibling rivalry.

After examining all the folktales of the six tribes we find that irrespective of varieties and local peculiarities the primary features of most of the folktales often coincide and share a common pattern. The general motifs extracted from all the folktales are given in the Table 8.2.

**Table 8.2**

**Motif Behind the Folktales (in number)**

| No. | Motif | Bhil | Barela | Korku | Munda | Oraon | Santal | Total |
|---|---|---|---|---|---|---|---|---|
| 1 | 2 | 3 | 4 | 5 | 6 | 7 | 8 | 9 |
| 1. | Animals perform the task of man | 2 | 2 | 1 | 3 | 1 | 1 | 10 |
| 2. | Be honest giving moral | – | 3 | 4 | – | 2 | 1 | 10 |
| 3. | Abandoned in forest | 2 | 2 | – | – | – | – | 4 |
| 4. | Cruel stepmother | 1 | 2 | – | 1 | – | – | 4 |
| 5. | Cruel sister-in-law | – | 1 | – | – | – | 1 | 2 |
| 6. | Getting something by luck | – | – | 1 | 2 | – | 1 | 4 |
| 7. | Secret overheard by animal/bird | – | – | 1 | 2 | – | 2 | 5 |
| 8. | Ordinary boy marries princess | 1 | 3 | – | 1 | 3 | – | 8 |

*(Contd...)*

| 1 | 2 | 3 | 4 | 5 | 6 | 7 | 8 | 9 |
|---|---|---|---|---|---|---|---|---|
| 9. | Ordinary girl marries prince | 2 | – | – | – | 1 | 1 | 4 |
| 10. | Reincarnation in plant/tree growing from grave | – | | – | – | – | 4 | 4 |
| 11. | Showing smartness by stealing goods or making others fool | 4 | 2 | 1 | 1 | – | 3 | 11 |
| 12. | Man or woman defeats or kills demon | – | 3 | 1 | – | – | 1 | 5 |
| 13. | Only for fun | – | 5 | – | 1 | 5 | 1 | 12 |
| 14. | Darling sister | – | – | – | 1 | – | 1 | 2 |
| 15. | Tribal and non-tribal contact | 7 | – | – | – | – | – | 7 |
| 16. | Knowledge of animal's/bird's language | 8 | 3 | 1 | 7 | 3 | 5 | 27 |
| 17. | Animals grateful to rescuer | – | – | 1 | 3 | – | – | 4 |
| 18. | Magical object (ring, doll, beds) | 1 | – | 1 | – | – | 1 | 3 |
| 19. | An imposter takes wife's/husband's place | – | – | 1 | 1 | – | – | 2 |
| 20. | Selected by an elephant | 1 | – | 1 | 1 | – | – | 3 |
| 21. | In answer to prayer | 2 | 1 | 2 | 1 | – | – | 6 |
| 22. | Flying cot | 1 | 2 | 1 | – | – | – | 4 |
| 23. | Princess married to boy who cured her | 1 | 1 | 1 | – | – | – | 3 |
| 24. | Task assigned to get rid of hero or to choose brave man | 2 | 1 | 3 | 2 | 1 | – | 9 |
| 25. | Origin Story land/plough/tree | 2 | 1 | – | 2 | 1 | 1 | 7 |
| 26. | Clever wife/daughter | 3 | – | 1 | – | – | – | 4 |
| 27. | Helpful birds/animals | 2 | 3 | 2 | 3 | 3 | 3 | 16 |
| 28. | Animals win wives | 1 | – | – | – | 1 | 1 | 3 |
| 29. | Recognize by hearing life history | – | 1 | – | – | – | – | 1 |
| 30. | Victorious younger son | – | 1 | 1 | – | 1 | 2 | 5 |

*(Contd…)*

| 1 | 2 | 3 | 4 | 5 | 6 | 7 | 8 | 9 |
|---|---|---|---|---|---|---|---|---|
| 31. | Angry king punished younger daughter | 1 | – | 1 | – | – | 1 | 3 |
| 32. | Taking revenge | 3 | 1 | – | – | 1 | 1 | 6 |
| 33. | Conception by eating fruits | 1 | – | 1 | 1 | – | – | 3 |
| 34. | Dead person comes alive | – | – | – | – | 1 | 1 | 2 |
| 35. | Flood/drought | 2 | – | – | – | – | 1 | 3 |
| 36. | To celebrate rituals | 2 | 2 | 1 | 5 | 4 | 7 | 21 |
| 37. | To celebrate festivals | 4 | – | – | 2 | 2 | – | 8 |
| 38. | Woman turns witches | 2 | – | – | 1 | – | 1 | 4 |
| 39. | Man turns ogre | – | – | – | 1 | 1 | – | 2 |
| 40. | Morals by animal tales | – | – | – | 1 | 1 | – | 2 |
| 41. | Revenge by fun | – | 5 | – | – | – | 1 | 6 |
| 42. | Animal/bird gives birth to human child/god/goddess | 3 | – | – | – | 1 | – | 4 |
| 43. | Human gives birth to animal/bird | 1 | 1 | – | – | 1 | – | 3 |
| 44. | Importance of good company | 1 | 1 | – | 1 | – | – | 3 |
| 45. | Day dreamer | – | – | – | – | – | 2 | 2 |
| 46. | Gushing up of milk in mother's breast | – | 1 | – | 1 | – | – | 2 |

Stories about the origin of man, growing of some plants, animal stories about the supposed cleverness of jackal and monkey, the mischief of crow and chicks, helpful parrot, stupid tortoise and royal magnanimity of the tiger are found in the folktales of every tribe. The life of a single sister among her seven brothers, the jealousy of brothers, the cruelty of step mother, the wickedness of ogre and witches, the simplicity of the poor villager, the ultimate triumph of goodness and virtue, happiness after all the trials are some of the basic common features of folktales of tribal people. In fact these features are not only common in tribal folktales but in the folk stories of non-tribal people as well (Chaudhary 1994). Not only this, folktales also include warnings to rulers such as a simple villager can kill a king in disguise, a rat or rabbit defeats a tiger. Such stories help preserve tradition and avoid certain taboos. In every tribe there are folktales behind the celebration of certain rituals and festivals. Such tales said during festival times or before celebrating any ritual give solid base of justification for there celebration and enhance community feeling (Lourdusamy and Sahay 1996, Sahay 2010).

In India the people of dominant culture believe that god, the guardian of cosmos takes care of every individual. God, *sadhu* (saint man), or even animal comes to rescue the people from sufferings and punish the wicked. These stories generate a sense of hope in the life of poor man (Sahay 2005). In tribal society as well, we find such stories where either *sadhu* or animal or even god comes to rescue people in pain. It seems that the limitations of human life and the similarity of its basic situations necessarily produce tales everywhere which are much alike in all important structural respects.

The similarities between the different elements of the folktales of different regions were first noticed by Tylor (1871) and Lang (1974), the theorists of cultural evolution. They developed a theory for explaining these characteristics, known as parallelism, arguing that several cultural elements evolve in parallel and almost simultaneously in different societies. The universal human psyche transcending the limits of time and geographical boundaries forms the most logical basis for explaining such similarities in the folktales of different regions. The essence of the universal psychic unity lies in a similar human to his surroundings under similar socio-cultural conditions. On the other hand the anthropologists (Boas 1881, Frazer 1922, Benedict 1935) also argue that the transmission of folktale incidents from tribe to contiguous tribe took place by diffusion at points of cultural contact.

Some of the basic features of the tribal folktales which make those stories different from the folktales of non-tribal people are related with their socio-economic and cultural condition. Tribal people even after working hard live in economic hardship. They find the marriage with any rich person as one of the easiest ways of coming out of their misery. Marriage of a poor girl with a prince or a poor boy with a princess is one of the common features of their folktales. Some of their stories reveal that they think they are very clever. They think that with their cleverness and power they can control and influence the wild animals and can make any one fool specially the non-tribal people. Perhaps their suffering at the hand of non-tribal people in the past has influenced their folktales. They satisfy their emotions by doing such things in their tales which they could not do in reality.

In tribal folktales we do not find a king in a chariot and the queen resting on a luxurious bed. Their king works in field and queen goes to collect fuels in forest. In general their stories are more about poor villagers, the forest, wild animals and even about ogre and witches.

In their mythological tales the gods and goddesses, even if immortal, are not thought of having existed. Stories are told about their origin, birth, and family relations. Myths dealing with the origin of animals and of mankind are often intimately connected. It is especially found in connection with the system totems in which particular animals and plants are regarded as ancestors.

We need people from different background such as literary critics, anthropologists, historians, psychologists, and aestheticians if we try to find out why folktales are made or invented, what art is used in their telling, and how they grow and change. After going through all the folk tales collected we find that the primary motif of each folktale is emotional healing of the story teller as well as the audience and it is the emotional healing which is responsible for the creation and propagation of the folktales. The forefathers of Bhil tribesmen had suffered badly due to severe drought in their area. If in their folktales the Bhil tribesmen harass Megh Raja (King/God of clouds) responsible for rain they feel happy. Similarly poultry is one of the important methods of livelihood for the tribal people. Jackal and fox, the enemy of chicken create problem for them by stealing their chicken. Many of their folktales deal with the subject of how they had fooled the jackal or the fox. Such stories which are full of entertainments satisfy their emotions too.

Thus, we find folktales like other genres of folklore of any society; reflect emotions, needs, conflicts and other aspects of human psyche that people acquire as a result of growing up in a specific culture. Folktales are probably the most crystallised and apt expression of human thoughts. The study of folktales prevalent in a society helps understand the common universal elements on one hand and certain characteristic traits specific to that society on the other.

# Bibliography


Anderson, G. (2001). *A New Classification of South Munda: Evidence from Comparative Verb Morphology, Indian Linguistic, 62*. Poona: Linguistic Society of India.

Anderson, J.D. (1895). *Kachari Folktales and Rhymes*. Assam: Secretariate Printing Office.

Archer, W.G., & Soren, G.S. (1943). Dasar Hat. In D. Seren & H.S. Reak (Eds.), *Bena Gariars*. New Delhi: The Mission Press.

Aurora, G.S. (1972). *Tribe, Caste, Class Encounters*. Hyderabad.

Avari, G.J. (1957). *Adivasinchin Lokgeetan*. Nasik: Sarvodya Kendra.

Babulkar, M. (1964). *Garwali Lok-Sahitya ke Bibechanatmak Adhyayan*. Prayag: Hindi Sahitya Sammelan.

Bannerman, H.D. (1902). *The Rajputana Gazetter*. Calcutta

Bascon, W. (1955). Verbal Art. *Journal of American Folklore, 68*, 245-252.

Benedict, R. (1935). *Zuni Mythology*. Columbia: Columbia University.

Bhandari, N.S. (1946). *Snowbalss of Garhwal*. Lucknow: Universal Publishers.

Bhatt, H.D. (1962). Folksongs of Garwal. *Folklore, 12*(3).

Bhowmik, P.K. (1957). Lodhas and their Folksongs. *Vanyajati, 4*.

Boas, F. (1981). Dissemination of Tales among the Natives of North America. *Journal of American Folklore, 4*, 13-22.

Bodding, P.O. (1925). *Santhal Folktales 3 volumes*. Hass: Oslo and Cambridge.

Bompass, C.H. (1909). *Folklore of the Santhal Parganas*. London: David Nutt.

Brahma, M.M. (1960). *Folksongs of Bodos*. Guahati: Publication Department

Campbell, A. (1891). *Santhal Folktales*. Orissa: Mission Press.

Chakrabarti, B. (1994). *A Comparative Study of Santhali and Bengali*. Calcutta: K.P. Bagchi.

Chettiar, S.M.L.L. (1973). *Folklore of Tamil Nadu*. New Delhi.

Cole, F.T. (1875). Santhal Folklore. *Indian Antiquary, 4.*

Crooke, W. (1909). Under Bhils II *Encyclopedia of Religion and Ethics*. Edinburgh.

Dalton, E.T. (1872). *Descriptive Ethnology of Bengal*. Calcutta: Government Printing Press.

Damant, G.H. (1875). The Two Brothers of Manipur. *Indian Antiquary, 4.*

Damant, G.H. (1877). The Story of Khamba and Thobi. *Indian Antiquary, 4.*

Das, K. (1953). *A Study of Orissan Folklore*. Santiniketan: Vishwa Bharti Publishing Deapartment

Das, M. (2010). Study of Nutritional Status of Korku Tribes in Betul District of Madhya Pradesh. *Tribes, 8*(1), 31-36.

Deliege, R. (1985). *The Bhils of Western India*. New Delhi: National Publishing House.

Deogaonkar, S.G., & Deogaonkar, S. S. (1990). *The Korku Tribals: Castes and Tribes of India*. New Delhi: Concept Publications.

Deva, I. (1972). *Folklore Studies: A Trend Report*. Bombay: Popular Prakashan.

Dhan, R.O. (1972). Poetry in Oraon Songs of Bihar. In L. P. Vidyarthi (Ed.), *Essays in Indian Folklore*. Cacuttá: Indian Publication.

Dundes, A. (1965). *The Study of Folklore*. N. J.: Prentice-Hall.

Edward, R.E. (1990). The Tribes and Castes of Bombay. *Asian Education Service, 1*, 195-198.

Elwin, V. (1948). Notes on the Juang. *Man in India, 1 & 2.*

Elwin, V. (1954). *Tribal Myths of Orissa*. Bombay Oxford University Press.

Elwin, V. (1958). *Myths of the North East Frontiers of India*. Shillong: North East Frontier Agency.

Ember, C. R., & Ember, M. (1993). *Anthropology* (6th ed.). New Delhi: Prentice-Hall of India Private Limited.

Emeneau, M. B. (1940). *A Classical Indian Folktale as a Reported Modern Event, The Brahman and the Mongoose.* Paper presented at the Proceeding of the American Philosophical Society.

Emeneau, M.B. (1941). The Faithful Dog as a Security for a Debt. *Journal of the American Oriental Society, 71.*

Frazer, J.G. (1922). *The Golden Bough* (3rd ed.). New York: MacMillan.

Fuchus, S. (1973). *The Aborginal Tribes of India*. New Delhi: McMillan.

Fuchus, S. (1988). *The Korkus of the Vindya Hills*. New Delhi: Inter India Publication.

Gariola, T.D. (1926). Folklore of Garhwal. *Vishwa Bharati Quaterly, 4.*

Ghosh, A. (2003). *History and Culture of the Oraon Tribe: Some Aspects of Their Social Life*. New Delhi: Mohit Publication.

Ghurye, G.S. (1973). *The Scheduled Tribes of India* Bombay: Popular Prakashan.

Ghurye, G.S. (1980). *The Scheduled Tribes of India*. New Jersey: Transaction Publishers.

Goswami, P.D. (1949). Abor Tribes. *Man in India, 9*(2).

Goswami, P.D. (1958). Naga tales. *Eastern Anthropologists, 8*(2).

Gulab, S. (1954). *Panduwani: Pradhan Git Katha Matha*. Chindwara: Adimjati Anusandhan Ayaur Parikshan Sanstha.

Gupta, U.N.D. (1923). *Folktales of Orissa*. Calcutta: S. K. Lahiri and Co.

Haekel, J. (1963). Some Aspects of the Social Life of the Bhilala in Central India. *Ethnology,* 2(2), 190.

Hoffmann, J.B. (1937). *Encyclopaedia Mundarica* Patna.

Hougton, B. (1893). A Folktale of the Lushais. *Indian Antiquary,* 22.

Islam, M. (1985). *Folklore: The Pulses of the People*. New Delhi: Concept Publishing Company.

Kabiraj, S.N. (1962). Jhum Cultivation of the Garos and Rains. *Folklore,* 3(1 & 2).

Kapp, D. (1986). A Parallel Motif in Lepcha and Barela-Bhilala Mythology. *Asian Folklore Studies, 45*, 259-285.

Kluckhohn, C. (1965). Recurrent Themes in Myth and Mythmaking. In A. Dundes (Ed.), *The Study of Folklore* (pp. 158-168). New Jersy: Prentice Hall.

Langness, L. L. (1974). *The Study of Culture*. San Francisco: Chandler and Sharp.

Lourdusamy, S., & Sahay, S. (1996). The Mythological Concept of Gayasura and the Performance of Sradha Yajna in Gaya: Belief and Behaviour Patterns of Hindus. *Studies in Folklore and Popular Religion, 1*, 197-203.

Lourdusamy, S., & Sahay, S. (Eds.). (2004). *Lok-Kathayen I, II, III*. Indore: Sat Prachar Pradesh.

Majumdar, D. N. (1950). *The Affairs of a Tribe*. Lucknow: Universal Press.

Malhotra, R. (1992). *Anthropology of Development*. New Delhi: Mittal Publications.

Malinowski. (1925). *Magic, Science and Religion*. New York: Doubleday.

Malinowski, B. (1926). *Myth in Primitive Psychology*. New York: W.W. Norton.

Mann, R.S. (1978). Religious Attributes of Bhils. In N.N. Vyas, R.S. Mann & N.D. Choudhry (Eds.), *Rajasthan Bhils*. Udaipur: Tribal Research Institute.

Mitra, S.C. (1922). On A Birhor Folktale of the Wicked Queens Type. *Journal of Anthropological Society of Bombay, 14*.

Mitra, S.C. (1928). Notes on a Birhor Legend About Ravana's Abduction of Sita. *Journal of Bihar and Orissa Research Society, 14*.

Narayan, J.S. (1942). Khasi Folklore. *The New review, 16*.

Nath, K. (1958). Daughter of Kangana Folk-Songs. *March of India, 10*.

Nath, Y.U.S. (1960). *Bhils of Ratanmal: An Analysis of Western India Community*. Baroda: M.S. University.

Orans, M. (1965). *The Santal: A Tribe in Search of a Greater Tradition*. Wayne: Wayne University Press.

Pandey, T. (1962). *Kumaun ka Lok-Sahitya*. Agra: Almora Book Depot.

Parkin, R. (1992). *The Munda of Central India: An Account of their Social Organisation*. New Delhi: Oxford University Press.

Patnaik, N. (2002). *Folklore of Tribal Communities: Oral Litreature of Santhals, Kharias, Oraons, and Mundas of Orissa*. New Delhi: Gyan Publishing House.

Prasad, O. (1985). *Santhal Music: A Study in Pattern and Process of Cultural Persistence*. New Delhi: Inter India Publications.

Punia, D. (1993). *Social Value in Folklore*. New Delhi: Rawat Publications.

Rafy. (1920). *Folktales of Khasi*. London: MacMillan Press.

Rangamathu, D.S. (1960). *The Folktales of Garos*. Gauhati: Department of Publication.

Redcliffe-Brown, A.R. (1933). *The Andaman Islanders*. England: Cambridge University.

Riccio, M.E., Nunes, J.M., Rahal, M., Kervaire, B., Tiercy, J.M., & Sanchez, A. (2011). The Austroasiatic Munda Population fron India and its Engimatic Origin: A HLA Diversity Study.

*Human Biology, 83*(3), 405-435.

Roy, S.C. (1912). *Munda and their Country*. New Delhi: Asia Publications House.

Roy, S.C. (1916). The Divine Myths of Munda *Journal of Bihar and Orissa Research,* 2.

Roy, S.C. (1999). *Oraon Religion and Custom*. New Delhi: Gyan Publishing House.

Roy, S.C. (2010). *The Oraons of Chotanagpur* (3rd ed.). Ranchi: Crown Publication.

Russell, R.V. (1916). *The tribes and catses of the Central Provincess of India*. London.

Russell, R.V., & Hiralal. (1976). *Tribes and Castes of Central Provinces of India III*. New Delhi Cosmo Publications.

Sachchidananda. (1963). Some recent Evidence of Human Sacrifice. In L. K. B. Ratnam (Ed.), *Anthropology on the March: Recent Studies of Indian Beliefs, Attitudes, and Social Institutions* (pp. 344-351). Madras: The Book Centre.

Sachchidananda. (1964). *Culture Change in Tribal Bihar: Munda and Oraon*. Calcutta: Bookland Private Limited.

Sachchidananda. (1979). *The Changing Mundas*. New Delhi: Concept Publishing Company.

Sahay, S. (2000). Janjatiye Kala aur Sanskriti: Bhil Janjatiye ke Nirtya aur Sangeet ka ek Addhyan. *Vanayjati, XLVIII*(3), 37-42.

Sahay, S. (2001). Folktales of Bihar: An Anthropological Perspective. *Folklore, 13*, 93-102.

Sahay, S. (2002). *Tribal Women in the New Profile*. New Delhi: Anmol Publications Pvt. Ltd.

Sahay, S. (2004). Forward Notes. In S. Lourdusamy & S. Sahay (Eds.), *Loksahitya Paschmi Madhya Pradesh*. Indore: Sat Prachar Press.

Sahay, S. (2005). Folk Tradition and the People of Bihar. *Encyclopedia of World Folklore, 2*, 24-30.

Sahay, S. (2010). The Heavenly Cow Rupan and the Festival of Ceremonial Torture Gai-Goheri: Myth, Rituals and Sacrifice among the People of Bhil Tribe of of Western India. *Folklore, 45*, 45-60.

Sahay, V.S., & Singh, P. K. (1998). *Indian Anthropology*. Allahabad: K.K. Publications.

Satyarthi, D. (1951). *Meet My People*. Hyderabad: Chethna Prakashan.

Satyarthi, D. (1953). Gaddi Folk-Songs. *March of India, 5*.

Shukla, H. L. (1986). *Tribal Heritage of Madhya Pradesh*. New Delhi: B.R. Publishing Corporation.

Srivastava, M. (2007). The Sacred Complex of Munda Tribe. *Anthropologists, 9*(4), 327-330.

Srivastava, S.K. (1949a). The Diwali among the Tharus. *Man in India, 29*.

Srivastava, S.K. (1949b). Spring Festival among the Tharus. *Eastern Anthropologists, 2*(1).

Srivastava, S.K. (1958). *The Tharus*. Agra: Agra University Press.

Srivastava, S.K. (1974). *Folk Culture and Oral Tradition*. New Delhi: Abhinav Publications.

Stiglmayr, E. (1970). *The Barela-Bhilalas and their Songs of Creation*. Wien.

Thompson, S. (1951). *The Folktale*. New York: The Dryden Press.

Tod, J. (1920). *Annals and Antiquities of Rajasthan. Volume 1*. London: Rutledge and Kegan Paul.

Tribhuwan, R.D. (2003). *Fairs and Festivals of Indian Tribes*. New Delhi: Discovery Publishing House.

Trigunayat, J. (1957). *Bansuri Baj Rahi*. Patna: Bihar Rashtrabhasa Parishad.

Troisi, J. (1976). *The Santhals: A Classified and Annolated Bibliography*. New Delhi: Manohar Book Service.

Tylor, E.B. (1958). *Primitive Culture*. New York: Harper Torchbooks.

Venkatachar, C.S. (1933). *Census of India*. New Delhi: GOI.

Vidyarthi, L.P. (1961). *Sacred Complex of Hindu Gaya*. Bombay: Asia Publishing House.

Vidyarthi, L.P. (1963). *The Maler, A Study in Nature Man-Spirit Complex of Hill Tribe*. Calcutta: Bookland Pvt. Ltd.

Vidyarthi, L.P., & Rai, B. K. (1985). *The Tribal Culture of India*. New Delhi: Concept Publishing Company.

Vishnupuran. (1990). (16th ed.). Gorakhpur: Geeta Press.

Vyas, N.N., Mann, R. S., & Choudhary, N. D. (1978). *Rajasthan Bhils*. Udaipur: Tribal Research Institute.

W. Kopper, & Jungblut. (1976). *Bowman of Mid India*. Wein.

West, B.A. (2009). *Encyclopedia of the Pepole of Asia and Oceania* (Vol. 1). New York: Infobase Publishing.

# Glossary

Acculturation: The process of extensive borrowing in the context of super-ordinate- subordinate relations between societies.

Achieved Qualities: Those qualities a person acquires during his or her life time.

Ancestral Spirit: Supernatural beings who are the ghosts of dead relatives.

Animatisms: A belief in supernatural forces.

Animism: A belief in a dual existence for all things—a physical, visible body and a psychic invisible soul.

Bride Price: A substantial gift of goods or money given to the bride's kin by the groom or his kin at or before marriage.

Catastrophism: The theory that extinct life forms were destroyed by cataclysms and up heals and replaced by new divine creations.

Chief: A person who exercises authority, usually on behalf of multi-community political unit.

Clan: A set of kin whose members believe themselves to be descended from a common ancestor; often designated by a totem.

Crime: Violence not considered legitimate that occurs within a political unit.

Domestication: the cultivation or rising of plants and animals that are from wild varieties.

Dowry: A substantial transfer of goods or money from the bride's family to the groom, or the groom's family.

Exogamy: The rule of specifying marriage to a person outside one's own kin group.

Folklore: All the lore myth, fairy tales, superstitions, riddles and game of a culture; generally orally transmitted, but may also be written.

Genetic Drift: the change in frequency of a gene variant in a population due to rapid sampling.

Ghost: Supernatural beings who were once human, the soul of dead people.

Gods: Supernatural beings of nonhuman origin who are named personalities.

Hunter-Gatherers: People who subsist on the collection of naturally occurring plants and animals.

Incest: the crime of sexual relations or marriage taking place between a male and female who are so closely linked by blood or affinity that such activity is prohibited by law.

Magic: The performance of certain rituals that are believed to compel the supernatural powers to act in a particular ways.

Marriage: A socially approved sexual and economic union between a man and a woman that is presumed, both by the couple and by others, and that subsumes reciprocal rights and obligations between the two spouses and their future children.

Nocturnal: Active during the night.

Polyandry: The marriage of one woman to more than one man at a time.

Polygyny: The marriage of one man to more than one woman at a time.

Priest: A male intermediary between humans and gods.

Religion: Ant set of attitudes, beliefs, and practices pertaining to supernatural power.

Shaman: A religious intermediary, whose primary function is to cure people through sacred songs, pantomime, and other means.

Shifting Cultivation: A type of horticulture in which the land is worked for short periods and then left to regenerate for some years before being used again.

Siblings: A person's brother and sister.

Slaves: A class of persons who do not own their own labour or the products thereof.

Sorcery: The use of certain materials to invoke supernatural powers to harm people.

Spirits: Unnamed supernatural beings of nonhuman origin who are beneath the gods in prestige and often closer to the people; may be helpful, mischievous, or evil.

Taboo: A prohibition that, if violated, is believed to bring supernatural punishment.

Tribe: A type of political system characterized by kin or non-kin groupings that can informally and temporarily integrate a number of local groups into a large whole.

Witchcraft: The practice of attempting to harm people by supernatural means, but through emotions and thought alone, not through the use of tangible objects.

# Botanical Index

| HINDI | ENGLISH | BOTANICAL |
|---|---|---|
| *Aam* | Mango | Mangifera indica |
| Aalu | Potato | Solanum tuberosum |
| Adrak | Ginger | Zinziber officinale |
| Aphim | Poppy | Papaver somniferum |
| Amla | Myrobalan | Phyllantus emblica |
| Arendi | Castor | Ricinus cpmmunis |
| Baigan | Egg plant | Solanum melongena |
| Bajra | Millet | Pennisatum typhoideum |
| Bans | Bamboo | Bambuseae poaceae |
| Bargad | Banyan tree | Ficus indica |
| Bel | Hard apple | Aegle marmelos |
| Ber | Jujube tree | Zyziphus jujube |
| Champa | Pagoda tree | Michelia champacca |
| Chana | Gram | Cicer arietinum |
| Chandan | Sandal | Santalus flavus |
| Chawal | Rice | Oryza sativa |
| Dabh | Raw coconut | Cocos nucifera |
| Dhatura | Datura | Datura alba |
| Gajar | Carrot | Daucus carota |
| Ganna | Sugarcane | Saccharum arundinaceum |
| Imli | Tamarind | Tamarindus indica |
| Jau | Barely | Soraghum vulgare |
| Juhi | Jasmine | Jasmimum anriculatum |

| | | |
|---|---|---|
| Kachari | A small fruit | Cucumis madras-patanus |
| Kaddu | Pampkin | Cucurbita moschata |
| Kamal | Lotus | Nelumbo nucifera |
| Kapash | Cotton | Gossypium herbaceum |
| Karam | A tree | Adina cordifolia |
| Karanj | Karanja | Pongamia glabra |
| Karela | Bitter guard | Memordica charantia |
| Kela | Plantain | Musa paradisica |
| Keri | Small raw mango | Mangifera indica |
| Kesar | Saffron | Crocus sativus |
| Khajoor | Date palm | Phoenix dactylifera |
| Lahsun | Garlic | Allium sativum |
| Lawang | Clove | Pipper cubebe |
| Mahuwa | A tree | Bassia latifolia |
| Makka | Maize | Zea mayis |
| Masur | Lentil | Lentilla lens |
| Matar | Pea | Pisum sativum |
| Mehandi | Myrtle | Lawsonia alba |
| Mirch | Red pepper | Capsicum frutescens |
| Muli | White root/radish | Raphanus sativus |
| Mung | Muni tree | Phaseolus aureus |
| Munhphali | Ground-nut | Arachis hypogagea |
| Narangi | Orange | Citrus sinensis |
| Nariyel | Coconut | Cocos mucifera |
| Neem | Margosa tree | Azadirachta indica |
| Nibu | Lemon | Citrus limon |
| Paan | Betel | Piper betle |
| Palak | Indian spinach | Beta vulgaris |
| Palash | Kino tree | Butea frondosa |
| Papeeta | Papaya | Carica papaya |
| Parash peepal | Portia tree | Thespesia populnea |
| Peepal | Sacred tree | Ficus religiosa |
| Phulgobhi | Cauliflower | Brassica oleracea |
| Rai | Black mustard | Brassica juncea |
| Sabai | Grass | Ischaemum angustifolium |
| Sal | Sal | Shorea robusta |
| San | Jute | Corchorus tiliaceae |

| | | |
|---|---|---|
| Shaljam | Turnip | Brassica rapa |
| Supari | Betel-nut | Areca catechu |
| Tamatar | Tomato | Lycopersicum esculentum |
| Tambakku | Tobacco | Nicotiana tabaccum |
| Til | Sesamum | Sesamum orientale |
| Timru | A fruit tree | Carissa carendas |
| Tuar | Lentils | Cajanus inclicus |
| Tulshi | Basil plant | Ocymum sanctum |
| Urad | Lentils | Phaseolus mungo |

# Index


**A**

*Abba kulchi*, 90
Aestheticians, 251
After the cataclysm, 83
Air, 133
Animal friends, 191
Anna raja, 26, 27
Anthropologists, 247
Assam, 215
*Asur*, 169

**B**

Backward Regions Grant Fund Programme, 5
Bada Damor, 10, 11
Banana tree, 241
Baniser raja and onkha kumari, 61
Bapsi dev, 56, 57
Barela, 85
Barwa, 40, 54
Beggars, 237
Bengal, 147
Bhada garden, 17
Bhajans, 39
Bhanzgerio, 52
Bhil, 2, 7, 84
Bhil boy and the king, 65
Bhil farmer and the god, 69
Bhil tribesmen, 251
Bhilala, 84
Bhilji bhil, 57
Bhima, 38
Bhola and bhunda, 108
Bhola Ishwar, 49
Bhola oraon, 192
Bhondu barela and his son, 110
Bijashni, 110
Biri, 182
Black cobra, 242
Blacksmith, 102
Bongas (spirits), 187
Bongas, 236
Boy named son-in-law, 196
Boy, the dragon and the monkey, 171
*Brahmin Guru*, 50
*Brahmin*, 84
Brave prince, 122
British Colonists, 216
British officials, 183
Brother born again, 209
Brother in a mandolin, 189
Buddhu, 17
Budhna oraon, 203
Bull and the tiger, 91
Bullock cart, 117

**C**

Carpenter, 103
Cattle worship, 206
Cave, 109
Chamars, 9
Chatak bird, 69

Christianity, 5
Clever boy and the bear, 235
Clever chicks, 217
Clever farmer, 136
Clever girl, 77
Clever sablu, 100
Cock, 39
Common universal elements, 251
Conceited, 131
Cotton tree, 236
Cow named rupan, 29
Creation and propagation of the folktales, 251
Creation of land, 148
Creation of world, 183
Crocodile and the jackal, 228
Culprits, 122
Cunning jackal, 208, 243
Cunning step mother, 74
Curiosity, 246
Cursing of a cow, 134

**D**

Damor clan, 8, 33
Dancing mouse, 190
Darling sister, 233
Dassai, 182
Day dreamer, 218
Death of a demon, 101, 141
Deceitful rabbit, 231
*Dharam*, 126
*Dharmesh*, 182
*Dharmi raja*, 24
Dhinchiri, 101
*Dhoti*, 49
Dishonest oilman, 223
Dog, 92
Dona, 210
Donkey, 87
Dream of a potter, 224
Drought, 251
*Duda Dutiya*, 17
*Dudi megh* and *bhada* garden, 63
*Duniyari*, 110

**E**

Earthworm, 149

**F**

Farmer, the bull, and the justice, 89
Fig (*Ficus indica*), 223
Fight, 133
Fire, 133
Fish, 243
Flying cot, 102
Folktales of Barela, 85-117
Folktales of Bhil, 7-84
Folktales of Korku, 118-146
Folktales of Munda, 147-181
Folktales of Oraon, 182-214
Folktales of Santal, 215-245
Foolish man, 186
Foster parents, 175
Four fools, 137
Four friends, 201
Fox, 140
Frog, 81
Frog and the fish, 179

**G**

Gabbin, 140
Game of luck, 120
*Ganga teli* and *Bhlat dev*, 99
*Gappa* and *sappa*, 97
*Gaura*, 183
Genetic drift theory, 3
Ghee, 176
Gift, 226
Girl inside a drum, 224
Girl named sonbai, 114
Girl refused to marry, 229
Goat, 39

God, 134
Golden bull, 96
Golden haired boy, 116
Gond tribe, 118
Gond tribesmen, 118
Great drummer, 165
Greedy brothers, 136
Greedy tigress, 195
Guard a corpse, 212
Gullible man, 194
Guru-Dakshina, 8

**H**

Hag and her daughter, 31
*Halun sorya*, 21
*Handiya* (rice beer), 200
Hanuman, 110
Helpful wolf, 180
Hinduism, 5
Hindus, 73
Hindustani Classic Music, 215
Historians, 251
Holi, 57
Howan mata, 19
Hunipurti clan, 160
*Hura* and *pura*, 81

**I**

Ill-begotten earnings, 130
Imposturous exorcist, 175
Introduction, 1-6
    Jhabua, 4-5
    Khandwa, 5
    locale of the study, 4
    methodology, 6
    organisation of data, 6
    present book, 4
    Ranchi, 5
    rationale behind selection of locale, 5-6
    rationale behind selection of tribes, 2-3
    studies on tribal folktales, 3-4

J

Jackal, 153
Jadur, 182
Jahma mata, 41
Judgement, 231
Jukhari, 110

**K**

Kachari, 43
Kajali van, 29
Kaliya khet, 23
Kalua the barber, 129
Kana, 53
Kanya kumari, 45
Karam, 147
Karhi, 71
Karma and balma, 237
Karma raja, 197
*Karma*, 182
*Katha*, 145, 146
Khokha and Kassumar Dev, 33
King and his four sons, 155
Korku, 118
Kumari, Onkha, 62
Kurukh, 182
Kurus or kauravas, 118

**L**

Lal bai mata, 19
Likhari, 110
Lion and the jackal, 212
Literacy crisis, 251

**M**

Madhya Pradesh, 4, 118
Mage, 147
*Mahabharata*, 3, 118
Mahadeva, 28, 29
Mahak, 115
Maharashtra, 118

*Mahua* (*Bassia latifolia*), 38, 101
*Mandap*, 51
*Mantras*, 13, 92
Megh raja, 12, 45
Milk man, 159
Miseries, 246
Monkey friend, 173
Monkey, 94
Moon of *jalmata*, 80
Moon, 28, 29
Moving room, 59
Munda, 2, 147
Myths, 250

N

*Nastik*, 112
Nature and forms of the folktales, 246-251
motif behind the folktales, 247
structural classification of the folktales, 246
Neegasher, 132
New exorcist, 230
New pair of shoes, 207
NGO, 8
Nostril of the minister, 89

O

Ogre, 188
Old couple and seven children, 95
Old couple and the Jackal, 166
Old couple, 152
Old woman, 172
Oraon, 2, 182
Origin of the world, 221
Orissa, 118
Ornaments and sweets, 238

P

Parents of *Gaura*, 52
Parrot and the sparrow, 105
Patal, 49
Peepal Dev, 135
Petha, 72
Pewit and the thieves, 106
Phagu, 147
Pigeon, 31
Plough, 154
Potha, 49
Pottery, 168
Psychologists, 251

R

Rabbit and the girl, 72
Rajput, 84
Rama, 84
Ramiya and Shaymiya, 112
Ramu and Shamu, 219
Rat and the female mouse, 106
Realization of the mistake, 125
Revenge of a jackal, 200
Ringiya and Jingiya, 85
River, Tapti, 118
Roasted birds, 237
Running dog, 202
Rupan, 83

S

*Saat bhowani mata*, 52
*Sabai* grass, 220
*Sadhu*, 250
*Sal* tree, 240
*Salar mata*, 19
Santal, 215
Santhal, 2
*Sarhul*, 147
*Saubhagya*, 232
*Sawan Mata*, 9, 38, 45
Search of fortune, 75
Seth, Meegal Moti, 33
Seven brothers, 92
Seven fruits, 119

Seventh queen, 161
She-elephant, 163
Shinning dark hair, 184
Shiva, 119
*Shorea robusta*, 241
*Sing-bonga* (supreme deity), 150
Snake and the girl, 202
Sohari festival, 149
Sohrai festival two, 170
Solve a riddle, 127
Somara and budhna, 168
Somara, 70
Somara, 76
Sparrow chicks, 85
Speaking bed, 239
Steal the wealth of Kalua, 130
Stupid tortoise, 152
Sun, 28, 29

T

Tadvi, 56
Teaching of a Brahmin, 113
Teer-Kaman, 5
Tiger and the king, 216
Traditional instruments, 182
Tribal people, 247
Trick of a father, 221
Trick of a woman, 82
Two brothers, 142
Two friends, 187

V

Vaan, 110
Vayu, 110
Vayuser, 132
Veracious, 144
Verbal Art, 2
Vilash, 92
Vinyari, 110
Vrishbha, 7

W

Waiting for the god, 139
Water, 134
Well wisher parrot, 155
Wicked sisters-in-law, 173
Wild buffaloes, 150
Wise jackal, 158